THE INDUSTRIALIST AND THE MOUNTAINEER

WEST VIRGINIA AND APPALACHIA

Edited by Ronald L. Lewis, Ken Fones-Wolf, and Kevin Barksdale

TITLES IN THE SERIES

Memorializing Motherhood: Anna Jarvis and the Struggle for Control of Mother's Day
Katharine Lane Antolini

Working Class Radicals: The Socialist Party in West Virginia, 1898–1920
Frederick A. Barkey

"They'll Cut Off Your Project": A Mingo County Chronicle
Huey Perry

An Appalachian Reawakening: West Virginia and the Perils of the New Machine Age, 1945–1972
Jerry Bruce Thomas

An Appalachian New Deal: West Virginia in the Great Depression
Jerry Bruce Thomas

Culture, Class, and Politics in Modern Appalachia
Edited by Jennifer Egolf, Ken Fones-Wolf, and Louis C. Martin

Governor William E. Glasscock and Progressive Politics in West Virginia
Gary Jackson Tucker

Matewan Before the Massacre: Politics, Coal, and the Roots of Conflict in a West Virginia Mining Community
Rebecca J. Bailey

Sectionalism in Virginia from 1776 to 1861
Charles H. Ambler

Monongah: The Tragic Story of the 1907 Monongah Mine Disaster, The Worst Industrial Accident in US History
David McAteer

Bringing Down the Mountains: The Impact of Mountaintop Removal on Southern West Virginia Communities
Shirley Stewart Burns

Afflicting the Comfortable: Journalism and Politics in West Virginia
Thomas F. Stafford

Clash of Loyalties: A Border Country in the Civil War
John W. Shaffer

The Blackwater Chronicle
Philip Pendleton Kennedy; edited by Timothy Sweet

Transnational West Virginia: Ethnic Communities and Economic Change, 1840–1940
Edited by Ken Fones-Wolf and Ronald L. Lewis

THE INDUSTRIALIST AND THE MOUNTAINEER

The Eastham-Thompson Feud and the Struggle for West Virginia's Timber Frontier

RONALD L. LEWIS

WEST VIRGINIA UNIVERSITY PRESS
MORGANTOWN · 2017

Copyright 2017 Ronald L. Lewis
All rights reserved
First edition published 2017 by West Virginia University Press

ISBN:

cloth	978-1-943665-50-1
paper	978-1-943665-51-8
epub	978-1-943665-52-5
pdf	978-1-943665-53-2

Library of Congress Cataloging-in-Publication Data is available from the Library of Congress

Cover design by Than Saffel / WVU Press

CONTENTS

Acknowledgments   vii

Introduction   1

1. The Incorporation of West Virginia   11
2. Modernizing the Law   32
3. Robert W. Eastham, the Early Years   52
4. Eastham in West Virginia   78
5. Who Were the Thompsons?   94
6. Setting the Stage for Trouble   114
7. The Struggle for Control   135
8. The Shoot-Out and "Lawyers by the Dozen"   161
9. Jury Selection and the Appeal   191
10. On Trial for Murder   212

Epilogue   242

Notes   255

Bibliography   285

Index   297

ACKNOWLEDGMENTS

In many respects both Robert W. Eastham and Frank E. Thompson were ordinary men, and neither of them left the kind of personal papers or records historians generally consult to reconstruct the past. Most of the primary research was conducted in the Tucker County Circuit Court where I consulted the case files from the several trials involving Robert W. Eastham and Frank Thompson, most importantly the testimony and depositions given in evidence. My goal was to gather enough evidence to reconstruct the events that led to the death of one of Tucker County's leading businessmen. Large gaps remain in the biographies of Robert Eastham and Frank Thompson, and since the feud occurred nearly one hundred and twenty years ago, even descendants of the participants are only vaguely aware of it. This effort to reconstruct the Eastham-Thompson feud has, therefore, frequently been frustrating, but always intriguing. That it finally came together is testimony to the generous assistance from some very helpful people.

First and foremost, I must express my deep gratitude to two Eastham relatives. While traveling to Charlottesville, Virginia, in 1992, I stopped to visit Robert Eastham III, of Flint Hill, Virginia, the great nephew and namesake of the principal subject of this book. There he entertained me with Robert Eastham stories and provided family information that was of great value in trying to understand the man who was charged with murder, and the impact this episode had on the Eastham family. Mr. Eastham died in 1995, and I have regretted ever since that I did not have the opportunity to spend more time with him. Edwin I. Eastham III, of Huntly, Virginia, another relative of Robert W. Eastham, has provided me with invaluable assistance in understanding the context of Rappahannock County, Virginia, the place Robert Eastham called home. The houses Eastham lived in are still inhabited. He also showed me important sites associated with the Civil War exploits that have become legendary in Rappahannock County, arranged for me to meet with others who shed light on the personality of Robert Eastham, and shared photographs of family heirlooms. Louise King Eastham graciously shared her stories and allowed me to take photographs of the gravestones of Robert, his wife Mary, and daughter Eliza which have been preserved in a garden at her beautiful old plantation home, Ben Venue.

Of the Thompson family, Sarah Thompson Fletcher, of Canaan Valley, Tucker County, has provided the kind of information that historians find most useful, family papers. Frank Thompson had no direct descendants, but Sarah's grandfather, George B. Thompson, continued as general manager after the lumber operations were sold to another company. He recorded the company's history, made an effort to reconstruct the Thompson family history, and most importantly never discarded anything. Sarah's father, Benjamin F. Thompson, also preserved family documents and photographs, and he bequeathed everything to her. She graciously gave me full access to this collection, which is now in the West Virginia and Regional History Center. Without her help it would have been impossible to provide background information on the Thompson lumbermen who, after leaving West Virginia, scattered across the country. Another distant relative of Frank Thompson contacted me and shared what she had uncovered in her own reconstruction of the family's history. Unfortunately, I never met Mary Beausoleil of Lyndonville, Vermont, self-described as Frank's first cousin thrice removed;

our communications were by e-mail. However, I appreciate her willingness to share family information, especially the photograph of the Thompson family mausoleum.

County courthouses are a treasure trove for historians who have the patience and skill to use the records effectively, which happens only with the assistance of a knowledgeable staff. Back in the 1990s, before the courthouse was upgraded and the clerk's facility was constructed, I was very fortunate to have the cooperation of former Tucker County Circuit Court clerk Alan Judy. He allowed me to make my own arrangements for photocopying the stacks of case files involving Robert Eastham, especially *R. W. Eastham v. Blackwater Lumber Company*, *Blackwater Lumber Company v. R. W. Eastham*, and *State v. R. W. Eastham*. Without that documentary foundation this story could not be told. I would also like to acknowledge the assistance of current Tucker County Circuit Court clerk Donna Jean Bava, Tucker County clerk Sherry Simmons, and Rappahannock Circuit Court clerk Margaret Ralph.

At West Virginia University, I am in constant debt to the library staff, especially Jo Brown, and Christelle Venham in the West Virginia and Regional Research Center. Judy Tole at the Rappahannock County Historical Society also was very generous with her assistance. Robert Bastress, professor of law at West Virginia University, deserves my thanks for his advice and assistance in retrieving relevant records from the West Virginia Supreme Court of Appeals. Similarly, I am appreciative for the helpful assistance of WVU law librarian and archivist Mark Podvia. I am also grateful to West Virginia University and the Department of History for supporting emeritus faculty members who continue to research and write.

My deepest appreciation goes to my wife Susan E. Lewis who, doing what she does so well, copyedited the entire manuscript.

All the assistance in the world, however, does not absolve me from the responsibility of presenting my historical subjects as fairly and as accurately as possible.

Ronald L. Lewis
Morgantown, West Virginia

INTRODUCTION

A cool drizzle was falling high in the Tucker County seat of Parsons, West Virginia, that evening on March 17, 1897, as passengers boarded the train for the short journey up the line to Davis. Daylight was fading, and the coach was lighted for residents returning to Davis after attending a court proceeding in the county seat. Davis businessman Frank E. Thompson boarded with a friend and they took their seats, followed shortly by famous outdoorsman Robert W. Eastham. As he walked up the aisle, Eastham stopped at Thompson's seat, swore at him, and slapped his face. He had taken two steps past him when Thompson jumped to his feet, pistol drawn, and fired point-blank at Eastham. The intended victim returned fire, and within a few seconds seven or eight shots echoed through the car; passengers instinctively ducked for cover. Eastham's wounds were not serious, but Thompson was mortally wounded in the abdomen and died the following day. The sheriff arrested Eastham and locked him up in the county jail. The press declared the ensuing trial one of the most sensational in the state's history. Twice a grand jury was impaneled and dismissed before a third complied with the presiding judge's order and charged Eastham with murder. In the end, a petit jury convicted Eastham of involuntary manslaughter rather than murder. The state's case very quickly became ensnared in a larger political struggle that far surpassed the charge of murder in historical significance.

Thompson and Eastham both were well-known, popular figures, but they represented two different cultures within the county and people quickly took sides. The feud between Eastham and Albert and his son Frank Thompson began with a dispute over the Thompsons' purchase of a lumber mill in which Eastham had a financial interest and escalated over logging contract disputes that resulted in each party filing lawsuits against the other. The ensuing trials were a local version of the national legal struggle for control over America's natural resources between the emerging corporations and individual property owners. In short, the Eastham-Thompson feud bore the hallmarks of a battle between David and Goliath, which is exactly how it was regarded by those who supported Eastham the small landowner against the Thompson "lumber barons."

One of the more arresting features of the trial was the array of legal talent that converged on tiny Parsons to try the case. The state fielded eight attorneys, among them a congressman, a former congressman, and a future governor. The defense mounted a team of eleven lawyers put together at the behest of Henry G. Davis, a U.S. senator and the state's leading industrialist. They included two of Davis's own counselors, another powerful lawyer-industrialist, a recent U.S. solicitor general, and three of the most eminent defense attorneys in West Virginia and Virginia. One might ask why so many prominent attorneys had assembled in the recently established county seat, with a population of 1,200, in the backwoods of West Virginia? The courthouse had yet to be constructed, requiring the trial to be held in the social hall on the second floor of the Knights of Pythias building without the benefit of electric lighting. And one might also ask why an avalanche of reporters, representing all of the regional newspapers and many of the large eastern city dailies, descended on Parsons? People from the surrounding countryside also arrived to witness the excitement. The hotels were filled and so were the saloons.

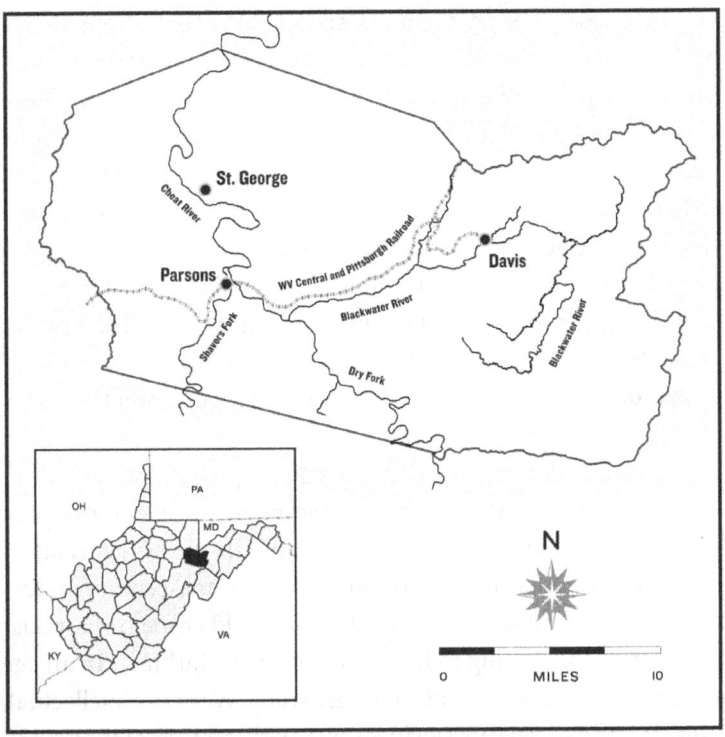

Tucker County, West Virginia. Map by Jim Schindling.

Although neither Thompson nor Eastham were natives of the mountains, the press undoubtedly hoped the trial would be the beginning of a new story of Appalachian violence. After the headline bonanza generated in the 1880s by the Hatfield and McCoy feud and subsequent trials, newspapers and magazines were well aware that stories of Appalachian violence increased their sales. The Thompson-Eastham shoot-out occurred during the most productive period in the creation of Appalachian stereotypes, one of the most prominent and persistent being that Appalachians were inherently violent. That stereotype was deeply rooted in earlier decades. During the Civil War both Confederate and Yankee armies pillaged the Appalachian countryside, and guerrilla warfare, bushwhacking, and brutal retaliatory violence tore families and entire neighborhoods apart. The "moonshine wars" of the 1870s, a result of the federal government's effort to enforce the regulation of homemade liquor, turned a minor mountaineer sideline into a major criminal activity. The ensuing violence between revenue agents and moonshiners offered plenty of fuel for the pens of newspaper and magazine writers. The Appalachian feuds of the late nineteenth century provided further confirmation of the mountaineers' preference for guns over the courts in settling personal disputes.[1]

Two generations of scholars since the "Appalachian revival" of the 1970s have demonstrated that the negative stereotypes were constructed from the desire of urban middle-class Victorians to validate their own recent arrival in turn-of-the-century industrial cities by stressing the benefits that would ensue from industrialization. According to historian Anthony Harkins, "In an age of faith in American, and more generally Western, intellectual, cultural, and social superiority over the other 'races' of the world," these stereotypes were intended "to show not cultural difference so much as cultural hierarchy—to celebrate modernity and 'mainstream' progress."[2] Taking the law into one's own hands was emblematic of "premodern" America and, therefore, had to be stamped out to make way for the "modern" America where disputes were to be settled by legal professionals in the courts.

The reporters who thronged to Parsons during the summer and fall of 1897 looking for an incident that would feed the public hunger for feud stories like that of the Hatfields and McCoys of the previous decade would be disappointed. Although reporters reflexively looked for the stereotypically violent mountaineers to be involved in the Eastham-Thompson gunfight, both men came to Tucker County as adults from regions beyond the mountains. When Robert Eastham moved to Tucker County from the Shenandoah Valley of Virginia in 1876, the county court system resembled Virginia's on which it was modeled. The county was divided into five smaller districts with a magistrate elected for each district. The magistrate was not necessarily an attorney, but he upheld the law and the standards of social behavior expected among his neighbors. Therefore, personal knowledge of the families and individual residents was an important consideration when a problem arose. Traditionally the county court was a comprehensive, autonomous institution with judicial, legislative, and administrative functions responsive to local needs, but in February 1881 the state legislature restructured the entire county court system. Judicial decisions were to be made by an experienced professional attorney who was appointed judge for a circuit that included several counties. Cases were to be tried in a distant county seat by professional attorneys before a trained judge, rather than by the district justice of the peace known and trusted by his neighbors. This shift signaled the emergence of the new merchant-lawyer-industrialist elite.[3]

Conflicts between small landowners and the new elites over land and timber, the predominant type of civil dispute in Tucker County, were now heard in the county court at Parsons controlled by the new elites. Many local small farmers logged their land to supplement their subsistence. Generally they used the Blackwater River to transport their logs to the mill in Davis. When the Blackwater Lumber Company blocked free access to the river on Frank Thompson's direction, the company threatened the farmers' ability to sustain themselves. The festering dispute between Thompson and Eastham was over just such an issue, and the trial revealed the emerging class chasm between the new elites and the traditionalists who resisted modernization in an effort to protect their customary rights of access to life-sustaining resources. Robert Eastham and his supporters did not oppose industrial development. Indeed, they wished to participate in that development, but as independent local farmer owners unhindered by the monopolistic practices of encroaching corporations. Significantly, even though Eastham attempted to participate in the business activity generated by industrialization, his behavior, social attitudes, and values did not transcend the traditional culture that had shaped him.

The Eastham-Thompson feud demonstrated how the different cultural worlds of the nineteenth and the twentieth centuries were imprinted on individual social behavior. Thompson was a northern Yankee, an active Republican, and a corporation man who threatened to alienate the land and resources from the smallholders. Eastham was an ardent Democrat, a former Confederate soldier, and outdoorsman of repute who was admired by the backwoodsmen. Thompson and those who prosecuted Eastham on his behalf were agents in the "wars of incorporation" that were in full stride in the 1890s, transforming society through the aggregation, consolidation, and centralization of power in a national market system buttressed and protected by a new emphasis on property-oriented law and authority.[4] Eastham and those who defended him resisted incorporation into the national market system. They sought to retain control of their lives through small government, local political control, the preservation of local markets, strategies of economic self-sufficiency, and the support of personal and family networks that traditionally had been the vital support system for rural people.

The reporters who congregated in Parsons also might have come looking for a classic face-to-face gunfight that the public associated with the law-and-order movement in the vast empty lands west of the Mississippi River, in what historian Richard

Brown calls the "Western Civil War of Incorporation."⁵ Modernization of the West required business, industry, and a top-down social structure featuring a narrow band of elite capitalists at the top. A diverse middle class composed of businessmen, professionals, ranchers, farmers, and skilled tradesmen occupied the middle rungs of the social hierarchy. At the bottom of the class structure was a "large, unruly element of the alienated," people who opposed the new elites, particularly the rugged independent cattlemen and cowboys. Those who resisted incorporation often were socially attuned to combat and violence, Brown observes, and were "not offended by disorder." These were social values which "more cosmopolitan citizenry in the growing towns and cities saw as antiquated and harmful" to capital investment. Also among those at the bottom of the pyramid were Native Americans who had to be killed or moved onto reservations with the help of the U.S. cavalry. Mexicans, particularly in the Southwest, also had to be marginalized and barred from power as the territories became states.⁶

By the 1890s the popular demand for stories about taming the "Wild West," in which the heroes of law and order took on and subdued the evil men of disorder, was already embedded in American popular culture. The showdown gunfight at high noon involving "good" gunfighters against "bad" gunfighters that became the formula for western novels and motion pictures had already achieved a mythical status. Town merchants and professionals with an eye to modernization hired "conservative incorporation gunfighters" to enforce the law against the rowdiness and disorder created by "dissident resister gunfighters" who rejected the law and order measures imposed by businessmen. From these confrontations came famous gunslingers such as Wild Bill Hickok and Wyatt Earp, and the infamous gunslingers like Jesse James and Billy the Kid. In this Western Civil War of

Incorporation the cow town merchants and residents wanted the profits generated by the unruly cowboys, but did not want the drunken disorderly behavior. There is more to this animus. According to Brown, those who favored progress were generally Northern Unionists during the Civil War, and Republicans. The cowboys, on the other hand, were overwhelmingly Southern Rebels, and Democrats. Hatred between the cowboys and the Yankees who controlled the towns was multilayered and sometimes erupted into outright warfare.[7]

Reporters might be forgiven, therefore, if they were predisposed to see features of the western wars of incorporation (although they would not have used the term) in the Eastham-Thompson confrontation. The mythologizing of western gunfighters as men who stood their ground was well established among the reporters who swarmed into Parsons to cover the Eastham trial. The popularization of the western gunfighter by sensationalizing newspapers, popular magazines, and dime novels overlapped their creation of "violent Appalachia" as the home of demented moonshiners and blood-thirsty feudists.[8]

The western wars of incorporation are more familiar than those that took place in West Virginia and Central Appalachia. In some ways Appalachia resembled the frontier, but West Virginia was already a state with an established governmental structure. There were no Indians to be removed or Mexicans to be marginalized or dispossessed as in the West. Open-range cattle ranchers were not present either, although small self-sufficient farmers grazed their animals in the forest commons "open range" style. Industrial and commercial development was confined primarily to the eastern panhandle and the Ohio and Kanawha river valleys, but in the interior back counties of the state, the hand of government rested lightly on a culture founded on informal community consensus. The western model for imposing law and order through violence when necessary by capitalist elites was more readily apparent in West Virginia's southern coalfields where the railroads and coal companies hired "gunslingers" through the Baldwin-Felts Detective Agency to protect their property, police their towns, and keep out the undesirables. The mine wars triggered by that suppression are reminiscent of the western conflicts of the same period as was the suppression of recalcitrant feudists like Devil Anse Hatfield.[9] In the interior counties where the lumber industry dominated, the struggle for control was largely a political/ideological one between those who sided with the incorporators and those who resisted. The lumber companies generally did not employ gunmen to impose their dominance; they insured compliance through economic power and dispossession of obstinate small landholders. As traditional farmers either abandoned or were forced off the land, they became dependent on jobs with the lumber companies or left for opportunities elsewhere. Nevertheless, the process of incorporating the rural back counties into the national market system did not proceed unchallenged even though the locals were at an overwhelming disadvantage.

The pent-up hatred of two strong-willed men exploded in the Thompson-Eastham shooting when the pressures could no longer be restrained. For most Americans the violence in this drama echoed the Appalachian variant of the popular mythology of "gunslinging" in the Wild West. Eastham prompted the shoot-out when he confronted Frank Thompson on the railway coach, and then slapped him across the face. As a man of the Old South, Eastham would have understood that act as a challenge to Thompson's honor, which he had verbally questioned on numerous previous occasions. The younger Thompson was more likely to have understood it as a personal affront to his masculinity and, skipping the preliminaries, went straight for his gun.

The final curtain came down in the personal drama between Eastham and Thompson with the gunfight that cost Thompson his life. This was not the last act, however, for the trial of Robert Eastham ended in his conviction by a jury of his peers for the misdemeanor of involuntary manslaughter rather than the capital crime of murder. It was a victory for Eastham, but a temporary one, for it marked the end of the nineteenth-century traditional culture on West Virginia's "timber frontier." The resisters won the battle, but the twentieth-century modernizers whom Thompson represented ultimately won the war. Unlike the well-defined reputations of gunfighters in the Old West, deciding which man in the Eastham-Thompson drama filled the role of hero and which the villain is contingent on the sympathies of the reader.

1

THE INCORPORATION OF WEST VIRGINIA

Incorporators and Resisters

The United States, a nation of diverse regions with their own unique historical experiences and cultural identities, underwent a profound social, economic, political, and cultural transformation during the late nineteenth and early twentieth centuries. During this watershed period the dozen or so American regions were drawn together into a unified whole by a process Alan Trachtenberg has aptly described as "the incorporation of America."[1] At its core was "the conservative consolidating authority of capital—the urban, industrial, often corporate forces" that moved unevenly and ignited strident class conflicts. Opposing factions and individuals with a stake in the status quo resisted, sometimes violently, through strikes, feuds, and vigilantism.[2]

The "old order" was rooted in the conditions of the nineteenth century, while the "new order" was grounded in the power relations of the twentieth century, producing conflict between what some contemporaries referred to as the "old men" and the "new men." The social hierarchy in the countryside featured a narrow elite at the top, a small middle class of business and professional men, farmers, ranchers, and skilled craftsmen, and below them a large amorphous base of landless, unskilled, and the poor. Diffused throughout the rural areas were those who resisted the "aggressive men of capital" who sought to impose "property-oriented law and authority." Those who resisted often displayed a tenacious allegiance to what were essentially highly traditional, even premodern, social values: law and order per se was much less prized than personal and family relationships, violators of which, in accordance with traditional values, were punished by the use of violence. As one scholar observed, "They were not offended by disorder." They had little interest in or sympathy for the incorporating process, which emphasized "the aggregation of wealth, the consolidation of capital, and the centralization of authority at the local, the state, and the national levels." Locals had a clear understanding of community standards, one historian observes, and they often rose up in defense of "community values."[3]

Traditionally, farmers, artisans, and rural merchants shared a sense of personal control grounded in the capacity of traditional households to grow or make the goods their members required. The face-to-face transactions between individual consumers, artisans, and local merchants resulted from the integration of production and consumption that prompted traditionalists in the old order to believe that the price of products should be determined by local rather than the impersonal distant markets. Farmers in the old order required unimproved land, the habitat for fish and game on which rural people depended to sustain their self-sufficient lives. According to one scholar, "The survival of the traditional unity of life and work depended on the survival of local markets, self-sufficiency, and personal networks as the central economic facts of life. Those realities remained powerful where the market remained local," and those who identified with the "old order" resisted efforts to change it.[4]

Industry-oriented public officials had promoted economic development even before West Virginia became a state in 1863 and the promotion of natural resource extraction industries became official state policy. Indeed, in 1906, the *Manufacturer's Record* reported that "the entire machinery of State government" was employed "to attract capital to the State to develop its railroads, its coal, and its timber interests."[5] The incorporators of the "new order" believed they were the torchbearers of civilization. Newspaper editors, who generally favored the increased population and the increased pace of business activity that would accompany modernization, scorned the unambitious resisters as "Rip Vanwrinkles" who were satisfied with the stagnant old ways of self-sufficiency. "We must help our people out of the woods," proclaimed one editor.[6] Another booster of the "gospel of progress" asserted in 1902 that the entire state was ready for the incorporators: "Even in the heads of the hollows, the 'moss-backs' are being hustled out of their hibernation" and jostled awake "by industrial developers with money to buy land and natural resources."[7]

The incorporators offered a new social vision that departed dramatically from that of the resisters. Their new world encouraged the "progressive" elements in society to shed the restraints imposed by local traditions for a new life founded on economic rationality and growth rather than mere self-sufficiency. Once freed from local constraints and linked to national markets they would enjoy more of everything: money, time, material goods, education, opportunities, and freedom. However, the new order required that local markets be absorbed into the national market system so that "the price and quality of goods would no longer be restrained by local consumers."[8]

The promotion of railroads became an obsession among new local elites after the Civil War. Most of these promoters owned large investments in land and natural resources whose value would skyrocket with the arrival of the railroad. On the other hand, failure to attract railroads would reduce the value of their investments and their communities would become backwaters. Ambitious men of property, therefore, found it necessary to suppress local resisters whose inertia inhibited the "the modernizing of society and the incorporation of power and authority."[9]

The new order collided with the old in West Virginia between the 1880s and the 1920s, and the state acquired a national reputation for conflict as a result of the mine wars brought about by the desire for unionization and the Hatfield and McCoy feud. Both were prime illustrations of the "wars of incorporation." Both incorporators and resisters attempted to control political parties which could serve as instruments for gaining hegemonic power over public policy and the law, and to block popular resistance. The national political parties in particular united state representatives in loyalty to a single organization that could compel its members to follow the party line. Politicians who would subordinate policy to winning office were readily persuaded by corporations to adopt favorable business policies "by providing parties and candidates with the money and troops to win elections."[10]

Like West Virginia generally, Tucker County was divided during the Civil War between supporters of the Union and the Confederacy. Many residents alive in the 1890s had fought in that war, and the attending cultural conflicts seriously aggravated the growing postwar struggle between incorporators and resisters. The industrial transition during the decades before and after the turn of the century was led by West Virginia's most prominent industrialist-politicians. Democratic senator Johnson Newlon Camden (1881–1887, 1893–1895) was a lieutenant of John D. Rockefeller and his Standard Oil trust, and also developed railroads, coal, and timber enterprises in the northern and central sections of the state. Another leader of the Democratic Party, Senator Henry G. Davis (1871–1883), also a developer of coal, timberlands, and railroads, was one of the most powerful industrialists in the state. To control the party apparatus, especially the selection of candidates for office and the distribution of patronage, the factions had to be brought into line with the policies supported by the leaders. Davis and Camden were not only political allies, they were fast friends, and usually they exerted influence by helping one another.[11]

Earlier in Davis's and Camden's careers, during the post–Civil War years, the state Democratic Party remained divided "between those who looked to the future and those who dwelt on the past." As leaders of the party, Camden and Davis, devoted significant time and resources to maintaining a governing coalition within the party among three major, mainly rural, traditional factions. "Redeemers" were generally former Confederates or sympathizers, and were represented by lawyers schooled in the land law inherited from Virginia. According to one state historian, the Redeemers "spoke for the southern and eastern West Virginia strongholds of Confederate sentiments and Virginia traditionalism and were usually conservative in their economic views; in fact, they yielded nothing to the industrialists in their anxiety to attract—and profit from—the investment capital needed to develop West Virginia's natural resources."[12] The "Agrarian" faction was composed of anticorporation and antimonopoly resisters. Notwithstanding their Southern leanings, they made a poor showing in the backwoods counties. Their greatest strength was located in northern and western counties along the Ohio and Kanawha river valleys and along the Baltimore & Ohio (B&O) Railroad. John J. Davis, a leading Agrarian, had been a Copperhead who opposed secession and was a firm advocate for the southern approach to racial issues. Old Virginia provided their cultural frame of reference, and they still mourned the Lost Cause. They saw Camden, Davis, and Republican leader Stephen B. Elkins as representatives of the outside incorporators, which, in fact, they were. The Agrarians seldom prevailed in intraparty skirmishes, but they occasionally stalemated a convention and forced the selection of compromise Democratic candidates. Another traditional-style political faction within the Democratic Party, the "Kanawha Ring," sympathized with the Confederacy and its heritage. State historian John A. Williams succinctly characterized the leaders of this faction, who were based in two prominent Charleston law firms, as adeptly combining "the traditional face-to-face style and political sympathies of circuit-riding lawyers in the southern interior with the practice of land and corporation law." In other words, they plied both sides of the fence, appealing to traditional southern farmers and Confederate sympathizers as well as the railroad corporations that were expanding into the interior sections. The Kanawha Ring represented, therefore, a hybrid of traditional and modern political styles.[13]

Underlying these intraparty tensions was a contest over how the business of politics should be conducted. In the words of one of the most astute scholars of West Virginia's politics during this era, "Entrenched in the interior counties and in tradition-minded districts along the Virginia border was a pre-industrial political system, whose social basis was kinship, propinquity, and deference to neighborhood and district notables. It rested on face-to-face communications, with linkages provided by lawyers and other itinerants who followed the rough mountain trails through settlements whose residents were scattered along the watercourses, isolated even from nearby neighbors by the difficult character of the terrain."[14]

Opposing the traditional political factions were the "Regular" Democrats led by Camden and Davis. The expansion of railroads, lumber camps, and coal mines during the 1880s and 1890s gradually eroded the traditionalists' political system and supplanted it with a modern one. "Among its features were centralized and continuously functioning machinery for the recruitment of candidates and the conduct of election campaigns," Williams observes. "Against the pre-industrial networks of information and influence that survived in West Virginia, Camden and Davis manned the axes of modern communications." They invested in Democratic newspapers, contributed financially to like-minded candidates, provided jobs, railroad passes, legal work, and other forms of private patronage to supporters. To control the party's position on issues of importance to them, Camden and Davis Regulars held a firm grip on the committees that controlled the nominating conventions, awarded credentials, constructed party platforms, and distributed campaign literature and funds. Either Camden or Davis led the West Virginia delegations to every Democratic National Convention from 1868 to 1892.[15]

The Democratic coalition finally began to break down in 1887 when Camden lost his seat in the U.S. Senate, opening the door for Republican Stephen B. Elkins to enter the state's political arena. Elkins successfully led the resurrection of the Republican Party and its ascent to power in the election of 1894. By the mid-1890s, therefore, the industrialists had gained power in both political parties. This state of affairs has been described as "a bipartisan 'merger' operated by and for the leading business interests of the state.... All were business and political associates or allies of integrated industrial concerns operated from Baltimore, Cleveland, Pittsburgh, or New York."[16]

It was at this exact point in the power struggle between the incorporators and resisters that their surrogates, Frank Thompson and Robert Eastham, confronted each other in the passenger car at the Parsons depot.

Bird's-eye view of Davis, West Virginia, and lumber mills along the Blackwater River. Courtesy of Sarah Thompson Fletcher.

Railroads

Early loggers floated timber down the state's streams to be gathered by distant log booms. They utilized hand tools readily available to backcountry farmers, but production was limited by manual labor, and transportation to the mills downstream depended on seasonal flooding from spring rains and snow melt. With timber between six and twelve feet in diameter, exploiting the vast virgin forest of the interior mountains required the steam-powered technology and heavy equipment which could only be brought to bear by the railroads. Development of the interior forests was only a dream until the east-west trunk lines of the B&O Railroad were laid through northern West Virginia in the 1850s, and then the Chesapeake & Ohio Railroad bisected southern West Virginia in the 1870s.

After these two trunk lines were in place, numerous small independent railroads sprouted out from the main lines. Along with more than 600 logging railroads, they completed an elaborate web of rails connecting the cutting face deep in the forest, the processing mills along the main lines, and the nation's markets. Even excluding the small logging and tram roads, track mileage in the state doubled in the 1880s, doubled again in the 1890s, and covered 3,705 miles in 1917.[17]

Where previously there had been only a thinly scattered farming population, the coming of the railroads caused small towns to spring up along the lines like wildflowers. According to James Morton Callahan, a prominent state historian writing at the peak of the timber boom in 1913, the railroads "carried into the silence of the primeval woods the hum of modern industry," bringing forth "gigantic lumber plants" and bustling new towns.[18] As the lines penetrated ever deeper into the forest, lumber towns were constructed as processing centers and staging areas for the final assault on the timber at the highest mountain summits where Tucker County awaited the age of steam power.

In northern West Virginia a smaller regional system connecting Cumberland, Maryland, to Parsons and Elkins, West Virginia, was established and operated by two of the state's most prominent industrialist-senators, Henry G. Davis and his son-in-law, Stephen B. Elkins. During the Civil War, Davis had quit his job as station agent for the B&O at Piedmont, Maryland, and entered business for himself selling cross ties and other supplies for the war effort. A loyal Unionist, and supporter of separate statehood for West Virginia in 1863, Davis served in the West Virginia legislature and then as U.S. senator from 1871 to 1883. His superior knowledge of the timberlands which he acquired during the search for war supplies prompted Davis to initiate a plan to drive his own railroad into northern West Virginia after the war. He began by purchasing options on timber and coal lands in Mineral, Grant, and Tucker counties. No ordinary businessman, Davis personally explored the northern mountains on horseback, searching out resources and buying lands, always with an eye to the best routes for railroad construction.[19]

With his brother Thomas and son-in-law Stephen Elkins, Davis raised the capital for a new enlarged road, the West Virginia Central & Pittsburgh Railroad (WVC&P), from other businessmen in politics. As a result, the list of stockholders in the new company read like a "Who's Who among the business-minded politicians." In fact, the line was popularly referred to as the "Senatorial Railway" because so many senators purchased stock, as did prominent congressmen, several cabinet members, and other powerful national figures.[20]

Davis's and Elkins's political connections extended as far as Washington and New York, but also down and into state politics as leaders of their respective parties, which was a great strategic advantage for their entrepreneurial projects. The West Virginia legislature approved the West Virginia Central and Pittsburgh Railroad charter on February 23, 1881. A very liberal document, the charter granted Davis and Elkins a flexible route, and the right to condemn land necessary for the construction of the railroad should the company encounter resistance from reluctant landowners. Davis was named president of the company, and Elkins vice president.[21] The WVC&P opened a line beyond the Piedmont, West Virginia, junction on the B&O, up the North Branch, and passed over the divide at the headwaters of the Potomac. In November 1884, the rails reached Davis in the heart of the Tucker County forest. The WVC&P tracks were then advanced to Parsons and finally reached Leadsville in the summer of 1889. A hamlet of a few houses in 1888, Leadsville changed its name to Elkins as a tribute to Stephen B., and city lots were laid out and land set aside for erecting the necessary railroad shop buildings. By 1895, the population of Elkins had grown to a few thousand, the town had a substantial business district, including the general offices of the WVC&P, and Davis and Elkins had established their permanent residences there.[22]

Prior to the arrival of the WVC&P, the northern mountain counties remained almost completely undeveloped. Even though the first settlers had arrived a century earlier, these counties remained so inaccessible that very few people had settled there. In 1913 state historian James M. Callahan observed that the mountain counties had remained in a wild and unsettled condition as a result of the difficulty of making mountain roads and the distance from railroad connections. The streams as a rule were not navigable for boats and were too swift for any use except floating timber. Consequently, this high, rugged region had been "neglected while the tide of investment and immigration passed by to the far west." With the arrival of the WVC&P all of that changed. According to Callahan, "The new road . . . expressed its material usefulness in gigantic lumber plants and rich coal mines, and in newly made and growing towns" that attracted "a good class of merchants who increasingly attracted trade from the surrounding country."[23]

Completion of the WVC&P into the higher elevations of Tucker County furnished an outlet for timber that was previously unexploitable. Numerous independent railroads shot out from the main line into the deepest heart of the high forest, followed by sawmills, pulp mills, tanneries, and lumber camps. Steam whistles broke the solitude that had reigned in this wilderness from its botanical birth, and sounded the death knell for West Virginia's most awesome primeval forest, and the beginning of the end of that traditional culture that had been secure since the first settlers had arrived. The railroad stimulated the development of lumber mills, pulp mills, tanneries, and secondary wood product manufacturers, but farmers also quickly turned to the railroad to ship livestock out of the counties through which it passed.[24]

Lumber

Railroads stimulated the convergence of technology, heavy transportation facilities, natural resources, and the national markets. Mountain mill towns became processing outposts of the expanding capitalist economy. An impressive number of band sawmills, the most technologically sophisticated operations, were established in West Virginia between 1890 and 1910. Single, double, and triple band mills operated one to three endless strips of steel saw blades, which could cut timber of up to eight feet in diameter. These mills were capable of cutting 100,000 to 140,000 board feet of lumber in an eleven-hour day.[25]

Within two decades a remarkable number of band mills were erected in the previously inaccessible mountain back counties. Towns proliferated wherever the great mills were constructed, flourished for a time, and then declined when the timber was cut out and the mills were closed. Over the entire forty-year period from 1890 to 1930, an estimated two hundred band mills cut through the West Virginia woods. The mountain counties of Tucker, Randolph, Pocahontas, and Nicholas, with the state's highest elevations and fewest people, led the state in the number of large mills and in the production of lumber. At the peak of production in 1910, 26,000 employees earned direct annual wages of more than $16 million in West Virginia's forest industries.[26]

Natives with small amounts of capital to invest, such as Robert W. Eastham, generally organized contracting companies and hired independent woodsmen to deliver timber to lumber mills. In the early stage of the timber boom, contractors were timbermen from the northern woods who brought a core of experienced woodsmen with them to West Virginia. Accustomed to working in the woods, local men soon predominated among the crews and contractors alike. Many of the operators who migrated to West Virginia from the northern states, disproportionately Pennsylvania, were working men looking for new opportunities. Information on conditions in West Virginia was transmitted through informal channels back to family and friends, attracting additional opportunity seekers. Other investors with access to substantially more capital also came from northern states and at least for a time became residents of West Virginia.[27] The dominant milling centers were established with external capital and by businessmen from other states, like the Thompsons, who had extensive experience and connections with the national markets.

One of the largest milling centers in the state between the 1880s and 1920s developed in Davis, Tucker County, around the triple band mill operated first by the Blackwater Boom and Lumber Company and then its successor, the Blackwater Lumber Company. The town was planned and carved out of the wilderness by Henry G. Davis in 1886, two years after Davis's WVC&P Railroad reached the site. Logging railroads went out from the mill center, even into the precipitous Blackwater Canyon itself. Albert Thompson reorganized the company as the Thompson Lumber Company and continued operation between January 1905 and June 1907, when the Babcock Lumber & Boom Company, a Pennsylvania firm, purchased the company and all of its subsidiary operations.[28]

This operation was only one of the major forest product plants in Davis, however. The Fairweather and LaDew Tannery, a New York-based company, was established in 1886, the same year that Jacob L. Rumbarger built the first sawmill. Hundreds of employees worked in the tannery and in the woods supplying the hemlock bark used in the tanning process. The Marshall Coal and Lumber Company, founded in 1888, operated a coal mine two miles away in Thomas, but also supplied timber for the mills of Davis. Between 1895 and 1920, the West Virginia Pulp and Paper Company operated a large pulp mill in Davis to supply its Maryland paper mill.[29]

In 1888, the Marshall Coal and Lumber Company acquired about 12,000 acres north and west of Davis owned by H. G. Davis and his brother Thomas. The organizers of this company represented some of the most influential industrial developers of their day: Augustus Shell, Jerome B. Chaffee, James G. Blaine, J. A. Condon, John R. McPherson, R. C. Kerens, William Windom, Thomas F. Bayard, Stephen B. Elkins, Thomas B. Davis, and Henry G. Davis. Thirty acres of this tract near Davis was subsequently purchased by the West Virginia Pulp and Paper Company, and they built their plant on this site.[30]

It is apparent, therefore, that when Robert Eastham took on the Thompsons it became a David and Golilath story in the making for the local populace in these back counties who identified with Eastham and traditional culture.

Commercialization

Many lumber towns were commercial centers in addition to being significant industrial sites, depending on their scale of operation. The mills not only brought in workers from outside the region, but also attracted job seekers from the countryside. As the population swelled, so too did the need for the social services required of a wage-earning population now dependent on others to produce their subsistence. A middle class of businessmen and professionals emerged to provide these services to the residents of the new towns and countryside. Stores of all description, hotels, banks, doctors, lawyers, teachers, and clergy increased dramatically in the lumber towns and commercial centers, all of whom had strong economic incentives to support the increased business activity.

The large mill towns attracted a comparatively large population, which in turn sparked a significant expansion in commercial and professional enterprises. Davis was incorporated on December 1, 1889, about five years after the railroad reached the site on November 1, 1884. Henry G. Davis owned all of the land, but he divided the town into lots and sold them fee simple. Most owners were responsible for constructing their own dwellings or other buildings.[31] Therefore, while he exerted substantial political and economic influence, Davis was uninterested in running a company-owned town.

In 1889 Davis had a population of 909, quickly stabilized at 3,000 during the next few years, and remained at that level until the late twenties. In its heyday Davis boasted Tucker County's first high school and first hospital; two national banks served the financial needs of the community, and two hotels provided rooms for travelers. Fourteen years after the electric light was invented, the Davis Electric Light Company was established to provide electricity for homes and businesses, and to light the streets. Two newspapers of different political persuasions served Davis, the *Davis Republican* and the *Davis News*, both founded in the 1890s. During Davis's sensational rise between 1886 and 1890, the town had three lawyers, three doctors, two dentists, two barbershops, two blacksmith shops, three butcher shops, two shoemaker shops, a printing office, a post office, two bakeries, two milliner shops, a harness shop, and numerous clothing, dry goods, and grocery stores. The

Presbyterians established the first church in Davis in 1886, and by 1900 four more churches opened their doors. In the mid-nineties an opera house was built with a 1,200 seat capacity and private boxes decorated in gold leaf. No lumber town would be complete without saloons; Davis officially listed six of them in 1910, but innumerable illegal saloons, or "pig ears," also operated in the neighborhood.[32]

Tucker County historian Homer Floyd Fansler claimed that "the Town of Davis struck awe into the rustic bumpkins of Canaan and Dry Fork." Fansler reproduced the following poem by an unknown author in his county history that suggests what proud town dwellers believed was the influence of the changes on isolated rural people in the countryside surrounding Davis:

Jes In Frum Caynane
I jes cum in frum the valley of Caynane,
An I heered the folks up thar a sayin
Bout this bein sich a peart like town,
I got on my hoss an thot I'd cum down
An seed for myself if what they said is true,
Bout havin steam injuns an water works tu.
Wall stranger I never wus in har afore;
It sprises me an I tell yer what's more,
If I hadn't cum down I'd never a knowd
How big yer town wus but I'll be blowed!
Jes seed the houses, tu fine fer me I own;
An dash my britches if thar aint one uv stone.
What's em ropes fer hung up on a pole,
An all em glass things, ell bless my soul;
What's that thing bangin up in the street?
It looks right smart, but stranger I'm beat;
Lectricity! An yer say it makes a light?

By gosh I'm gonna seed it if it takes all night.
Is that the thing that pulls out the train?
It must be, fer they say up in Caynane
That it cums to town a puffin an a blowin,
Wus than a hoss when he cums in frum mowin;
Oh! It's an injun, an has a tender behin,
An all em cars a standin in a line!
Do I rub snuff? Wall I reckon I do;
I been a hankerin all day for a chew;
Say, if yer don't keer, I'll take sum home
Fer the gals an my ole woman, Siloam;
She be the best critter an strong as a hoss,
Our kids air all gals an she be the boss.
Now my farm is jes tolable, yer see,
My ole woman says I can't pick a pea,
So her an the gals do the plantin an hoein
An I lay aroun an see the stuff growin;
Course sum days I pick up an go to the brook
An tote home any fish that gits on my hook.
I be bliged tu yer stranger, fer showin me aroun,
An I'll know more next time I cum tu yer town;
The roads up the mountain air powful rough,
Yer reckon yer could spare a little more snuff?
I be bliged agin an I be off fer home
An next time I cum I'll bring Siloam.[33]

Fansler and his poet exaggerated the power of boomtowns such as Davis as well as the rusticity of the backwoods "bumpkins." Nevertheless, the scale and immediacy of a town like Davis rising overnight out of a pervasive wilderness certainly made a profound impression. Throughout the mountain counties of West Virginia hundreds of lumber towns sprang up overnight.

Even though most of them thrived only so long as the timber held out, for decades they influenced the lives of town and country dwellers alike by providing employment, binding the country people to the cash economy, and radiating the expanding consumerism of the modern American economy and the professionalization of services. In the larger commercial and service centers, the general store was eclipsed by the department store and specialized shops, such as hardware, clothing, and drug stores. The mill town attracted people out of all proportion to its size because there were so few towns in this vast, rugged land clothed in dense forest. Whether they came for business or pleasure, people needed a place to sleep, so hotels were among the first businesses to spring up spontaneously in lumber towns. Even insignificant logging towns often had more than one hotel established not to serve townsfolk, but rather business travelers, railroaders, woodsmen, and rural mountain farmers in town for supplies or recreation. Banks were another indicator of the economic development that accompanied hand in glove the industrial transition in the mountains. Before the logging boom, and indeed throughout most of the state's history, the lack of banking facilities was perceived by West Virginians as a serious handicap to the development of the state. Business directories for 1891 indicate no banks in the logging towns of Tucker County, and even after a decade of rapid industrial expansion, only the large mill town of Davis and the county seat of Parsons supported their own banks. From a local contemporary perspective, banks in the nearby large towns and county seats represented a major advance over conditions that had prevailed before incorporation into the national market system. Not surprisingly, lawyers oscillated toward the county seats where court business was transacted or to the larger lumber towns, and physicians were found almost universally in the lumber towns as well. Davis was served by two lawyers and two physicians in 1891, and four lawyers and three physicians in 1906.

The burgeoning business and professional services found in the new towns required utilities previously unknown in the mountains. Most of the significant lumber towns had electricity, telephone service, and since towns hugged the railroads, Western Union telegraph service also was available as was railroad express service through the railroad depot. For residents and others who lived in the countryside, the lumber towns also represented a social center where people found recreation and entertainment. Generally, this meant activities that appealed to male timber workers in town to blow off steam with alcohol, gambling, prostitutes, billiards, and bowling, all popular pastimes in many lumber towns.

Davis boasted an opera house, which brought in live entertainment, normally musical follies or dramatic troupes. In fact, music played a much more important role in the lives of lumber towns of all sizes than might be expected, and not just the rowdy music associated with saloons and bawdy houses. Amateur bands and orchestras were popular throughout rural America during this period, and the lumber towns of Tucker County were no exception. Davis had a cornet band in 1902, and by 1906 Herbert L. Blaker had begun his long career as the leader of the Mountain City Band.[34]

Railroads and lumber mills also refocused services provided by government. With the penetration of capitalism, business and government merged in realigned county seats. St. George in Tucker County was a typical rustic mountain county seat of the preindustrial era. It had a population of three hundred in 1891, with little in the way of outside connections except through Parsons, seven wagon-road miles away on the WVC&PRR, and the nearest bank was twenty-four miles away in Philippi. Serving a farming population, the town had four general stores, a shoemaker, a blacksmith, and a grist mill. As the county seat, it had need of the four hotels, eight lawyers, and one physician. St. George never was much of a commercial center, but after the county seat was moved to Parsons in 1893, it lost all signs of its previous importance. Twenty years later a few artisans continued to serve local farmers and loggers, but all of the hotels had closed their doors, and not a single lawyer or physician hung his shingle in the community.

What a difference in the new county seat of Parsons, just upstream on the Cheat River, at the junction of the WVC&P Railroad. The new town was developed as a shipping center and the removal of county government to Parsons brought additional power and commerce. In 1891, even before the county seat was moved to Parsons, business directories described the town as "the distributing point for a large section of country," and as "one of the most prosperous towns on the [WVC&PP] road."[35]

The population of Parsons quadrupled between 1892 and 1902, from 300 to 1,200, mostly because it achieved county seat status in 1893, and its role as a commercial-industrial hub continued to expand. In 1902, less than a decade later, the two largest lumber-related operations were the Milton Tannery Company and the Parsons Pulp and Paper Company. A large flouring mill continued to process grains from the countryside both for domestic use and export. Commerce also was booming now with eight general stores, two meat markets, three restaurants, a clothing store, one grocer, a druggist, confectioner, and other artisan-related businesses found in most towns of this period. Perhaps most telling of its new status, however, were the eight lawyers, six physicians, three hotels, a national bank, and two weekly newspapers, the *Tucker Democrat* and the *Parsons Advocate*.[36]

The railroad connected the lumber mill towns to the national markets and opened the way for economic development. Prosperity was welcomed, but incorporation into the larger world also challenged traditional cultural values that did not necessarily keep pace with changes in the political economy, all pointedly illustrated by the Eastham-Thompson feud.

2

MODERNIZING THE LAW

Making Capital Secure

While the desire for industrial development was strong among West Virginia's statehood leaders, the institutional mechanisms necessary to realize that goal simply were not in place. Before the dream could be fulfilled another kind of revolution was necessary, one that would transform the law into a progressive partner in industrial development rather than a protector of the traditional local autonomy that was woven into the fabric of backwoods culture. The legal revolution would have to start with the Constitution of 1863. The founders of West Virginia seceded from Virginia in 1863, and the state's Republican Party, which existed in name only before the Civil War, swiftly rose to power and then just as swiftly declined after the war. With the return of former Confederates to the polls, however, it seemed inevitable that the party that had "Yankeefied" government, delivered the vote to Lincoln in 1864, and secured ratification of the Thirteenth, Fourteenth, and Fifteenth amendments, would be doomed to an ignominious death in a state where approximately 40 percent of the population had supported the Confederacy.[1]

The election of 1870 marked the end of Republican rule in West Virginia, an interlude swept away by the resurgent tide of a revitalized Democratic Party. The Democratic ascendancy, which lasted from 1870 until a new Republican Party emerged to take control in 1896, marked the reestablishment of governmental control by the older, landed local elites and their lawyers. Their triumphal return was dramatized in the theater of the Constitutional Convention of 1872.

Whereas the Republicans held the liberal view that free markets would produce the desired economic transformation of West Virginia, the "Bourbon Democrats" who replaced them accepted the views of their antebellum forbears that the elites should control government in order to control the economy. Even though the Democratic Party harbored several major political factions, they all exhibited a faith in the railroad as the engine of that hoped-for economic transformation.

West Virginians during this period were deeply engaged in a new political struggle for control of an expanding capitalist economy. On the one side stood the older, conservative, agrarian world of the nineteenth century, and on the other stood the emerging industrial world of the twentieth century. The industrialists would eventually vanquish the agrarians, but the ideological contest was not between the Republican and Democratic parties, for both parties were converts to the development faith. The struggle was fought along philosophical lines defining the role of government in the economy, and the kind of legal system that would adjudicate conflicts between the competing cultures of the "old" and "new" orders.

Investment placed a heavy demand on capital, and as production improved, technology became increasingly more expensive. But like their counterparts elsewhere, West Virginia lumbermen also demanded that the law should assist them in overcoming their lack of capital in order to develop the state's resources. Transportation presented perhaps the greatest problem. The improvement of streams and the construction of railroads required the mobilization of capital on a scale that individuals could not accomplish on their own. Therefore, corporations were granted privileges to dam streams or change their flow which required the permission of the law, and without the special power of eminent domain, railroads were vulnerable to the recalcitrant landowner who refused to sell a right-of-way.

Direct public indebtedness to sponsor business projects was unconstitutional in West Virginia, as it was in Virginia, but that did not stop the state from providing indirect subsidies to major industries such as railroads. Public subsidy to improve water transportation for lumber was never undertaken in West Virginia, especially in comparison with the public assistance provided to railroads. The lumber industry during this period developed no giant corporations that could compare with the railroads, and so its ability to exert political power was comparatively limited. It was through indirect stimulus that the law promoted investment in the lumber industry, which conformed to the principal theme of nineteenth-century policy.[2]

The desire to encourage industrial development in the nineteenth century by releasing individual initiative from state interference, and the contemporary view that this served rather than exploited the public, is amply illustrated by the privileges granted to entrepreneurs by West Virginia legislators. While mill-dam and timber-boom operators were granted permission to construct dams across streams, for example, they were not permitted to build them in waters navigated by steamboats, or to be built in such a way as to block the streams used by other logging companies. Similarly, the legislature granted mill and boom companies the power to condemn land under eminent domain that was needed to operate their businesses. Nevertheless, the thrust of these public franchises, given the government's inability to enforce them, was to bolster the development of business by placing industrial organizations in a much stronger legal position relative to traditional users of the streams. The same laws regarding condemnation under eminent domain pertained to a range of industries in addition to timber, including the railroads, quarries, mills, salt wells, and lime kilns, among others.[3]

Similarly, public support for the timber industry is evidenced in the protection granted to companies from financial losses through the theft of logs being transported downstream to booms. The state required that each company file a brand with the clerk of the county court, and logs bearing the company's mark were admissible as evidence of ownership. If logs washed up on someone else's land, the company was given sixty days to remove them; to disturb them during this period was a misdemeanor. To steal a branded log worth ten dollars or more was grand larceny, punishable by one to five years in prison.[4]

Some legal scholars have argued that nineteenth-century courts gave so many advantages to industry in disputes with traditional users of the land as to actually "subsidize" industrialization. Whatever the case elsewhere in America, this definitely was not the way courts behaved in nineteenth-century Virginia, dominated as they were by conservatives who wanted a common law grounded in custom and tradition rather than science or economics. The roots of this tradition reached deep into the colonial period. Local gentry and justices of the peace maintained their power in Virginia, and the law continued to be a profession practiced in county courthouses before local juries with decisions based on common law and natural rights philosophy. The system required that government be limited and decentralized, and did not sanction using the law as a lever to reform government, society, or the economy.[5]

This preference for the common law and local government, a style characterized as "country over court," had evolved in a planter-dominated society confronted periodically with debt problems. In this society, the common law practiced by local lawyers before juries made up of their neighbors was considered the "shield of liberty" against strong "foreign" government or debtors suing to take away the farmers' land. Juries of farmers supported their neighbors in such cases because they believed that retention of the land was a more fundamental right than a merchant's right to collect on a debt. Thus in Virginia the county government was ruled by local gentry who served in the state legislature in order to protect local interests. Judges of the Virginia Supreme Court of Appeals buttressed this system by rejecting attempts to break down the power of the local courts in order to foster industrial development, and time and again they interpreted the law in favor of the agrarian landowners in contests with capitalists. In Virginia, the gentry dominated a government to insure that political power remained at the county level.[6]

West Virginia retained this decentralized, static approach to government and the law when it emerged as a separate state in 1863. One important point of difference between the new state and its eastern relative was that nearly everybody in West Virginia wanted internal improvements, yet they were much more ambivalent than Virginians about how the costs should be allocated. West Virginia subsidized industry through special privileges and tax breaks, but the courts proved resistant because of the legal tradition on which decisions were based. In a transition of personnel and judicial philosophy that has not been duplicated since, the West Virginia Supreme Court of Appeals experienced a "legal revolution" in 1889–1890. Resistance to industrial development evaporated on the high court as a generation of judges who adhered to Virginia traditions was replaced by a new generation reflecting a modern, positivist legal philosophy.

The change in approach to industrial development from the Old Court to the New Court was so dramatic as to constitute a watershed event. After 1890 the court abandoned the traditional strict liability principle favoring agrarian over industrial users of the land and adopted an approach that accepted multiple economic uses for the land. The timing of this pivotal redirection is explained in part by the rapid influx of capital into railroad, timber, and coal development. The older system was simply incapable of withstanding this deluge of capital, which accentuated the inadequacies of the traditional approach and then dissolved it. In the late nineteenth century, lawyers and judges still rode the circuit in West Virginia's rural, isolated countryside, except for the approximately one-third of the state represented by the old settled town and farm areas.

The West Virginia Supreme Court of Appeals has gone through several distinct political transitions since statehood. The first court of the 1860s was composed of statehood leaders, men who had been active in the movement and could be depended on to defend the new state from its Virginia enemies. The Republicans who led the drive for separate statehood identified with the Union rather than the Confederacy and the commercial culture of the North rather than the traditional agrarianism inherited from Virginia. As the former Confederate Democrats regained power in the 1870s, the new members who took seats on the court overwhelmingly were men who had supported secession and the emphasis on common law tradition that favored traditional landowners.

The emergence of large corporations in West Virginia did not begin until the 1880s, but when they did arrive, they produced social and economic problems that forced the old system into bankruptcy. The New Court of 1889–1890 finally made a complete break with Virginia legal tradition and reinterpreted the law to favor, rather than hinder, industrial development. A major study of nuisance cases by legal scholar Jeffrey Lewin concludes that, until the Civil War, American courts staunchly supported the legal rule of *sic utere tuo ut alienum non laedas* ("so use your own as not to injure that of another") in cases that involved conflicts of property rights emanating from industrial nuisances. Lewin argues that American jurists generally viewed property as a "natural right"; therefore, property owners should enjoy legal protection against any interference with the use of their property. This reasoning, of course, protected a status quo dominated by agricultural interests, which represented the overwhelming majority of Americans in the early nineteenth century. Over the course of the nineteenth century, however, industrial growth forced judges to shift away from natural rights and to adopt a more dynamic approach to the nuisances created by industry, such as fire, smoke, noise, pollution, flooding, and other damages.[7]

This was not the evolution of legal history in Virginia, however. Throughout the nineteenth century the Virginia Supreme Court adhered to a "static" theory of property rights that focused on maintaining the rights of agricultural plaintiffs in disputes with industrial defendants. Early West Virginia nuisance decisions rendered by the Supreme Court of Appeals generally conformed with Virginia legal tradition by upholding the plaintiffs' right to be free of interference in the enjoyment of their property.[8]

After 1890, the Supreme Court of Appeals judges abandoned the static view of their Virginia-trained forbears and, to the great relief of business and government leaders, adopted a dynamic theory that recognized the economic use of property for commercial and industrial enterprise as well as for agriculture. The significance of this transformation of nuisance law became readily apparent to farmers, who represented about two-thirds of the state's population in 1890. For them the new approach revealed itself in how jurists applied the law in fencing cases, in assessing damage liability for livestock killed by locomotives, and in cases involving fires ignited by sparks from locomotives or other steam engines employed on logging and lumber operations. But the New Court was so bold in reversing the strict liability standard in nuisance and negligence cases that its decisions can only be interpreted as the judicial subsidization of industry to the disadvantage of other segments of society. The failure of natural rights theories to resolve the tensions created by industrial uses of the land prompted the new court to adopt a "reasonable use" rule recognizing the rights of both agriculture and industry in nuisance disputes. This approach focused on *how* property was used on a "scale of reasonableness" defined by the circumstances. If the court determined that plaintiffs contributed to the damage, for example, then their "contributory negligence" shifted some of the absolute liability away from defendants who acted "reasonably." In effect, the court adopted the concept that industry and agriculture represented competing interests, although both had a right to the enjoyment of their property.[9]

This concept fit into the broader philosophical boundaries of "legal positivism," which replaced the "natural rights" focus of the court at the turn of the century and substituted a utilitarian criteria quantified by a kind of social cost-benefits analysis to determine what was in the public interest. Thus the intentional invasion of another's right to the use and enjoyment of property was defined as "unreasonable" unless the resultant public good outweighed the gravity of the harm. This was a radical departure from traditional reasoning. Whereas natural rights rested on a foundation of normative, universal principles, legal positivism assumed that costs and benefits were related and should be weighed quantitatively in order to determine what was in the public's interest.[10]

In addition to the multitude of railroad cases that passed through the Supreme Court of Appeals during the industrial transition, a number of cases related to logging and boom companies also came before the court. These cases demonstrate the dynamic approach taken by the judges in conflicts over industrial activity. The reasonable use rule applied by the New Court was most often associated with cases involving riparian rights and stream flow. Perhaps the most important precedent-setting case heard by the court during the transition was *Gaston v. Mace*, which established the legal rights of the lumber interests to use non-navigable mountain streams. In fact, the central issue of this case pivoted around the question of whether the common law interpretation of navigable streams as public highways was applicable to non-navigable streams in the back counties where the big timber was located. In *Gaston v. Mace* the court simply altered the definition of a public highway as the term applied to watercourses.

The case itself involved the owner of a mill dam on Stone Coal Creek, Lewis County, who sought damages for the destruction of his water-powered mill and dam by logs driven downstream in November 1884. The defendants claimed that the stream was navigable, that they therefore had a right to float timber on it, but the plaintiff had obstructed the stream with his mill dam by refusing to construct a sluice. The jury rejected the mill owner's claim for damages in July 1885, and sided with the defendants. Arguing his case before the Supreme Court of Appeals, the mill owner claimed that he had prior rights to the use of his mill and dam because it had been in continuous operation since 1818, on a stream that was not navigable except in the occurrence of floods from rain or melting snow. The plaintiff argued for his common law right to continue using his property without interference and asked that the defendants be held to strict liability for damages to the mill. The circuit judge determined otherwise, however, and emphasized to the jury that the real issue was whether the stream was navigable, and whether a dam or getting the products of the country to market was more beneficial to society.[11]

The high court affirmed the lower court's verdict, but rejected the argument that the stream's navigability was the central issue, declaring that, even though the stream was *not* navigable, it was a "floatable" stream. The court held that the rights of the public and riparian property owners in such a stream was governed by "reasonable use," and declared that the test to be applied in such cases was not whether a stream was navigable, but whether it was capable of floating vessels, rafts, or logs for purposes of commerce. Traditional users of watercourses who had always relied on a natural rights defense could take little comfort from the court's reasoning that time alone was no determinant of riparian rights. The plaintiff's dam, constructed without a sluice, and for most of the nineteenth century regarded as a benefit to society, was now deemed a public nuisance because it did not accommodate the industrial use of the stream.[12] The Supreme Court affirmed the circuit court's ruling, but took the opportunity to move the argument beyond traditional terms by implementing a more dynamic theory of the law's role in shaping society, one which directly benefitted industry over agriculture. How riparian law would be applied was, therefore, undergoing a dynamic reversal just at the time when Robert Eastham and Frank Thompson began suing and countersuing each other in county court over use of the Blackwater River.

The Courthouse War

Industrial development profoundly altered West Virginia's prevailing political culture. Before the 1880s, political affiliation was aligned along the traditional axes of Democrat-Confederate-agrarian versus Republican-Unionist-industrial sympathies. With industrialization, however, economic interests marginalized all other concerns within both political parties. The traditional political factions within the Democratic Party became secondary but did not disappear entirely, surfacing during intraparty power struggles and elections. At the local level political realignment is clearly revealed in the more than twenty West Virginia county-seat wars, primarily struggles among local elites to relocate old county seats along the transportation corridors where economic development would follow.

Charles Ambler, the noted state historian, alluded to this realignment as a contest between "Bourbon Agrarians" and "Ironheaded Industrialists," a conflict between those who wanted to maintain the dominance of agrarian life, republican values, and the personal political style that prevailed in nineteenth-century Virginia against those "progressives" who looked to the industrial, market-oriented twentieth century, and political parties that became loyal cadres who followed orders from the top—the "Republican Party Army."[13]

Another state historian, John A. Williams, elaborated on this theme by demonstrating that the preindustrial elite who owned the land were drawn from the circuit-riding lawyers who traveled to back-county courthouses in the conduct of their business. Therefore they were well acquainted with the people, and politics evolved into a personalized agrarian style. These networks of personal acquaintances grew into courthouse cliques, which in the back counties were likely to be traditional Virginia Democrats in politics, and became a major source of resistance to separate statehood and the Union. After statehood, the separatist leaders, usually Republicans, denounced these courthouse cliques as bastions of resistance to modernization.[14]

The founders of statehood constituted a new mélange of Whigs, Republicans, and Union Democrats who were more economically utilitarian than they were party faithful or political radicals. They lived in the economically developed industrial and commercial farming counties of northern and western West Virginia where "the politics of kinship and deference, isolation and parochialism" had given way to modern communications, bureaucratic organization, and a literate electorate with a partisan press to unify their adherents. In other words, Williams argues, they established the "modern party system" during their relatively short reign between 1863 and 1872.[15] They also approved a state constitution that eliminated the county court system.

The Democrats regained power in the elections of 1870, and the grievances that grew out of the war and the treatment of ex-Confederates were quickly resolved by a Democratic Party–controlled convention in 1872, which approved a new state constitution. The first order of business was to restore the county court system, thereby reestablishing "the most important institutional means by which local notables sustained themselves in power and influence," according to Williams. The inevitable result was the restoration of those "courthouse cliques" so important to traditional Democrats. Future Republican industrialist-politicians also learned to control them in the 1890s.[16]

Arrival of the railroad was sufficient to stimulate political realignments in the back counties as the old courthouse cliques, and the location of the county seat itself, came under pressure from those who sought to benefit from commercial and industrial development. In a state that was highly sectionalized, and where the rugged terrain determined that politics would be local, the location of the county seat was a leading source of factional conflict. Since the county seat usually was the commercial, social, governmental, and geographical center of the nineteenth-century mountain county, an inaccessible county seat was a significant handicap to residents. Most people traveled by horse, and with roads often little more than bridle paths, travel was always difficult and sometimes impossible. Accessibility, therefore, was the most common, and legitimate, rationale for establishing a new county seat.

Much was at stake in who controlled the county seat. The courthouse itself was the symbol of dominance in this contested terrain, for the side that ruled the courthouse also controlled official functions, such as law enforcement, court proceedings, tax collections, and school administration. The railroad completely changed the spatial significance of the county seat from geographic center to business center where revenues that sustained the county's institutions were generated. "Center" came to mean location in the transportation and communication network that connected the county and its hinterland to the national market system.

Although physical control translated into real material advantages, possession of the courthouse also was symbolically significant for the contesting political cultures. The elections for removal usually involved a long bitter struggle waged to win the hearts and minds of the people. In this contest the industrialists and their local boosters, such as the shopkeepers, professionals, and land developers, all stood to benefit financially from the economic transition. These were the agents of change in the timber-rich mountain counties. Penetration by the West Virginia Central and Pittsburgh Railroad transformed the social and economic landscape in Tucker County and shifted the center of local political power. As in the other mountain counties, the showdown between the Ironheads and the Agrarians to control the county seat was emblematic of how the "old" republican-agrarian culture was pushed aside by the "new" culture of industrial capitalism.

The Tucker County seat of St. George suffered an irreversible setback in 1888 when, instead of coming down the Cheat River through St. George to Rowlesburg, the WVC&P Railroad bypassed the county seat on its way to Elkins by following Shavers Fork River. Just eight miles away, at the confluence of Shavers Fork and Black Fork rivers, the new town of Parsons began to grow, and was incorporated in June 1893. Parsons's rapid growth was matched by St. George's precipitous decline.[17]

From its inception the developers of Parsons planned that their town would become the county seat. Parsons boasted a population of less than fifty people on February 12, 1889, when a group of town developers headed by Ward Parsons, the primary booster and the town's namesake, filed a petition with the county court requesting that the people be canvassed on the issue of relocating the county seat from St. George to Parsons. It took several more petition drives and elections until, in the special election held on April 28, 1893, the voters finally sided with the developers in making Parsons the new county seat. Bids were opened for moving the records, furniture, and other county property from St. George to a temporary courthouse in Parsons. St. George would not be vanquished so easily, however, and the St. George men continued to resist the removal. Adam C. Minear, an ex-sheriff from St. George's most prominent family, filed a bill of exceptions with the county court protesting election irregularities. When the court overruled this bill, Minear and William M. Cayton, a St. George resident and the county clerk, secured an injunction from the State Supreme Court of Appeals to prevent the removal.[18]

The Parsons faction received this information with great irritation, realizing that an injunction might delay removal perhaps for years. Drastic action was called for, and Ward Parsons and his most trusted partners in the removal enterprise decided to take matters into their own hands by forcibly removing the county property from St. George. Forming an "army" of about two hundred armed men, with wagon teams and horse-drawn buggies, the men assembled in Parsons on the evening of August 1, 1893, for a march on St. George to liberate the court records. The train brought about seventy men from Davis enlisted by Robert W. Eastham whom the county historian described as a "swashbuckling . . . local bigwig of Davis."[19]

The invaders arrived at St. George at about 9:30 P.M. where they met defenders who also were armed. The St. George defenders apparently were intimidated by the much larger force from Parsons, however, and they withdrew. Sheriff Will E. Cupp ordered the crowd to disperse, but he was ignored. Because the courthouse was locked, entry was gained through a broken window, and the doors thrown open from within. All of the county records and furniture were loaded onto wagons, including the bell which hung in the steeple, and the boisterous procession began its withdrawal to the more friendly confines of Parsons.[20]

The sun came up on the morning of August 2, 1893, to find the Tucker County seat in Parsons, where the courthouse was established temporarily in the same building that housed the Knights of Pythias fraternal lodge. In 1900 the present Tucker County courthouse was completed and occupied. Reports of the episode went out over the wires, and newspapers throughout the state and nation reviled the participants and deplored the episode as an insult to law and order by backwoods ruffians.[21]

Following considerable political intrigue and legal jockeying the issue found its way to the West Virginia Supreme Court of Appeals. In *Hamilton et al. v. Tucker County Court et al.* the high court ruled in favor of the Parsons men. Justice Henry Brannon,

The "removers" of county seat records from St. George to Parsons, 1893. Robert Eastham is probably standing at the front and center of the photograph. Courtesy of the West Virginia and Regional History Center.

writing for the court, declared that no matter how the records were removed, the people of Tucker County had voted, and the county court had declared Parsons the new county seat. These proceedings had been lawful, and an earlier, forcible removal did not change that fact.[22]

In a special local dispatch a reporter claimed that the "best citizens" regarded the forced removal as "a disgrace to Tucker County," and one that was likely to "breed a feud which will be serious in its results." Just who the "best citizens" were is open to interpretation, but the reporter was either ignorant of the facts or did not regard the professionals and businessmen of Parsons and Davis as members of that group, for they were the most prominent figures in the removal. Among them were Ward Parsons, the major figure in the entire struggle to remove the county seat and one of the wealthiest landowners in Tucker County; Solomon W. Kaler, a trustee of the local Presbyterian Church who subsequently served as mayor of Parsons; C. G. Lashley, who served as the mayor of Davis in 1900–1901; Robert W. Eastham who was contracted to clear the land on which Davis was laid out, owned a timber supply company and a general store, and was one of Senator H. G. Davis's local lieutenants; Cyrus O. Strieby, a prominent lawyer from Davis; Dr. Bascom B. Baker, a graduate of the Baltimore College of Physicians and Surgeons with a medical practice in Tucker County; James P. Scott, a newspaperman who took up the law and became the Tucker County Prosecuting Attorney; and Samuel O. Billings, a partner in the prosperous Cheat River Milling & Feed Company who served as county clerk and as surveyor during this period. Biographies of the most active individuals involved in the three-year campaign to move the county seat, a total of twenty-nine individuals, reveal that they cannot be identified with the delineators of the old political system that pitted northern Unionist-Republican-statehood-industrialists against southern secessionist-Democrat-anti-statehood-agrarians.[23] Indeed, as a group the leaders in the movement project a highly diverse collective profile. Some of the removers were either former Confederates or their families took a strong stand for secession. Ward Parsons himself, the driving force behind the movement, was the most influential local secessionist, and his friend Robert W. Eastham of Davis was an unreconstructed Rebel. Riley Harper, who served as Tucker County sheriff from 1897 to 1901, also came from a family of Confederates. However, Sansome E. Parsons, Ward's half-uncle, was a strong Union man, as was Arnold H. Bonnifield, who had gone to California with his family after the state was redeemed in 1872 to escape the hostility directed against him for his Union stand.

Lorenzo Dow Corrick's father, the first settler on the land where the town of Parsons was constructed, and Ward Parson's neighbor, was known as a "rabid Unionist." Most of the men, however, were too young to personally identify with either side during the war. A few were not locally born so that little is known of their position on secession, the war, or statehood.[24]

As with attitudes toward secession and statehood, political affiliation is not a defining element in the profile of the Parsons faction. The Parsons family, one of the oldest and largest in the county, was equally divided into Democrats and Republicans, although Ward Parsons was prominent among local Democrats. Samuel O. Billings, a partner in Cheat River Milling & Feed Company who held the county offices of clerk and surveyor, was a Republican. On the other hand, Robert W. Eastham was a Democrat, as was Sheriff Riley Harper. John B. Jenkins, who succeeded Harper as sheriff and held other county offices, was the superintendent of the Cumberland Coal Company in Douglas, Tucker County, and a member of the Republican Party. James P. Scott, the newspaperman turned lawyer, later was elected prosecuting attorney as a Democrat. Cyrus O. Strieby, a Pennsylvanian who moved to West Virginia and established a prominent legal practice in Tucker County, also was a Democrat. But Arthur Jay Valentine, a corporation lawyer in Parsons who served as local counsel for the WVC&P Railroad, Mosser & Company, the Otter Creek Boom & Lumber Company, and the Hamilton Leather Company, was a Republican.

What was it, then, that drew this diverse group of men into a common cause? A general profile of the twenty-nine removers who can be identified from among the approximately two hundred participants in the removal of the county records demonstrates that nearly all of the promoters were native West Virginians, most of them locally born. Their average age was about forty, and so they were in the prime of their lives. Many held public office of some type during their careers, and fifteen of the twenty-nine held numerous local offices. Also, they were leaders in the community: four lawyers, one doctor, eleven merchants, five in the timber industry, one in the coal industry, and six large farmers. Fourteen of the men whose residences can be determined either lived in or near Parsons, or were residents of Davis. The only common delineators among this heterogeneous group of removers, therefore, are economic opportunity and personal gain.

H. G. Davis's WVC&P Railroad was completed to Davis in 1884, but throughout the 1880s tens of thousands of acres had been purchased in anticipation of railroad construction. Everybody knew it was coming, and a struggle for control of local politics ensued between the Ironheads and the Agrarians for control of the county Democratic Party. From the moment Davis decided to extend the railroad up the Dry Fork and down the Tygart Valley to Elkins, the industrialists had the motive required for supporting removal of the county seat to a location on the railroad, and Parsons was located on the most promising commercial real estate in Tucker County. No historical "smoking gun" points directly at Henry G. Davis, but he almost certainly was involved. Several key figures in the removal faction were Davis lieutenants: Valentine and Strieby, for example, handled the senator's local legal affairs, and Eastham, who led a large contingent of Davis residents who engaged in the forced removal of the court records, surveyed Davis's timberlands, laid out the town of Davis, and was a trusted friend and confidant of Davis's brother Tom. Although no direct link has been established between Davis and Ward Parsons, the industrialist certainly would have been more confident about doing business with a "heads-up" development booster such as Parsons than the St.

George farmers. Moreover, the commercial ambitions of the removers were in perfect alignment with Davis's understanding of progress.[25]

The movement to transfer the county seat in Tucker County was powered by local men with economic motives, and undoubtedly supported by the invisible hand of H. G. Davis. The struggle to control the courthouse in neighboring Randolph County was openly supported by Davis's Republican son-in-law and business partner Stephen B. Elkins. Explaining the battle to his readers, a Pittsburgh newspaper reporter observed that "under other circumstances a county seat war might be a mere passing event," but on the ground "it stood for everything. It was the meeting of the old and the new civilization," a conflict between "tradition with all of its sentiment and modern industry with all of its disregard for tradition." It was a "collision between the young men who believed in business . . . and the old men who have veneration for their home and the bones of their ancestors." The contest was so spirited because it was "the ruthless assault of nineteenth-century progress upon the posterity of the pioneers" who settled in the mountains generations ago.[26] "Old" and "new" pulled in the same direction during the county-seat wars in Tucker and Randolph counties, but the reporter did not understand that, even though both sides wanted industry, they wanted to control it for quite different ends. The feud between Robert Eastham and Frank Thompson reveals this broader truth as it impacted individuals on the ground.

3

ROBERT W. EASTHAM, THE EARLY YEARS

Among the great outdoorsmen of his time Robert Eastham was a legend. He moved into the Canaan wilderness of Tucker County in 1876 with little more than a rifle and an axe and succeeded in carving out a prosperous life. His Civil War service to the Confederacy as a member of the intrepid Mosby's Rangers brought him equal portions of admiration from Confederate sympathizers and deep disdain from Yankee detractors. In the folklore that grew up around Eastham's numerous exploits, it is nearly impossible to separate fact from fiction, but to those who knew him any tale of derring-do seemed plausible.

Family History

Robert Woodford Eastham descended from a very long line of Easthams in Virginia. The first ancestor in the colony of Virginia was born in England in 1621 and immigrated in 1637. A son, George Eastham (born 1663), was father to the very first Robert Eastham born in 1705 in Gloucester County. Robert bought 1,000 acres of land in King and Queen County from one Thomas Guy in 1728, and, according to local legend he acquired the plantation house on that land by winning a gamble. Fortunately, legends do not require evidence for there is none either to support or reject this story. In 1742, Robert Eastham was commissioned a captain in the Virginia militia, and in 1755 Governor Robert Dinwiddie promoted him to the rank of colonel. He served in the French and Indian War protecting the British forts built along the eastern ridges of the Appalachians as a line of defense against Indian attacks on the eastern settlements. Colonel Eastham also held the position of Justice of Orange County in the 1750s. His wife Anne Lawson gave birth to a son, William Eastham, in 1734, and he married Frances Byrd in 1753. Their son, Byrd Eastham, born in 1762, married Lucy Chapman, and in the 1790s they became the first Easthams to settle in Rappahannock County. Their son, Benjamin Franklin Eastham (1813–1887), "Captain Frank" as he was universally known, married Lucy Elizabeth Browning (1818–1858) in 1841, and together they raised a large brood of ten children on Buena Vista farm. The eldest of them was Robert Woodford Eastham.[1]

Captain Frank owned five slaves in 1840, but, as his estate grew over the next decade, so did the number of slaves. In the 1850 U.S. Federal Census Slave Schedules, Frank was listed as a farmer whose real estate was valued at $12,000, a substantial portion of which was tied up in seventeen slaves. With such a large household to manage, Captain Frank could not wait long to find a partner after his wife Lucy died in 1858, and in November 1859 he wed Sarah A. Wall, a widow. For reasons now unknown, by 1860 the slave schedules show that Benjamin F. Eastham no longer owned slaves.

The Civil War

Fact and legend are sometimes indistinguishable when referring to R. W. Eastham's role in the Civil War. Certainly his entire family experienced the war that raged at their doorstep.

Including Robert Eastham's close relatives, it is claimed that fifteen Easthams fought in Stonewall Jackson's Brigade.[2] The family seat in and near Flint Hill, Rappahannock County, was but a few miles from Front Royal. Armies of the North and South crisscrossed the area throughout the war so it would have been impossible for the Easthams and their neighbors to avoid the bloodshed and devastation.

Franklin Dabney Eastham (born 1843), Robert's junior by one year, nearly died from battle wounds. Known by his middle name, Dabney, he joined his brother Robert Woodford in enlisting in the 6th Virginia Cavalry, Company B, which sent the Union army into retreat toward Winchester at the Battle of Front Royal. At the Battle of Cedarville, Company B was at the point of the cavalry charge and took heavy casualties, including Dabney who was severely wounded. He was taken to the old stone house that served as a field hospital (and still stands on state route 522). Determining that he was near death, they laid him in the field next to the hospital and sent word to his father. When Captain Frank and a slave came to get him, Dabney's blood had matted with the ground so they dug up the ground around him. Placing him on a garrison wagon, they took him back home to Flint Hill where he was nursed back to health by his first cousin Jennie Eastham. Dabney subsequently married her.[3]

Brother Philip Byrd Eastham (1845–1933) was only sixteen when the Civil War began. Captain Frank would not give him permission to enlist unless Robert, who was three years older, took care of him. He enlisted in the 7th Virginia Cavalry, Company E, and then joined the 43rd Battalion, Virginia Cavalry, Company B, when Mosby's Command was established in 1863. Mosby's Rangers were involved in many harrowing escapades during the war, but his brother Robert W. was in Company D and could keep a watchful eye on his younger brother. According to

Robert's great nephew and namesake, the late Robert Woodford Eastham III, Philip always looked up to his older brother and claimed that he lived through the war only because he "taught him the tricks of guerrilla warfare." After the war Philip married Mafie Deatherage (1872–1947) and the couple had two children. Philip was killed in an unfortunate accident when a car struck him in Front Royal in 1933. Both he and his wife are buried in Prospect Hill Cemetery, Front Royal, Virginia.[4]

Robert Woodford Eastham (February 28, 1842–April 7, 1924), one writer claims, "decided to secede even before the state of Virginia did." True in sentiment, but not factually exact. President Lincoln called for 75,000 volunteers to suppress the southern rebellion on April 15, 1861, prompting Virginia to secede two days later on April 17. Robert Eastham left home for his county seat of Washington shortly thereafter and enlisted in the Rappahannock Cavalry, also known as the Old Guard, commanded by Captain John Shackelford Green. Military records described Eastham as a nineteen-year-old farmer, six feet two inches tall, with "auburn hair, fair complexion, and blue eyes." He used his middle name rather than his first, signing on as "Woodford Eastham," a practice he adopted throughout his military experience. The company was ordered into service at Fairfax Court House on May 20, 1861. Eastham arrived for duty with his horse "Steamboat" and personal property valued at twenty-five dollars. His unit was assigned to General Richard S. Ewell, designated Company B of the 6th Virginia Cavalry, and dispatched to Camp Pickens near Alexandria. In a report dated April 22–June 30, 1861, Captain Green stated that Company B possessed sixty-two sabers but no firearms other than personal property.[5]

Since they were not appropriately armed, Company B was restricted primarily to scouting and picket duty for General Ewell and J. E. B. Stuart. Robert Eastham was with Stonewall Jackson's forces during the First Battle of Bull Run (First Manassas) on July 21, 1861, participated in the Second Battle of Bull Run (Second Manassas) August 29–31, 1861, and on September 1, 1861, his Company B engaged federal troops in a skirmish at Sangster's Crossroads in Fairfax County. They saw little action for the rest of the year other than the constant drilling and picket duty. Eastham's company was then quartered at Alexandria, Virginia, until the Confederates were driven out by the Union army and heavy shelling by the USS *Pawnee*. On May 23, 1862, Eastham's regiment destroyed the Manassas Gap Railroad near Front Royal, and then marched to Cedarville where Company B launched an attack against the Federals at the McKay house. Eastham was also present when his regiment supported General Lee's retreat across the Potomac River on September 18, 1862, following the Battle of Sharpsburg.[6]

Eastham also served with Major Chatham Roberdeau Wheat's "Louisiana Tigers," a battalion of 500 "hard men" pulled together by Wheat in New Orleans. The "Tigers" served in Jackson's Valley Campaign and the Peninsula Campaign in 1862. When Wheat was mortally wounded at the Battle of Gaines's Mill in June 1862, according to a historian who interviewed Robert Eastham in 1883, Eastham was offered the opportunity to take his place. For whatever reason, Eastham declined. At this time, the Confederate army permitted units to elect their officers, and the "Louisiana Tigers," who were known as "street toughs" short on discipline but good fighters in a battle, might well have regarded R. W. Eastham as a good replacement. He too was tough, daring, and like Wheat a large man; both were described as tall and muscular.[7]

During this period Eastham was primarily assigned to scouting duty and served under the command of Colonel William E. Jones's 7th Virginia Cavalry; in September 1862 Jones was promoted to brigadier general and assigned command of the 4th Brigade of General J. E. B. Stuart's Cavalry Division in the Army of Northern Virginia. Composed entirely of Virginians, it contained the 6th, 7th, 11th, and 12th Virginia Cavalry regiments, and the 35th Battalion of Virginia Cavalry. The 4th Brigade was made up of veterans who were accustomed to hard marching and tough fighting and considered one of the best cavalry brigades in either army.[8]

On April 21, 1863, General Jones left his base at Lacey Spring for a coordinated raid into western Virginia with Brigadier General John D. Imboden. Their primary mission was to destroy bridges and tunnels of the Baltimore and Ohio Railway west of Cumberland, Maryland, encourage volunteer recruits, confiscate livestock, and generally harass the provisional government of West Virginia, which officially did not become a state until June 21, 1863. Robert Eastham was with the 6th Cavalry and his brother Philip was with the 7th Cavalry in Jones's brigade, and both of them participated in the raid. Robert Eastham would have been riding in a forward position as he scouted the way for Jones's troops. Eastham related to acquaintances that he first entered Tucker County, West Virginia, while scouting for the raiders. Jones and Imboden split their forces in a two-prong invasion with Jones proceeding along the Northwestern Turnpike to Oakland, Maryland, and across the mountains to Rowlesburg, Kingwood, Morgantown, and Fairmont, destroying railroad bridges and confiscating provisions and livestock along the way. He then proceeded to Burning Springs and Cairo, where his forces destroyed the oil-producing facilities and burned the stocks of oil, creating a blaze that could be seen for miles. Jones's command headed south to White Sulphur Springs, crossed the Jackson River, and camped in security behind Confederate lines at Warm Springs before marching northward up the Shenandoah

Valley to the Laurel Hill headquarters of the Department of Northwestern Virginia. In one month Jones's troops covered 700 miles and completed the most destructive Confederate raid ever made into northwestern Virginia. The raid was unsuccessful in destroying its primary target of the B&O bridge over the Cheat River at Rowlesburg where the Yankee resistance was too much to overcome. However, in confiscating 2,200 head of cattle and horses, taking 700 prisoners, and destroying 16 railroad bridges, train cars and engines, and the oil field, at the cost of only 10 killed and 42 wounded, the raid must be considered a tactical victory.[9]

Exactly when Robert Eastham joined Mosby's Rangers is not known. Company D of Mosby's Rangers, where he served, was organized on March 28, 1864. It is not known whether he accompanied General William E. "Grumble" Jones on the Gettysburg campaign in the summer of 1863, but he was listed as absent from Company B, 6th Cavalry Regiment after October 12, 1863. He resurfaced in the records in 1864 as an enlisted man in Company D, Mosby's 43rd Battalion Virginia Cavalry again using his middle name, Woodford. Some have speculated that Eastham might have known Mosby prior to joining his partisans since Mosby had joined the "Washington Rifles" in Abingdon, which Jones had formed and commanded for a time.[10] Colonel John Singleton Mosby's Rangers remained in the Shenandoah Valley to control the critical gaps in the mountains to the west and east, and to screen the Army of Northern Virginia's rear guard as it advanced toward Pennsylvania. Robert E. Lee authorized Mosby to organize the unit in January 1863 after the Confederate Congress authorized the formation of irregular units under the Partisan Ranger Act of 1862. Officially Mosby's 43rd Battalion, Virginia Cavalry, was formed on June 10, 1863, and acted under the authority of generals J. E. B. Stuart and Lee. By the summer of 1864

Mosby's battalion consisted of six cavalry companies and one artillery company totaling about 400 men. Irregular units caused problems for the regular army because the partisans tended to be undisciplined and some degenerated into marauding bands. The CSA revoked the authority of the partisan bands in February 1864, but made exceptions for two of them: Mosby's Rangers and John H. McNeill's Rangers, which operated in the borderland of Virginia and the Union stronghold of northwestern Virginia (now Grant and Hardy counties, West Virginia).[11]

Whatever the actual date when Eastham joined Mosby's Command, he spent the rest of his career as a Confederate soldier with Mosby. The Rangers' operational methods allowed Robert Eastham to take full advantage of his personal and physical attributes. Utilizing from twenty to eighty men who could penetrate federal lines undetected, they usually made small raids, swiftly executed their mission, and achieved a speedy exit. The troops then dispersed into a countryside friendly to the Confederate cause where sympathetic farmers protected them. To facilitate their ability to melt into the population, members of Mosby's command did not wear Confederate uniforms. The only prerequisite was that they wear something gray, no matter how small. Mosby's field of operations was in northern Virginia from the Shenandoah Valley to the west, along the Potomac River to Alexandria to the east, and above the Rappahannock River in the south. The center of operations was, in other words, in an area Eastham and his comrades had known since birth, and seldom exceeded a radius of twenty-five miles from Middleburg, Virginia.[12]

Eastham would have been attracted to Mosby's Rangers because many of their raids depended on the bravery and cleverness of the individual, and Eastham was the model for Mosby's profile of the perfect Ranger, described by one former partisan as someone motivated by the glory and valor of fighting, and the allure of booty. But also required was an eye for military intelligence, and overall resourcefulness. Above all Mosby wanted youth. He believed, claimed one former Ranger, "that boys make the best soldiers . . . mere boys, unmarried and hence without fear or anxiety for wives or children."[13] Each man carried two .44 Colt army revolvers worn in belt holsters, and some carried an additional one tucked down into their boots. Sabers and carbines were too awkward for close-up combat. Mosby trained his men to hold their fire until they could see the eyes of their opponent. Artillery also proved cumbersome for hit-and-run tactics on horseback. Mosby's men were of necessity all excellent horsemen; they had been born and raised in the section of Virginia renowned for raising good horses, and the men were devoted to them. In this kind of fighting, where speed and surprise were the secrets to success, the men would quickly exhaust a horse, so each man had at least two quality mounts.[14]

This was a life in which R. W. Eastham was prepared to excel. As a guerrilla combatant he became popularly known as "Bob Ridley," an alternate name that he assumed for the rest of his life. "Bob Ridley" and the name of his horse, "Steamboat," were adopted from a popular song that he often sang while playing his fiddle to entertain his comrades. "Old Bob Ridley" was a standard of the American blackface minstrel stage of the mid-nineteenth century, although there were many variations. In all versions of the song, "Bob Ridley" was a black caricature who does the impossible in a humorous way. One version went as follows:

> Now white folks I'll sing you a ditty,
> I'se from home but dat's no pity,
> Oh, to praise myself it am a shame,
> But Robert Ridley is my name.

Oh, white folks I hab cross'd de mountains,
How many miles I did'nt count 'em,
O, I'se left de folks at de old Plantation,
'An come down here for my education.

De first time dat I eber got a lickin,
'Was down at de forks ob de cotton pickin,
O, it made me dance, it made me tremble,
By golly it made my eye-balls jingle.

Philadelphia am a mighty fine city,
For beauty and location it ain't behind 'em,
Oh, de ladies all look so sweet and Gidley,
Wonder dey don't fall in love wid old Bob Ridley.

Chorus following each verse:
Oh Bob Ridley ho, Oh Bob Ridley ho,
Oh Bob Ridley! Oh!! Oh!!
Robert Ridley, HO![15]

The Eastham family was famous for its horsemanship, and Robert was no exception. In a letter to the editor appearing in the *Northern Virginian* in 1933, J. William Yates Jr. wrote that he remembered hunting with Robert and his younger brother Charlie Eastham. Yates described "Bob Ridley" as an "interesting character." Robert and Charlie were "the sons of Capt. Frank Eastham, a veteran foxhunter and one of the first flight men of that section of Virginia. The Easthams were manly, splendid fellows . . . [who] were daring, fearless riders."[16]

Standing six feet four inches tall and weighing close to 250 pounds, Eastham was a very imposing figure in his day. Most descriptions of Eastham described him as tall, athletic, well-proportioned, and muscular. Hu Maxwell, a Confederate sympathizer who interviewed Eastham for his 1884 history of Tucker County, West Virginia, described him as "one of the most perfect men, physically, in the county, State, or the United States." In fact, Eastham presented "as fine appearance as ever Sam Houston did. He is active and athletic, walks with grace, and is a splendid rider." While he supported the Confederacy out of principle, Maxwell wrote, "the prospect of excitement and adventure had not a little to do in shaping his course," and his record during the war "hardly has a rival anywhere." Eastham was "seldom seen without a crowd about him. There seems to be some attraction in him for other people." In short, he was charismatic. "Fear has no part in his nature," Maxwell continued. "Indeed, his bravery may at times amount to rashness. His sense of honor is such that he will not do an unmanly act. . . . He hates a lie and cowardice and deceit as he hates everything that is mean; and, one who sins in this particular must, before again gaining his favor, wipe out the contamination of the iniquity in a multitude of praiseworthy acts." In short, he was a man with "southern honor." All of these attributes would have been welcomed by Colonel John Mosby, and importantly, he was not married and barely in his twenties when he volunteered for Mosby's Rangers.[17] Although another historian of Tucker County, unsympathetic to Eastham and the world he stood for, described him as a "huge 250-pound, 6-foot 4-inch goon," it is clear that among his many friends Eastham and his character traits were highly respected.[18]

Eastham's adventures during the war evolved into legends, and they have been retold in print and in popular lore. It is said, but cannot be confirmed, that his daring exploits prompted the Federals to put a price on his head, a price that varies depending on the source between $5,000 and $15,000. According to Maxwell, "He was hunted by the Yankees with a perseverance surpassed only by the perseverance with which he hunted them. They feared and hated him, yet respected him for daring."[19]

On the first day of the Second Battle of Bull Run Eastham was not engaged in combat, but he was there the following day when he and eleven other scouts rounded up sixty-five Yankee prisoners who had hidden in a thicket of brush. Eastham suffered a gunshot wound in the foot during the action. In another skirmish a bullet passed through the horn of his saddle, another perforated his belt, and one took off a coat button. Eastham himself preferred to use a "stout club" in a close-up fight.[20]

In another episode, Eastham and thirteen companions captured eighty-six Yankees who were retreating down a road that led to a partially destroyed bridge. The Union soldiers found themselves trapped on a bridge and were forced to surrender. On another occasion he and two other men captured thirty-six horses and twenty-three men in one day. These escapades began when he was still scouting for the 6th Virginia Cavalry under General "Grumble" Jones. The effort to capture him became even more intense after he joined the Mosby's 43rd Battalion.

Frequently "Bob Ridley" had to save himself by clever concealment. On one occasion, he was riding down a road at dusk and "met an old negro" whom he knew. On seeing him alive the old fellow reportedly exclaimed: "'Good heavens! Massa, de whole world am full of Yankees huntin' foh you.'" At that moment he heard galloping horses in the distance. After concealing his own horse, he took a grain-cradle and a basket which the slave was carrying, and climbed the fence into the field.

> He threw down a sheaf of wheat and sat upon it. The soldiers came by and saw him, but in the dusk of evening they did not recognize him. He watched them go by, and then mounted his horse and struck after them. He

followed them boldly into town, dismounted and entered into conversation with them. He went into a store and bought him some tobacco, and made free with all about him. None recognized him, until a little negro came along. The little scamp knew him and yelled out: "I do 'clah! tha's Bob Eastham!" Immediately the whole town full of Yankees started up and rushed at him. He sprang on his horse and dashed through them, knocked them down and rode over them, and finally reached the edge of the town. . . . He dashed up the mountain and escaped.

He once entered a house full of Yankee soldiers and ate dinner with them; another time he entered a barn where several Union soldiers were asleep and stole the officers' horses. He often hid in a pile of rails, lay flat in a potato patch, or next to a stone fence while the Yankees were looking for him. Somehow he always escaped, and of such stuff as this are legends born.[21]

Maxwell claimed that as a young man Eastham believed that he was invincible, an idea that only Eastham himself could have divulged. As an example, Maxwell relayed the story about how Eastham visited his father Captain Frank at his home, Buena Vista, near Flint Hill, Virginia, while there was a price on his head. From a back room he overheard two Union officers in an adjoining room talking about him, having no idea that he was in the house. When they sat down to dinner,

> he walked boldly into the dining room where they sat at the table. His father introduced him to them as "My son, Robert, the man you are looking for." They turned and looked at the tall figure before them, clad in full

Confederate uniform, and armed from head to foot. His belt gleamed with the hilt of a saber and with the handles of pistols. The officers evidently would rather have been excused from making new acquaintances that evening, but they had the presence of mind to make the best of the situation. They shook hands, and he sat down at the table with them, and talked two hours. They made no attempt or showed no disposition to capture him, and he was allowed to depart in peace.[22]

While it is possible that Eastham bragged about his exploits during the Civil War, and he did enjoy "pulling someone's leg," he was known for telling the truth as a matter of honor even when it worked to his disadvantage. Also, the stories so often repeated about his exploits passed down through other sources give them the ring of truth and are confirmed by other rangers in their reminiscences of their lives and experiences in Mosby's Command. For example, James J. Williamson, a veteran of Company A, described Eastham in a manner that is familiar in style and content to the legends. "Among the 'characters' in the Battalion was one Robert W. Eastham, familiarly known as 'Bob Ridley.' Of a restless, roving disposition, he was never idle. A fight or a foot race, a fox hunt or a raid, were equally gratifying to him. He would often start off with two or three companions, and seldom returned without prisoners and horses."[23]

One day, Eastham's scouting party captured two Union couriers with dispatches for Colonel George A. Custer. Another federal soldier was escaping when "Bob Ridley" suddenly "started from behind a bush and presenting his pistol," and called on the man to surrender. Returning on the road to Front Royal with his prisoner,

Eastham learned that a party of 37 Federal cavalry had passed but a little while before. As he had been joined by 4 troopers belonging to the Twelfth Virginia cavalry, he left a comrade in charge of the three prisoners and started in pursuit of the Federal cavalry. As soon as they came in sight Eastham and his little party charged with a yell. In the cloud of dust which enveloped them, the surprised and startled Federals could form no estimate of the number of their assailants, but naturally supposing the force superior to their own, broke and ran at break-neck speed. At a turn in the road one of the enemy's horses fell with its rider, and Eastham being too near to stop, attempted to jump over the prostrate horse and rider. As he did so, the horse started to rise, and threw Eastham's horse down the bank, both horse and rider being lamed in the fall. The pursuit was continued for some distance. Eastham then returned to Front Royal with the prisoners and 17 horses.[24]

Toward the end of the war, on March 30, 1865, Charles B. Wiltshire, a veteran of the regular service whom Mosby intended to promote to lieutenant in Company H, was ordered to take a few men and scout the route of the Winchester and Potomac Railroad. He, John Orrick, George Murray Gill, and Bartlett Bolling set out. Along the road they met Robert and Philip Eastham who were carrying a message to Colonel Mosby. Philip was sent on to deliver the message, but "Bob Ridley" joined the scouting party. The reconnaissance group traveled toward Berryville. Near there, Eastham and Bolling stopped at a house to make inquiries while the other three rode ahead. When the three came in sight of Colonel Daniel Bonham's house, they saw two Yankee soldiers making a dash for the barn. The men charged after the two Federals who took refuge inside the barn. As they galloped up, Wiltshire was shot from inside the barn door, and several more shots felled Gill, while Orrick's startled horse threw its rider to the ground. One of them, Lieutenant Eugene Ferris of the 30th Massachusetts, caught Wiltshire's horse, mounted it, and shot at the dying Wiltshire. Just as the firing began, Bolling and Eastham intercepted Ferris and his orderly attempting to make their escape. "Eastham started in pursuit of the two flying men, overtaking them before they reached their pickets."[25] By this time, Bolling was also wounded, but he seized the orderly and pulled him from his horse. Ferris then turned on Eastham, who fired at Ferris, grazing him slightly. Eastham then attempted to strike Ferris with his pistol, but the Union officer dodged the blow and set off again toward his camp. When Ferris avoided Eastham's attempt to cut him off and made his escape, Eastham returned to the dying Wiltshire just as Orrick and Bolling rode up shouting, "Get out quick, Ridley; the Yankees are coming!" The three rangers galloped off and avoided capture once again.[26]

Mosby's Rangers were involved in attacks on supply trains as well. In an earlier action, probably on January 31, 1865, "Jim Wilcher and Bob Eastham (alias Bob Ridley), with ten men, had attacked a train between Harper's Ferry and Winchester, without success. The engineer, however, fell from the train in his frenzied efforts to save his charge, and was instantly killed."[27] The best known of these efforts was their Berryville Wagon Train Raid of August 13, 1864, and "Bob Ridley's" presence was noted for more than his role in the action. Mosby learned that a large wagon train of supplies had embarked from Harper's Ferry for Winchester to supply General Philip H. Sheridan's Army of the Shenandoah, particularly its cavalry units, with precious stores. Too tempting to ignore, Mosby ordered companies A, B, C, and D, composed of between 250 and 300 rangers, to rendezvous at noon of August 12 at Rectortown. They found the wagon train, which consisted of between 500 and 600 four-team, canvas-covered wagons that stretched out for miles, stopped for a few hours rest and to water the animals. When the early fog lifted the mounted rangers attacked, and in the chaos the teamsters and the inexperienced Ohio infantrymen guarding them panicked and fled for their lives.[28]

Mosby's men attacked the rear portion of the train, and captured "over 500 mules, 36 horses, 200 head of fine cattle, 208 prisoners and 4 negroes." Mosby's men rummaged through the wagons and found feed for their horses and rations for themselves. The rangers also confiscated some fiddles, and as they rode away at least one of them began to play old plantation tunes.[29] The triumphal scene was later commemorated; in 1867, John S. Russell of Berryville, Virginia, and Mosby's chief scout during their campaigns, wrote to his former commander enclosing a photographic reproduction of a painting of the Berryville raid. "You will observe in the picture representing our return a figure on horseback playing a fiddle. It is Bob Ridley (Eastham). He got it from headquarters wagon. Bob is playing a tune to which he had danced—"Malbrook has gone to the Wars."[30] In 1876 a former Confederate, identified only as "Captain McAleer of Baltimore," visited the scene, made sketches, and acquired photographs of many of Mosby's men involved in the raid. He then travelled to Paris and commissioned three "distinguished artists" to create paintings of the raid. Afterward, illustrations of the paintings were widely circulated in France, England, and the United States. The painting, based on the photograph referred to by Russell, was created in 1868 by the French artist Charles Edouard Armand-Dumaresq and represented the rangers in a celebratory mood after the Berryville raid. The original painting

Robert Eastham, "Bob Ridley," mounted on the black horse in the foreground, plays a fiddle confiscated from a federal wagon train. Courtesy of the Museum of the Confederacy, Richmond, Virginia.

now hangs in the Museum of the Confederacy, Richmond, Virginia. In the forefront, and easily recognized by his trademark mustache, is a mounted "Bob Ridley" playing his newly acquired fiddle.[31]

The tune Eastham was playing was written on a false rumor that John Churchill, first Duke of Marlborough, had been killed in his 1704–1709 campaign during the War of the Spanish Succession. The lyrics, probably written by a French soldier, were sung to the tune of two other songs, "For He's a Jolly Good Fellow," and "The Bear Went over the Mountain." The song experienced a revival with the French Revolution, and then became extremely popular during the Napoleonic Wars in the Western world generally; the song is referenced in the works of numerous nineteenth-century artists, including Dostoyevsky, Tolstoy, and

Robert Eastham's army Colt and spur. Courtesy of Janet Eastham and Edwin I. Eastham III.

Robert Eastham, "Bob Ridley," attended the 1895 reunion of Mosby's Rangers. He is seated in the front center. Courtesy of the Warren Rifles Confederate Memorial Museum, Front Royal, Virginia.

Georges Bizet. The English corrupted the original French version of "Marlborough s'en va-t-en guerre" into "Malbrook the Prince of Commanders," and this is the version that would have been familiar to Eastham. We do not know if he was referring to the tune or Eastham's rendition, but one of the rangers, John Munson, described the music as "hideous."[32]

While life as a partisan was generally spartan, dangerous, difficult, lonely, afforded few amenities beyond the glory and occasional booty, and subjected the rangers to harsh weather, most of them were young enough to withstand the hardships. In February 1865, a blizzard postponed any forays they had planned. The drifted snow made the roads impassable, so the men found ways to amuse themselves. On this occasion fox-chasing was "proposed by some of the old hunters," and a "grand chase" was organized despite the eighteen inches of snow on the ground.

> Hunters came from the adjoining counties with their dogs. The foxes had become very annoying to the farmers in this portion of Fauquier [County], and as all kinds of business and work were suspended, it was thought an excellent time to terminate the career of some of them. The old hunters, Wm. Hopper, Reuben Triplett, Bob and Phil Eastham, Hand, and John Carr had the management of it. One hundred citizens and soldiers participated in the chase. There were one hundred hounds.... The chase commenced at ten o'clock A.M., and terminated at sunset. Five foxes were caught, and a large number chased to their caves.

Another of Mosby's rangers, Major John Scott, observed in his reminiscences of the war that Eastham would "preside as ringmaster of chicken and dog fights" to entertain the troops.[33]

Exploits involving "Bob Ridley" are still widely known and often repeated in the Flint Hill area of Rappahannock County. One of these stories centered on a farmhouse, currently owned by Jimmy DeBerg, and was passed down through the family along with the house. During the Civil War the property was owned by the Harris family. "Bob Ridley" was visiting when six Union cavalrymen rode up to the front of the house. Eastham went to an upstairs bedroom to hide. A very large trumpet vine grew up a tree next to a balcony at the back of the house, and Eastham climbed down this vine and ran to the barn where his horse was saddled. He dashed to the top of a small hill near the back of the house and yelled until the soldiers noticed him. Ever the daredevil, he taunted them to come get him, but they thought the better of it. Although the balcony has since been enclosed, the trumpet vine still survives next to the house and is as thick as a tree. History is close at every hand here.[34]

The good and the bad of the guerrilla life would not last, however, and soon men like Robert Eastham became part of the "Lost Cause" tradition in southern history. On April 9, 1865, Robert E. Lee surrendered to Ulysses Grant. Mosby attempted to negotiate a surrender of the 43rd Battalion with the Federal commander in Winchester, Virginia, but they could not come to terms. Therefore, twelve days later, late in the morning of April 21, 1865, Mosby mustered his battalion for the last time at Salem, Fauquier County, where it had been first organized. Company officers arranged the approximately 200 men in their eight companies according to the date of their formation. Among them was Robert Woodford Eastham and Company D, the "Darlings," in full dress. To this somber assembly, shrouded appropriately by a dense fog, Mosby read his farewell address: "The vision we have cherished for a free and independent country has vanished and that country is now the spoil of a conqueror. I disband your organization in preference to surrendering it to our enemies. I am no longer your commander."[35]

After the War

Nearly twenty years after the war, Robert W. Eastham informed an interviewer that he refused to surrender even after General Lee surrendered to Grant at Appomattox on April 9, 1865. In fact, he fought two battles after Lee's surrender, and remained with Mosby until the colonel disbanded the 43rd Battalion Virginia Cavalry. If Eastham informed his interviewer of when and where the battles occurred, this information was not shared with readers. During Eastham's trial for murder in 1897, newspapers frequently referred to his days as a ranger. For example, the Washington, DC, *Times* reported that "Col. Eastham was in the Confederate army and was a spy of prominence. He refused to surrender, was outlawed in Virginia and came to the Blackwater region, where he has become famous as a hunter and has acquired considerable property."[36]

Like other Confederate soldiers, the rangers were required to sign paroles officially accepting the defeat of the Confederacy. By the end of June 1865 some 779 of those who had served and were still alive were officially paroled. Robert Eastham was one of them. He signed his parole papers in Winchester on May 10, 1865, which required that he formally recognize that the United States had won the war, and returned to Rappahannock County. How soon thereafter he returned is unknown. Confederate general Joseph Johnston's army was still in the field, and after disbanding his battalion, Mosby and about a dozen of his men headed south to locate him. At this time Union general Winfield Hancock placed a reward for Mosby's capture of $2,000 which was increased to $5,000. Near Richmond, and learning of Johnston's surrender, the partisans rode west. Near Orange Courthouse, Mosby instructed his loyal followers to return to their homes. It is possible that Eastham was among that small group of diehards who followed Mosby south to find General Johnston. Ulysses S. Grant directly interceded on Mosby's behalf and by the end of June 1865 he had been paroled.[37]

Eastham returned to the farm in Rappahannock County, but it is not clear exactly when. What is clear, however, is that, like so many of his generation returning to civilian life, Eastham had a difficult time making the transition. Evidence appears in a report dated July 31, 1866, filed by an officer of the Freedmen's Bureau:

Capt. Wm. P. Austin
Supt. 1st Dist. Va.
Norfolk
Bureau of R. F. & A. L.
Office of Asst. Supt. Sub. Dist.
of Culpepper & Rappahannock
Culpepper C. H. Va. July 31, 1866
Bvt. Major
W. R. Morse
Supt. 4th Dist. Va.

Major:
 In compliance with circular No. 10 dated Hd. Qrs. Asst. Com. Va. Richmond, Va., March 12th, 1866, I have the honor to state that I attended the trial of Robert W. Eastham (not Esom as before reported) for the murder of Minor Menifus before the county court of Rappahannock County. The report of the case as the testimony disclosed was forwarded by Lt. Roth and myself. There was a large number present from all parts of the county and it was plainly seen that Eastham had all their sympathy. The Commonwealth's attorney stood alone doing all in his power to have justice done. Eastham was acquitted and allowed to depart. It would be well for the proper authorities to know who he is. I heard statements about this man that I believe can be proved. One is as follows:
 Mr. B. C. Macoy stated publicly in this place that Eastham & himself belonged to Mosby's Command and as they were riding along at one time they came up to a Union soldier (an old man) who was broken down and sitting beside the road his horse near him & his carbine

leaning on the fence. Eastham jumped off his horse against the remonstrance of Macoy took up the carbine and the old man began to plead for his life when he struck him dashing out his brains. Henry O'Bannon & U. T. Stark also made statements of like character. This man is considered in his county as a "gallant Southern Soldier."

No other cases have come under my notice during the month.

> I am Major Very Respectfully
> Your Obt. Servt.
>
> W. S. Chase
> 2nd Lt. 18th V. R. C. & Asst. Supt.[38]

Eastham was undoubtedly an implacable foe, but there is no other evidence to suggest that he was a vicious man, and no further evidence has surfaced to corroborate the episode reported to the Freedmen's Bureau by Lieutenant Chase. There is no mention of a trial in the Rappahannock County Law Books in the case of Minor Menifus, but it is entirely possible that the clerk did not enter cases against whites who committed crimes against blacks—especially in Rappahannock where the Easthams were one of the leading families. From the detailed description of the Freedmen's Bureau agent, however, the incident does appear to have occurred. Years later, it was reported in a few newspaper accounts of his 1897 trial that Eastham had "killed a negro [Menifus] whom he caught in some overt act. He was tried, but dismissed for this alleged offense."[39] Perhaps the court concluded that "rough justice" was appropriate during "rough times."

After Colonel Mosby disbanded the 43rd Battalion Virginia Cavalry, Robert W. Eastham returned to Rappahannock County and went back to farming. But after four years of constant movement and the adrenalin-rushes that accompanied life as a guerrilla fighter, Eastham found it difficult to settle down. Maxwell reported that "after his four years of war he could not feel satisfied with the tame existence of a farmer." He sold out and traveled to the South, roaming through North and South Carolina, Georgia, Alabama, and Tennessee. Because he was so rooted in the tradition of family and place, however, nomadic wandering ultimately could not sustain Robert Eastham. He returned to Rappahannock County and, on December 28, 1869, at the age of twenty-seven, married Mary Catharine "Mollie" Read, the daughter of Dr. Adolphus W. and Mary A. Read of the same county.[40]

4

EASTHAM IN WEST VIRGINIA

Move to the Canaan Wilderness

The Allegheny Mountain Upland Section presented settlers with their first great physical barrier to western migration. The forest contained timber of extraordinary diversity, size, and commercial value. Northern hardwoods, such as sugar maple, yellow birch, red maple, beech, basswood, and red spruce dominated the higher elevations. On the northern exposures, hemlock, which the tanning industry prized for its bark, was generally found mixed with the hardwoods. White pine and central hardwoods predominated in the lower elevations.[1]

Like many who lived in postwar ravaged Virginia, Robert and Mary suffered economically. They also lost an infant daughter, and perhaps thought they would start afresh. Always ready to take the initiative, Bob Eastham decided to seek new opportunities in the Canaan Valley, Tucker County, West Virginia. The Canaan Valley lies on a generally northeast-southwest axis, is about fifteen miles long and four to six miles wide, and rises to an elevation of 3,200 feet above sea level. The mountains on either side rise up to 4,200 feet and mark its longitudinal boundary. The valley covers an area of about 35,000 acres, and its climate is comparable with Quebec because of the elevation. Here the winters, along with a lot of snow, come early and stay late. On the other hand, the land is fertile, and in 1880 a towering virgin forest covered the entire county.[2]

Located in the Allegheny Mountain Upland Section, the Canaan Valley Eastham entered in the 1870s was still a wilderness and made a powerful impression on those who experienced it. Early settlers who encountered the rugged Appalachian wilderness did so with both awe and foreboding. A party of Virginians that included Colonel Peter Jefferson, Thomas Jefferson's father, climbed Cabin Mountain in October 1746 and looked out on the Canaan Valley spruce forest. The following day the men descended into the forest. Thomas Lewis, a surveyor, recorded in his journal that, from the moment the party entered the forest, they "did not See aplain Big Enough for aman to Lye on nor a horse to Stand," and soon found themselves ensnarled in an understory of rhododendron, or "laurel," eight to ten feet high. "Never was any poor Creaturs in Such a Condition as we were in nor Ever was a Criminal more glad by having made his Escape out of prison as we were to Get Rid of those Accursed Lorals," Lewis wrote afterward.[3]

David Hunter Strother, known professionally as "Porte Crayon," the mid-nineteenth-century writer and illustrator from Berkeley Springs, Virginia, enshrined the popular idea that the Canaan wilderness was "impenetrable." Describing a fishing trip to the Canaan Valley in 1857, Strother reported that he and his comrades had been "dodging the laurel-brakes all day," some of which stretched for miles and were so dense that even the deer could not pass through them. The party heard stories from locals about men who had spent days in the laurel-brakes, wandering in circles, and finally "perished from starvation."[4] Other observers were more awestruck by the Canaan wilderness. West Virginia novelist Rebecca Harding Davis wrote in 1880 that the total silence was as "strange and oppressive as noonday," and "human voices were an impertinence in the great and wordless meanings of the woods."[5]

In 1876 Robert and Mary Eastham appear in the Tucker County Land Books for the first time as owners of 500 acres of land in the Canaan Valley. On September 20, 1876, Mary's parents purchased 300 acres, recorded in Mary's name, and took a note for the debt. Robert purchased the other 200 acres, probably from his father-in-law, but the transaction does not appear in the Land Books.[6]

The first settler in the Canaan Valley was Henry Fansler who settled in 1803 at the mouth of the Blackwater River at the present site of Hendricks. Fansler was followed by Solomon W. Cosner who arrived in 1864, John Nine in 1870, James Freeland in 1872, and Robert Eastham in 1876. Nearly all of the land was still in virgin forest. In the early 1880s, only 40 of Eastham's 276 acres were "improved," meaning land cleared for use and included a farmhouse and other out buildings. Sometime during the late 1870s, while Robert and Mary were away, there was a fire in the woods that destroyed his house and virtually all of his possessions except for two horses, a cow, a dog, and a cat. He had "not a dollar left, nor even a coat to wear," Eastham told local historian Hu Maxwell. So Eastham borrowed a coat, went to Oakland, Maryland, where he bought a suit on credit, and went back to "Eastern Virginia where he had a little property."[7] The business that took him back to Virginia is unknown, but by 1881 he had returned to his Canaan Valley farm.

In 1882 Eastham sold 236 acres to Henry Jackson and Mary Margaret Randolph Cooper. Along with their seven young children, the Coopers left their home in Winchester, Virginia, behind them and relocated to the Canaan Valley. Their daughter Hattie Mae, "Myrtle," who was born in November 1882 in the Canaan, related to a local historian that her parents mortgaged their home in Winchester "in order to purchase at two dollars per acre three hundred acres of virgin timberland in an almost uninhabited area of West Virginia, which later became known as Cortland of Canaan Valley."[8] Henry was a friend of Eastham, whom he undoubtedly knew from the war. Henry J. Cooper served in Company A, 39th Battalion, CSA, as Robert E. Lee's bodyguard and messenger. According to Myrtle, "Our land was purchased from Col. Bob Eastham, a friend of father's from Front Royal, Virginia." Eastham had lived in the Canaan Valley for several years by then, and "he encouraged the move, assuring father that the soil was fertile; so fertile that all kinds of vegetables could be grown by merely clearing the land and planting the seeds." Berries were found in abundance, and fish and game also abounded. "On the other hand, bears, panthers, wildcats and wolves roamed the forests and the winters were extremely cold and the snow deep. No minor inducement was Mr. Eastham's faith that a railroad would soon be built which would make possible the transportation of the valuable timber to market. This and the fact that Mr. and Mrs. Eastham and, I think, two other families were there, made the opportunity irresistible to father and mother."[9]

They began their move to West Virginia on April 1, 1882, in covered wagons containing their food and possessions, and a spring wagon to convey the family. When they arrived, the Coopers "went to Mrs. Robert Eastham's and spent some time there. She was very kind to the family and helped them in every way she could to get them located and started.... The Easthams were very good to the family."[10] Upon their arrival, the Coopers "made their home in a log house on Mr. Eastham's land," and moved into their newly completed log cabin just a short distance on their own land. There were many hardships, but Mary Eastham shared them with Mary Cooper and they became "good friends." Henry Cooper's daughter remembered that Bob Eastham "often visited us and his experience there meant much to my father. He had a kind, tender, winning side that we children knew and loved." The

Easthams often shared with the Coopers, such as the day Bob Eastham showed up on his old horse "Jimmie" and delivered two deer he had killed for the family pot.[11]

Seeking Opportunity

In 1882, Mr. Eastham's belief that a railroad would soon be built to transport Canaan timber to market was based on solid information rather than "faith." During the 1870s, H. G. Davis and his brothers Thomas B. and William R. purchased 23,550 acres, and between 1880 and 1883 purchased another 34,806 acres of adjacent land. Eastham had been serving as a guide for H. G. Davis and helped to survey the route the new road would follow to Tucker County. Davis started building his railroad, the West Virginia Central and Pittsburgh Railroad, from Piedmont, West Virginia, on April 20, 1880, and completed the fifty-seven-mile line to the confluence of Beaver Creek and the Blackwater River, and the new town of Davis on November 1, 1884. On that date the first train consisting of a locomotive and two cars, arrived. Davis remained the western terminus for the railway until 1889 when it was completed to Elkins. Then the six-mile line from the mainline became known as the Davis Branch.[12]

Eastham was determined to get in on the ground floor of the development that was sure to follow. With foreknowledge of what was coming, and certainly the support of the Davis brothers, Eastham ran for a seat in the House of Delegates from Tucker County in the October 1882 general election. The popular outdoorsman came in third among the five candidates running for the seat, but carried his own Dry Fork District overwhelmingly.[13]

While the railway was under construction, Robert Eastham secured a contract from the Davis brothers to clear a town site.

Robert Eastham cleared the land of virgin timber for the town of Davis, West Virginia. Courtesy of West Virginia and Regional History Center.

After building a camp at the mouth of Beaver Creek and Blackwater River, his crew began clearing the timber on March 14, 1884. H. G. Davis deeded the first lot to him for one dollar, where he built the first log cabin in Davis. In 1889, Davis sold Eastham the second and third lots for one dollar and $250, respectively. Eastham subsequently built a combined general store and residence on William Avenue; his wife Mary served as the first postmaster. A portable mill was set up to cut logs from the site where the town of Davis would arise. As soon as the land was cleared, Eastham assisted James Parsons, a surveyor for Davis's railroad, in laying out streets and lots. The three main streets were named for Davis's founders: William, Thomas, and Henry. At first the locals called Davis "Stump Town" because there were so many tree stumps that, according to one contemporary, stepping from stump to stump, one could traverse the town without getting his shoes muddy.[14] The mental image of accomplishing

Robert Eastham laid out the town of Davis, West Virginia. Courtesy of the West Virginia State Archives.

this feat comes easier when we know that the tree stumps might measure from three to six feet in diameter.

In March 1884, at the same time that he began to clear the site for a town, Eastham began work on a road from the Canaan Valley to Davis. According to George B. Thompson, Eastham's crew chopped out a bridle path by September 1884, which gradually was widened and improved, and eventually became West Virginia Route 32. Myrtle Cooper Wiseman remembered that her brothers Charlie and Frank helped Eastham "a great deal in his road building and surveying, often camping for a week while surveying."[15]

With the arrival of the railroad and lumber mills, the town of Davis grew rapidly. Although Eastham helped to establish Davis as a thriving lumber town on the West Virginia Central and Pittsburgh Railroad, however, his heart still belonged to the Canaan Valley wilderness. In 1886 the *Graphic News*, of Cincinnati, Ohio, published a picture and accompanying story entitled

"Bob Eastham, Deer Hunter and Guide." Because the article reveals so much about Robert Eastham and his reputation as an outdoorsman, it is reproduced in full below:

> Among our illustrations this week is one of Bob Eastham and several of his dogs. Eastham is a famous Nimrod in West Virginia, and equally is a most eccentric individual. He is a native of the Old Dominion, and, like many of his countrymen, he has always experienced a liking for deer-slaying. He is nominally a contractor on the West Virginia Central Railway (the Hon. J. G. Blaine's road [Senator Blaine had purchased it from Senator Davis]), but really devotes all of his time to the gun. He has a natural weakness for solitude and prefers the quietude of the wild country in West Virginia and the companionship of his dogs to the pleasures of every-day city life. His business on the railroad named took him to the section referred to [they were mistaken], and in it seemed to be the Mecca he had been longing for, as he permanently located there. He says that it is out of the way of civilization and there he can enjoy the sport he so dearly loves with all the primitive glories of a deep forest to aid in making it still more enjoyable. He is of magnificent build, being six feet three inches in height and weighing 190 pounds. He is well educated, and, as far as worldly possessions go, has a goodly bank account. At Davis, which is nothing more than a clearing in the dense forests of West Virginia, he has a country store, where are dealt out the usual variety of calicoes, notions, sugars, etc. While his family attend to the plain ordinary duties of the store Bob lies in wait for the unsuspecting buck or doe, or devotes his time to piloting ambitious hunters through the new retreats of that animal.

He is wonderfully posted on the topography of the country and is in every way fit to be the hero of even that beautifully romantic tale, 'The Deerslayer.' During the late unpleasantness he was one of Mosby's most trusted lieutenants, and many of that guerillo's [sic] exploits originated with Eastham. At one time there was a price of $5,000 offered for his head.

He is very popular with the hundreds of hunters who visit West Virginia in quest of game and a number of the wealthiest Pittsburghers, great admirers of Eastham, have organized a fishing and hunting club after the eccentric guide. Among the prominent members are Captain Sam. Brown, the coal king, Harry Holdane, J. H. Flagler, E. C. Converse, B. C. Louth, J. R. Laughrey, Judge and Marsh Demshee, C. A. Beall, Bob Garrard, G. T. Rafferty, J. M. Pattison, and G. H. Johnston, while Jesse White, of Cincinnati, is one of the honorary members. Five miles from Davis this organization have a regularly located camp and here twice a year they make pilgrimages to it and enjoy a delightful fish and hunting [sic] under the tutelage of Bob Eastham, a rare treat. He has sixty-nine hounds, all admirably trained.[16]

Eastham moved to Front Royal for a time in 1889 and 1890, but had returned to West Virginia by 1891. Around this time he sold the general store to Thompson and Wilson, and perhaps with the proceeds he bought three lots in Front Royal, hoping to profit from the "town boom" currently sweeping the Shenandoah Valley. His brother Philip held the deeds for him and paid the annual taxes. He and his brother were close, and it is likely that Philip tried to entice Eastham to come home and go into business with him. Philip became a wealthy businessman in Front

"West Virginia—Bob Eastham, A Famous Deer Hunter." *Cincinnati Graphic News*, 1886. Courtesy of the West Virginia and Regional History Center.

Royal and an extensive property owner.[17] Clearly Eastham had entrepreneurial inclinations in addition to a desire for the isolation of the deep woods.

In 1894 he purchased a 300-acre tract adjoining his wife's property from the Davis lawyer Wilson B. Maxwell.[18] He testified in 1896 that when he purchased the land from Maxwell his property holdings and their values were: a house and lot in Davis worth $1,200 and 300 acres in the Canaan Valley "that I wouldn't take $15.00 an acre for." He also owned three lots in Front Royal, Virginia, for which he paid $1,900. Eastham also owned one-eighth of "a piece of land in the old home place in Rappahannock County, Virginia, subject to the dower. I don't know how many acres there are in it. The dower is worth about $20,000 and I own one-eighth of it." He also had pulpwood floating in the Blackwater River for the pulp mill that was worth $4,000 to $5,000.[19]

Confronting Trouble Head On

Eastham never seemed to "wear smooth" after the violence of the war, and the rough-and-tumble life of a lumber boomtown did little to change that. Writing in the early 1880s, Hu Maxwell, himself an unapologetic Confederate sympathizer who declared that he hated slavery but believed whites were superior to any other race, was unfailingly impressed by Eastham. On the other hand, Homer Fansler, another Tucker County historian, writing eighty-odd years later in the 1960s had nothing good to say about Eastham. He believed that the otherwise reliable Maxwell had been "deluded" in his assessment of Eastham. Whereas Maxwell portrayed him as a paragon of southern honor, Fansler described him as an oversized "goon, with hallucinations of grandeur," and a "boisterous and arrogant" personality.[20] We should take this into account when reading their descriptions of Eastham. An example is found in their characterization of a confrontation in 1881 at St. George, the original Tucker County seat, when two officers of the law tried to arrest Eastham on a minor charge. Eastham was willing to cooperate, Maxwell wrote, but a scuffle ensued during which Frank and Dock Pifer, the officers involved, "tore his coat off him, and someone else got his hat." Eastham had to go home hatless and coatless.[21] Fansler described this episode much more colorfully, and without documentation, stating that Eastham "made an issue" of it if anyone opposed him. In this case, "he carried a riding crop made from the dried copulation organ of a Hereford bull," which he used to beat up Frank S. Pifer, Dock S. Pifer, and James D. Griffith during a fight at St. George in 1881. "In attempting to pull him from his horse, each of the Pifer brothers seized his legs from opposite sides and pulled against each other, while he laid his riding crop shillelagh to the head of first one and then the other."[22] How Fansler knew that some eighty years later we do not know, and he did not elaborate. It is known that Frank S. was the deputy sergeant of the town of St. George who charged Eastham with beating and abusing Frank Pifer to his "great damage" and "against the peace and dignity of the State." The foreman of the grand jury indicted Eastham, but a motion to quash the indictment was sustained by the court in May 1881.[23]

The Tucker County lumber industry, sparked by the arrival of the West Virginia Central and Pittsburgh Railroad at Davis, began in 1885 when Jacob L. Rumbarger incorporated the J. L. Rumbarger Lumber Company in 1885. Rumbarger was an Indiana lumberman whose desire to cash in on the national lumber boom for cherry lumber in the early eighties brought him to St. George, Tucker County, in September 1883. He borrowed a horse to ride into the Canaan Valley where Robert Eastham provided him with lodging and acted as his timberlands guide. He purchased several stands of cherry timber, and in 1885 he brought in teams and equipment to skid the cherry logs to the Blackwater River, which he had improved to drive the logs down to Davis. There he built the state's largest band saw in 1886.[24]

Up to this point, Eastham had continued to farm his land. The arrival of Rumbarger, however, marked Eastham's entrance into the lumber business. Once his contract ended with H. G. Davis to lay out the town named for the industrialist, Eastham resumed cutting timber in the Canaan Valley, driving more than 700,000 feet of logs to the storage dam above Davis in 1887. In June 1887 Eastham became one of the original stockholders in the Blackwater Boom and Lumber Company, which was formed out of the restructured Rumbarger Company. The following year, the financially troubled company was sold to three investors headed by Albert Thompson the new company's president. In the interim, Eastham had acquired a 1,700 acre tract, known as the Norfolk tract after one of the previous owners, and contracted to supply Thompson's mill with timber from the tract in 1890 to a third party who had purchased the tract for Albert Thompson, an arrangement of which Eastham was unaware. The Blackwater Boom and Lumber Company was declared insolvent in 1893, and Eastham was forced to accept a settlement that he resented. A month later, the company was sold to William Osterhout, with Albert and Frank Thompson as the key managers of the new company. Eastham and his partners were the losing bidders, but Frank Thompson believed that Eastham was merely trying to drive up the price for a silent investor. Whatever the case, relations between Eastham and Albert and Frank Thompson went into a steep decline thereafter.[25]

Eastham sued J. L. Rumbarger in March 1888 seeking $1,000 in damages after the log boom constructed by Rumbarger backed up the Blackwater River and flooded his lot and dwelling in Davis. The boom was constructed near Eastham's house along the river, and the dammed-up river hindered the flow of "the excrement, filth, and water from time to time overflowing, inundating, and forming pools, stagnant water upon the plaintiff's lot and from running and proceeding therefrom into the said dwelling house." Eastham claimed that he "wrongfully and unjustly suffered large quantities of filth and water to penetrate issue and flow from and out of the said boom onto and into the said premises of the said plaintiff ... totally destroying and rendering worthless and valueless his lot" and made his house "uncomfortable, unhealthy and unwholesome and unfit for habitation."[26]

Rumbarger sent an attorney to Grospoint, Indiana, in February 1889, to take the deposition of D. C. Van Buskirk. He had been employed as a foreman by Rumbarger Lumber Company between 1884 and November 1886, and superintended the construction of the boom at Davis. He testified that Eastham had accompanied him while looking for the best location on the river, and in fact suggested the spot near his house because Eastham thought it would make a good pond and improve boating on the river. Van Buskirk and his family lived in Eastham's house [presumably renting it] between November 1885 and September 1886. Prior to that, he had boarded with Eastham in 1885 before his family joined him in Davis. Van Buskirk testified that neither the lot nor the dwelling had been damaged in any way by water overflowing the dam, nor did it cause stagnant or offensive pools of water on the lot or make the house unhealthy, even during the major floods of spring and summer 1886. In fact, the periodic inundations actually improved the banks of the river by washing away the filth which had accumulated along the stream, and gave the stream a better current. Van Buskirk provided testimony that colored the court's decision when he claimed that Eastham "told me on three or four different times that he had no deed for the lot. This he told me in connection with his recital to me of trouble between himself and his wife. Up to this time there was always a good deal of confidential talk between Eastham and me."[27]

As a consequence of Van Buskirk's testimony, both parties agreed to a dismissal of the case with the company paying the costs of the suit, and Eastham giving up his claim for a $1,000 in damages. By this time Rumbarger had sold the property to Albert Thompson, and the judgment declared that the outcome would pose no burden of liability on the new owner for the costs of the case.[28]

In May 1894, Eastham was once again involved in a physical conflict when he, Thomas Mouser, and Cal Davis were charged with assault and battery against Larra Rascals "by beating him and striking him with a gun and threaten[ing] to shoot him against the peace and dignity of the State." Justice of the Peace G. W. McIntire heard the case on May 11, 1894, and the three men plead not guilty. The JP discharged Cal Davis, but fined Eastham and Mauser ten dollars each and ordered them to pay for the cost of prosecution. They remitted the sum of $200 bond and appealed the case to the circuit court.[29] There is no reference in the Tucker County Law Books to what motivated the assault or to the outcome of the appeal.

Eastham never shied away from any dispute no matter what it was. He was one of fifty residents of Davis to sign a petition to the town council supporting two affidavits seeking to abate a nuisance. It seems the crowds, music, whistles, and steam discharges from "a steam riding gallery, commonly called a 'merry-go-round,'" disturbed the peace. Restating R. W. Eastham's testimony, the judge who wrote the opinion observed that Eastham "goes to bed early and gets up early; that he sleeps the best the first part of the night; that the noise of the merry-go-round interrupted him from sleeping; that his wife had the headache one night, and it annoyed her from sleeping; that the crowd around the merry-go-round hallooed and made a noise, and that the music annoyed him." When the council complied with the wishes of the petitioners, the case was appealed to the West Virginia Supreme Court of Appeals. Many witnesses testified that the merry-go-round was not a nuisance, but the high court declared that the council had the right to declare nuisances, and it was not a question requiring the court to overturn the lower court's decision.[30]

Even though Eastham did not go out of his way to avoid trouble and was jealous of his rights as he perceived them, it is also evident that he was considered a worthy citizen. When a dispute arose regarding the boundary line between Tucker and Grant counties, Circuit Court Judge Joseph T. Hoke appointed Eastham and two attorneys, Lloyd Hansford, and Rufus B. Maxwell, to serve as commissioners from Tucker County to meet with the commissioners from Grant County "to settle and adjust and determine the disputed boundaryline." It is interesting to note that Grant and Hardy counties were created out of old Hampshire and Mineral counties to separate Confederate South Branch agrarians and the Unionist railroad-industrial interests in Hardy County. As an outdoorsman and surveyor for H. G. Davis, Eastham knew this area very well. Moreover, Eastham was among the thirty names recommended as deputies for Tucker County sheriff Will E. Cupp. The court approved them, although only seven were present for swearing in. Eastham was not one of them.[31] Obviously not everyone considered Eastham a "goon."

5

WHO WERE THE THOMPSONS?

Family History

Like the Easthams of Virginia, the Thompsons of New England were an old established American family. Frank Thompson and Robert Eastham both descended from families who represented the two dominant, but divergent, national branches of the British family tree in nineteenth-century America. The Easthams traced their ancestry back to the earliest days of settlement in Virginia and evolved over subsequent generations within a slaveholding southern plantation society. The Thompsons' earliest roots are more ambiguous, but reach back to the early years of the Massachusetts Bay Colony. They evolved over the generations within the commercial, market-oriented society of New England. At the time of the Civil War, the Thompsons were antislavery Yankees in every feature that marked their region's political culture: business and market-orientation, economic rationality, and a belief in a moralistic political ideology. The Easthams were quintessential plantation slaveholders who became Confederates as naturally as the Thompsons became Yankee businessmen. Both families held elite positions within their respective societies. When Robert Eastham and Frank Thompson confronted each other in the close quarters of that railway car that fateful day in 1897, it is tempting to see them as the personification of America's grand political and cultural divide during the late nineteenth century.

Unlike the Easthams who have been members of the elite of Rappahannock County, Virginia, for centuries and, therefore, are much easier to document, reconstructing the ancestry of Frank Thompson's family presents a greater challenge. Responding to a relative's query regarding the family's history, Frank's cousin George Benjamin Thompson stated the problem: "The Thompsons had no family pride, that is, they were not very numerous and did not keep in contact with each other."[1] He might have added that they were very mobile, and for the most part West Virginia represented a brief interlude during their lives.

One historian of Norway, Maine, links the family to John Thompson who sailed from England to Plymouth before 1645. That same year he married Mary, a daughter of Francis Cooke, one of the Mayflower Pilgrims, and a member of the first Pilgrim church society at Scrooby, England. The principal Thompson families of New England have descended from this couple. Edward Thompson, of unknown relationship to John, was one of the passengers aboard the Mayflower in 1620. He died during the winter of their landing and is presumed to be the first Pilgrim buried in the New World. However, another source claims that the family can be traced back seven generations to the Reverend William Thompson (1598–1666) who came to colonial America, probably Massachusetts, from Winwich, Lancashire, England.[2]

Whoever the progenitor, Albert Thompson's family roots were very deep in New England soil. Benjamin Thompson, one of the first settlers in New Hampshire, was a resident of Concord. However, he was driven away by local patriots during the Revolutionary War for being an ardent loyalist. Two of his descendants settled and died in Norway, Maine: Belinda married General George L. Beal; Charles, who enlisted during the

Civil War in the Norway Company of the 1st Maine with the rank of lieutenant, was discharged in 1865 with a service-related disability.[3]

The Thompsons who engaged in the lumber industry at Davis were descended from the Berlin and Stark, New Hampshire, and Norway, Maine, branch of the family. The towns straddled the New Hampshire and Maine state line, and were not far apart. Six men in the Thompson family came to Davis to engage in the lumber business: Albert and his brothers John and Sumner, his son Frank Elmer, his nephew George B., and his brother-in-law Charles Blake. All of them were managers of the Thompson-owned Blackwater Lumber Company and its successor, the Thompson Lumber Company.

The Thompson brothers' grandfather, Samuel S. Thompson, enlisted at Gray, Maine, and fought in the War of 1812. He either lost a foot or the use of it at the battle of Sacketts Harbor, New York, and was disabled enough to be released with a pension. Samuel's son, Benjamin Thompson (about 1805–1881) married Sarah Wheeler (born about 1814). Both were natives of Maine who moved to Berlin, Coos County, New Hampshire, where Benjamin was a farmer, miller, lumberman, and operated a sawmill. In 1860 the value of his real estate was listed as $4,000 and his personal property as $1,000.[4]

Benjamin and Sarah Thompson had eight children according to the 1860 federal census, although county histories claim there were seven. Albert Thompson, who was born February 28, 1839, was the leading figure among the family of lumbermen. He was born in Berlin, Coos County, New Hampshire, but spent his youth in Stark. In 1851 the railroad passed through Berlin and a lumber mill was established on the Androscoggin River. Apparently, Benjamin recognized his opportunity to improve his family's fortune and he acquired rights to use the river for a lumber mill at Stark, New Hampshire, about twenty miles northwest of Berlin. Accordingly, he moved the family to Stark where Benjamin's sons worked in their father's mill and farmed on the side. Albert's plans for his future changed dramatically when, at nineteen, he suffered a serious accident in his father's sawmill. According to family history, he "lost a leg in a logging accident, and decided to study medicine. Later he became a dentist." Albert had attended the local public schools and then Gould's Academy, located in Bethel, Maine. After the accident, however, it was arranged that he would study dentistry with Josiah Heald of Portland, Maine. He practiced dentistry in Portland for a time before moving to Norway, Maine, where he practiced for another four years.[5]

While in Norway, Dr. Thompson married Mary Elizabeth Blake (1844–1925) of Bethel, New Hampshire, on June 20, 1861, and settled down in Norway, Maine. She was described as a "cultured and lovable lady" in the town history. Mary had attended a music school, probably the New England Conservatory of Music, where she and Albert later sent their daughter Sarah Maude.[6] After four years as a dentist in Norway, Albert's business imagination turned once again to the lumber industry. In 1865 Albert Thompson and G. T. Wheeler became partners in the lumber business at Ridgway, Elk County, Pennsylvania. Ridgway is in north central Pennsylvania on the southeastern edge of the current Allegheny National Forest. Wheeler was a cousin to Albert's wife on her mother's side; both men were born in 1839. Albert remained in Ridgway for four years before returning to New Hampshire to join his father in the lumber business. Back in his old hometown of Stark, Albert was elected in 1873 to a two-year term as delegate from Coos County in the New Hampshire House of Representatives, and reelected to a second term in 1875. In politics he was a "staunch Republican." Albert returned to Ridgway

Albert Thompson. Courtesy of Sarah Thompson Fletcher.

Frank E. Thompson. Courtesy of Sarah Thompson Fletcher.

in 1881 to take charge of an extensive lumber mill that produced more than six million feet of lumber a year.[7]

Albert and Mary had three children. Albert Jr. was a young boy when he was tragically killed on a train by a wild bullet fired by a drunken man. Frank Elmer Thompson, the second son, was born in Norway, Maine, December 19, 1861, and died in

Cumberland, Maryland, on March 20, 1897, from gunshot wounds at the hand of Robert Eastham. His remains were carried by special train back to Norway where they were interred in a mausoleum constructed by his sister Maude. He reportedly graduated from Dartmouth College in 1882, but a thorough investigation by archivists at that institution has revealed no record of Frank having ever attended Dartmouth. Whatever occupied him during that period, he joined his father shortly after Albert returned to Ridgway in 1881 as a lumber-mill operator. A local history published in 1890 after he made the move to Tucker County, West Virginia, described Frank E. as "a young man of considerable business ability" who had assumed the "entire charge of his father's lumbering interests in Ridgway" after his father's departure.[8] Another local historian declared that, like his father, Frank was a man of "sterling integrity and worth, being very popular with his associates and given to great charities."[9]

Albert and Mary Thompson's only daughter, Sarah Maude Thompson, was born in Stark, New Hampshire, in 1874. She was educated in the public schools of Ridgway, Pennsylvania, and then the New England Conservatory of Music in Boston, Massachusetts, where she graduated in 1895. Maude traveled extensively and studied for a time in Europe before returning to teach at the conservatory. A family friend described Maude as "charming and very talented musically." She had no known connection with West Virginia even after her family moved to Davis in the early 1890s. Nevertheless, through a generous bequest (discussed in the epilogue), Maude would play an important role in the development of Tucker County long after most of the family members had departed the state for new opportunities.[10]

The Thompsons also owned Rock Island in Lake Penneseewassee, Norway, Maine, where the family spent their summers.

While traveling between their permanent residence in Philadelphia and Norway, they often stopped over with friends in Somerville, Massachusetts. One of the family members who hosted the Thompsons remembered their visits well: "They were delightful people, warm-hearted, witty, full of fun and subtle humor. We always looked forward to their laughter-filled visits. Though millionaires they were unassuming, down-to-earth, comfortable friends."[11]

Sumner W. Thompson, born January 7, 1837, in Berlin, New Hampshire, was two years older than Albert. Like Albert, he moved with the family to Stark and was living at home in 1860 and probably working in his father's lumber business. He married Albina M. York in Stark on November 5, 1859, and the couple lived in Milan and Dummer, Coos County, New Hampshire before moving to Davis, West Virginia, with his brothers. Sumner served as the woods boss for the Blackwater Lumber Company and was responsible for timber operations at the time his nephew Frank E. was killed in 1897. He also directed the construction of the logging railroad on the south side of the Blackwater River and began the extension of a logging railroad to the head of the Blackwater Canyon.[12]

John Franklin Thompson was born June 29, 1851, in Stark and moved to Davis in 1888 with his brothers Albert and Sumner. When the Blackwater Boom and Lumber Company was organized in 1888, he took charge of the clapboard department. He also ran a lumber operation in nearby Bretz and remained in this position after 1893 when W. H. Osterhout of Ridgway, Pennsylvania, purchased the BB&L Co. and formed the Blackwater Lumber Company. John resigned in 1895 and moved to Harrison, Idaho, where he built a plant and manufactured clapboards and box shooks from local white pine. He returned to Davis in 1899 to become general manager of the Blackwater Lumber Company

John F. Thompson. Courtesy of Sarah Thompson Fletcher.

Charles G. Blake in the Thompsons' Philadelphia office. Courtesy of Sarah Thompson Fletcher.

now largely owned by his brother Albert. In 1905 John formed the Thompson Lumber Company, which purchased the holdings of the Blackwater Lumber Company. A talented builder, he constructed the Blackwater Lumber Company's narrow gauge logging railroad between Davis and Douglass and set up the company's log skidders to haul timber out of the Blackwater Canyon in 1904. According to family history, when the Thompson Lumber Company was sold to the Babcock Lumber Company of Pittsburgh, Pennsylvania, John moved to California where he built railroads and bridges for the mining industry.[13]

Albert Thompson's brother-in-law, Charles Gilman Blake, joined the Thompson exodus from Ridgway, Pennsylvania, to the new lumberman's paradise of Davis, West Virginia. His father, Jonathan Blake (1817–1902), served as a captain in the Norway Company of the 10th Maine during the Civil War. He married Elizabeth S. Crocket (1821–1908) of Norway, and they lived the rest of their lives in Norway, Maine. Charles Gilman Blake, born March 18, 1854, was one of four children from their union. He married Mary Addie Denison on October 16, 1878. Blake had worked in his father's business before joining his in-laws as the Blackwater Lumber Company bookkeeper and shipping clerk. The same year Blackwater Lumber Company was formed in 1893, Blake's fourteen-year-old son, George O. Blake, was killed by an "accidental discharge of a gun." When Frank E. was killed in 1897, Charles Blake assumed management of the company, and also found the time to serve as the mayor of Davis. In July 1902, however, he was sent to take charge of the company's Philadelphia sales office that Albert had established and never returned to West Virginia.[14]

The Thompsons played a strategically important role in the development of Tucker County, and particularly the boomtown of Davis, through their investment in logging operations, the lumber mill, and the jobs they created. In many ways, however, the youngest of them, Albert's nephew George Benjamin Thompson had a greater long-term impact on Tucker County than the other Thompson lumbermen because he and his descendants remained in the area and became prominent Canaan Valley residents for more than a century. George B. was born in 1871, the son of Hiram and Lucy Mason Thompson. Hiram was the brother of Albert and Sumner. They were, therefore, George B.'s uncles, while Albert's son Frank Elmer was a cousin. His father Hiram died at the early age of twenty-seven, and George B. was raised by his grandparents Benjamin and Sarah Thompson. Growing up as a member of the household, George was treated like a younger

George B. Thompson. Courtesy of Sarah Thompson Fletcher.

brother by his uncles. At the urging of his uncle Albert, George left school in 1893 as a young man of nineteen and joined his uncles in Davis to work in the Blackwater Lumber Company's office as a secretary and timekeeper. In 1900 he was living in his uncle Sumner's household, but shortly thereafter he married Elsie

Jane Pryor, a native of Pennsylvania. He and Elsie had five children.[15]

When the Thompson Lumber Company was sold to the Babcock Lumber Company of Pittsburgh in 1907, George B. became general manager and continued in that position until the company closed the operation in 1924. During this period he exercised a potent influence on the economic and political life of Tucker County. Running on the Republican ticket, he was elected to a term in the West Virginia House of Delegates in 1915–1917 and, on November 17, 1921, was appointed U.S. Postmaster of Davis.[16]

The Thompsons' Lumber Business

Albert Thompson had acquired extensive experience in the lumber industry prior to his arrival in Tucker County in 1887. He had worked in his father's lumber mill in Stark, New Hampshire, and extended his experience as a mill owner and operator in Ridgway, Pennsylvania, for several years. When he made his decision to explore his opportunities in West Virginia, he followed a well-trod path by Pennsylvania lumbermen who, in the last two decades of the nineteenth century, moved down the Appalachians in search of new timberlands.

In the 1880s nearly all of Tucker County was still covered by a towering virgin forest. A spur line of the West Virginia Central and Pittsburgh Railroad, extended from the mainline to Davis in 1884, provided an outlet for timber driven down the Blackwater River and opened the Canaan wilderness to development. Jacob L. Rumbarger, a native of Pennsylvania, was the first lumberman to establish an operation in the county. He was joined in the Rumbarger Company by his four sons John, Robert, Frank T., and Jacob Jr. In 1883 there was a national shortage of cherry lumber, and in Tucker County the senior Rumbarger expected to find a major supply. He arrived at Rowlesburg on the B&O train and rode a freight wagon to the county seat of St. George where attorney Wilson B. Maxwell informed him about the timber available in the Canaan Valley. Solomon J. Parsons loaned Rumbarger a horse and gave him directions to Robert Eastham's home in the Canaan Valley. With Eastham as his guide, Rumbarger spent the best part of the week inspecting the timber, and, by the end of the week, he had purchased several stands of valuable cherry. In 1885 teams of horses and equipment were shipped in, and a year later Rumbarger completed the construction of a sawmill along the river near Davis. The recently cleared town was on its way to becoming a major lumber processing center for timber cut in the Blackwater watershed and then shipped to the urban markets over the West Virginia and Pittsburgh Railway. Rumbarger's large bandmill was the second of its type to be erected in the state of West Virginia. He purchased only timber supplied by local contractors. The first log drive down the Blackwater River reached Davis on March 30, 1886, and Rumbarger quickly became "the foremost manufacturer of hardwoods in his day."[17]

Meanwhile, Albert Thompson had purchased a large acreage of timber along the Blackwater River, and obtained a charter, dated June 25, 1887, to build dams and booms to facilitate floating logs and rafts down river. Earlier that month, on June 9, 1887, he had obtained another charter incorporating the Blackwater Boom and Lumber Company. In 1888 Rumbarger sold his holdings to Thompson who immediately ceased construction of a sawmill he was erecting just below Davis and sold the framework to another lumber company. Thompson then rebuilt the Rumbarger mill to process spruce lumber; in March 1889 he contracted to cut the timber and pulpwood on a twelve-thousand-acre tract owned by the Marshall Coal and Lumber Company. The tract was strategically located at the confluence of the Blackwater River and Beaver Creek just above Davis, and the acquisition gave the company "a monopoly on all the timber in the Blackwater basin of Canaan Valley."[18]

The Blackwater Boom and Lumber Company found it difficult to reduce manufacturing costs and keep the mill stocked with a sufficient supply of logs to operate full time. Thompson attempted to resolve these problems by entering into a contract with his son Frank, who was at the time in charge of his father's mill in Ridgway, to manufacture the lumber. The contract continued in force until November 1, 1892. During this period, Albert contracted with the Blackwater Boom and Lumber Company to supply the mill with logs. He also extended a railroad to the Blackwater River in the Canaan Valley, and made extensive improvements on the river to increase its capacity to carry logs downstream to the mill. By 1893 the supply issue had been resolved, and the river was full of logs for twenty-five miles upstream from Davis to the upper Canaan Valley. Notwithstanding these improvements, the company continued to experience high production costs. In the middle of these persistent difficulties, disaster struck when the saw mill was destroyed by fire.[19]

Unfortunately, economic conditions did not provide a stimulus for the struggling business either. The Panic of 1893, one of the nation's most severe depressions up to that time, effectively killed the lumber market for several years. George B. Thompson related a story that illustrated how cutthroat the lumber business could be. In late 1894 and early 1895 the effects of the Panic of 1893 were still depressing the lumber market. A Mr. Quinn, the manager of the Export Lumber Company of New York, conceived the idea of combining the spruce manufacturers of West Virginia into an organization for handling the entire production. It was a feasible undertaking at that time because all the spruce was produced along the West Virginia Central and Pittsburgh Railway: "About the last of November in 1895, The Export Lumber Co. had placed an order with the Blackwater Lumber Co. of Davis for a cargo of lumber for South America and they were preparing to work on the same when [the company's agent Mr.] Quinn wired them to cancel the order unless they would cut the price .50 cents per million." Robert F. Whitmer, owner of the Condon-Lane Boom and Lumber Company of Horton, West Virginia, agreed to supply the lumber at the reduced price. Mr. Quinn then ordered the ship to come to Philadelphia to receive the cargo. Demurrage charges on this vessel totaled $100 per day for each day it was dockside without being loaded. However, when Quinn arrived at Horton he found that the gang saw was not in operation, and learned that the repairs would be delayed. Now desperate, he went back to the Blackwater Lumber Company and again offered the cargo to them. "Frank Thompson heard his tale of hardship and said he would consider taking the order for $1.00 per M. additional to the price offered him when they canceled the order on him. The Beaver Creek Co. told him they did not propose to play second fiddle to any one and would not be interested."[20]

Under the serious financial strain resulting from a dull market and high production costs, Albert Thompson sought a "white knight" and found him in an old acquaintance back in Ridgway, in the person of William A. Osterhout, proprietor of the Eagle Valley Tannery. A native of New York who grew up in the industry, in 1870 he moved to Ridgway and built the extensive tannery that included a store, a boarding house, and forty tenement homes to serve the 160 employees and local residents. Osterhout was engaged in many other businesses, however, and ranked as one of the state's most prosperous men.[21]

Undoubtedly Osterhout knew Albert and Frank well, and he demonstrated his faith in their managerial abilities by providing the capital to purchase the Blackwater Boom and Lumber Company holdings when it was sold at open auction on August 3, 1893. Frank Thompson represented Osterhout at the auction and was placed in charge of erecting a new sawmill on the site of the old one. Frank and his father Albert went to the World's Fair in Chicago to inspect the latest in sawmill machinery. Osterhout reorganized the company on January 26, 1894, and Frank E. Thompson, John F. Thompson, Sumner W. Thompson, George Benjamin Thompson, Charles G. Blake, and A. I. Wilson Jr., became stockholders. Frank Thompson was appointed general manager of the renamed Blackwater Lumber Company.[22]

Even though he was not a stockholder, Albert exerted considerable influence with the company, and he continued to accumulate land and timber rights to stock the company with logs. In some of these deals Frank joined him, as with the purchase of timber on what was known as the Dobbin Manor Tract which covered an area of 8,000 acres. The overstocked markets in 1894 and 1895 resulting from the continued effects of the 1893 panic was a serious concern for the Blackwater Lumber Company, especially since the company's logs filled the Blackwater River for miles upstream and were piled high at the railroad landing. When Frank died on March 18, 1897, from his gunshot wounds, as Frank's beneficiary, Albert once again acquired a direct interest in the company. Albert had decided to sell the property, but the failure of the jury to convict Robert Eastham for the murder of his son so upset him that he withdrew from an offer and instead purchased even more land and timber in the Canaan Valley, including the farm that had belonged to Robert and Mary Eastham. If he could not vanquish the farmers in court, he would have his justice by simply buying them out. Albert owned 8,400 acres and timber rights to another 12,000 acres prior to Frank's death. Afterward, he bought another 4,000 acres and timber rights to an additional 5,000 acres. By 1898, therefore, he either owned outright or controlled 29,400 acres of land and timber in Tucker County.[23]

With Frank dead, Albert's brother-in-law Charles G. Blake became the company's general manager. A few years earlier, Albert had opened a sales office in Philadelphia and his nephew George B. Thompson was transferred to that office. In July 1902, C. G. Blake was transferred to the Philadelphia sales office, and John F. Thompson became general manager. Sumner W. Thompson resigned in 1903, but subsequently rejoined the company when the roles of the Thompson family members within the organization were changed. In July 1902, Albert bought and then closed the Thomas Burger and Sons plant in Douglass, and extended the Blackwater's logging railroad from Davis to Douglass. Then, in January 1905, the Thompsons bought out stockholders of the Blackwater Lumber Company and chartered the entirely family-owned Thompson Lumber Company.[24]

Even more dramatic were the changes in the Thompsons' fortunes that occurred a few years later. In February 1907, the Thompsons had either decided to pull out of West Virginia, or received financial inducement that they could not refuse. Albert's brother John resigned in 1907 and moved to Long Beach, California, which was recorded as his home by the federal census takers in 1910; city directories for 1916 and 1932 list his occupation as mining. Since there is no mining in the greater Los Angeles area, he was probably an owner or consultant. On October 31, 1916, his wife Iola, whom he married in 1872 back in New Hampshire, died. John was interred next to her in the same mausoleum in Inglewood, California, upon his death December 30, 1935, at age eighty-four.[25] Albert's brother Sumner, who had resigned earlier

Thompson Lumber Company. Courtesy of West Virginia and Regional History Center.

in August 1903 because of ill health, joined his brother John in Long Beach, California, where he died a decade later on January 27, 1913. He was survived by his wife Albina, who lived on until 1922. Sumner and Albina are buried together in Sunnyside Cemetery in Long Beach.[26]

Albert's brother-in-law Charles G. Blake and wife Mary had moved to Philadelphia by 1910, but by 1920 they had returned to Norway where he was reportedly "carrying on the business of a lumber dealer." He was listed as a "widower" in the 1930 census. Charles himself died on March 25, 1932, and was buried in Norway Pine Grove Cemetery as was Frank E. Thompson.[27]

The Babcock Lumber and Boom Company headquartered in Pittsburgh was operated by four Babcock brothers who became titans in the lumber industry. The Babcocks took over all of the holdings and operations of the Thompson Lumber Company and the Albert Thompson Enterprises, including the sales office in Philadelphia. The extent of these operations is suggested by the properties acquired by Babcock: forty miles of standard gauge railroad, two sawmills, a planing mill, a box factory, 8.5 million feet of lumber stacked in the yards, 8.5 million feet of logs damned in the Blackwater River, and 46,000 acres of timber land, estimated at 450 million feet of lumber. The No. 1 (softwood) mill, located on the north side of Blackwater River, with two eight-foot and one six-foot band saws, was capable of cutting 100,000 board feet of lumber a day. The No. 2 (hardwood) mill, located on the south side of Blackwater River, with one eight-foot band saw, was capable of cutting 125,000 feet of lumber a day. At peak operation the Babcock Company employed five hundred men.[28]

The Babcock Company retained Albert Thompson's nephew, George B. Thompson, and appointed him general manager of these far-flung operations. He and his descendants remained in West Virginia to become leading citizens of Tucker County. The rest of the Thompson men and their families, however, scattered to other parts of the country.

6

SETTING THE STAGE FOR TROUBLE

Since purchasing the Blackwater Boom and Lumber Company (BB&L Co.) in October 1893, the Blackwater Lumber Company (BLC) had spent considerable time and money to improve the Blackwater River, repairing dams and booms, and constructing the new mill. In the transaction, the company acquired three storage booms in the river, one at the large mill in Davis, one a mile below the mill, and another about two miles above the mill. It also acquired approximately seventeen million feet of logs held by the storage boom two miles upriver from the mill, which choked the Blackwater River with logs for about sixteen miles upstream from the boom nearly to the river's source. Robert Eastham's land and timber lay along the river's upper reaches, and it was his inability to drive his logs to market that led to an escalation of hostilities between Eastham and the Thompsons.[1]

Eastham as Land Agent

Eastham was heavily involved in the timber business as an independent contractor supplying logs to the BB&L Co., and with his knowledge of the Canaan wilderness area, he also served as the local overseer for absentee landowners. One tract in particular lay at the heart of Eastham's conflict with BLC. This was the 444.4 acres of land near Eastham's own property in the upper Blackwater River owned by real estate investors C. Powell Grady of

Duluth, Minnesota, and Hiram Woods of Baltimore, Maryland, and for whom Eastham was serving as local agent. Since 1887 the owners had been trying to sell the timber, land, or both. As their local overseer, Eastham heard from them frequently seeking his advice. "Let me know when you think it will sell. I have to depend upon you entirely in this matter," Grady wrote Eastham in late 1887.[2]

Albert Thompson was one of the owners of the BB&L Co., but he also contracted to supply the mill with timber. In 1889, he made an offer, through Eastham, to Grady and Woods to purchase their timber. Woods wrote to Eastham urging him to use his "good offices in securing the best offer you can. I take for granted that Mr. Thompson is at present the only buyer, and that he has no competition." Consequently, "we must largely depend upon his liberality."[3] Apparently, a contract was concluded, and Thompson had cut the largest timber in 1889. Then he surprised Grady and Woods by going back on the tract in 1891 to cut the smaller timber he had passed over two years earlier. In December 1891, Woods communicated his strenuous objections to Eastham: for Thompson "to go back now upon the land and resume cutting we think entirely out of order. As you seem to be in association with the present officers of the Blackwater Boom & Lumber Co. we hope it may not be amiss for us to ask you to communicate these views to them."[4]

Eastham also contracted with Grady and Woods to cut the smaller and lower-grade pulpwood off their land at fifty cents per cord with a two-year limit, and by June 1893 he had cleared off from 1,000 to 1,500 cords. By the end of 1893, however, Hiram Woods was pressing Eastham for money, and Grady was reminding him that he had promised to have another 1,500 to 2,000 cords ready to drive by early January 1894, but Eastham was granted an extension of time.[5] Eastham alluded to the cause of his problem in getting the pulpwood to the mill when he informed Woods early in 1894 that he would then send the $500 since the buyer had "promised to pay up next week." However, Eastham continued, "I hope you all will not give the Thompsons any more privileges on the land as they are the ones that has [sic] caused all the damage to your timber and are now trying to hinder and cause me all the trouble they can in the way of selling and getting out any more.... I have never had to deal with [such] a set of Yankees before. I have come to the conclusion if all of them are like the Thompsons & Osterhouts I don't [want] any more to do with them than I possibly can help."[6]

Woods replied: "I note what you say about the Thompsons etc. Our contract with that party ceased long ago and I am at a loss to know how they are now in position to cause you trouble."[7] Eastham explained that he was unable to move any of his pulp wood because "the Thompsons have the river blocked and will not let my logs through." He was convinced that "their object is to freeze me out. He is the same one that first bought your timber and skinned you all. I will not be able to get what I had already cut and in the river down to Davis before late in the summer if then." Eastham surmised that Albert Thompson was "after some rights at the [splash] dam which is on your land just a few rods below mine which backs the water over more than 75 acres of my land."[8]

The issue had arisen earlier, but Grady informed Eastham that he did not "think the BB&L Co. ever asked for or got any permission to build a dam on our lands. Nor do I think they have ever paid anything for the right. I remember there was some correspondence about it when they were settling for the lumber and they said they would make it right with us, but that as I recall it was simply for timber that they had used in construction." Since they had not paid for its use, nor been given the rights, Grady wrote, "you might as well have the benefit of it. We certainly ought to have some concessions from them if they have enjoyed the benefit of our property."[9] Eastham notified the Thompsons that they were prohibited from using the splash dam in the future, explaining to Woods that it gave them "rights where they have none to stop me" from putting his logs into the river and driving them downstream to the mill in Davis. "I hope you will not give them any rights on the land whatever. If you do please notify me as I have bought the adjoining tract." Eastham lamented to Woods that "I have had trouble with A. Thompson." All the money Eastham possessed was invested in the pulpwood. Until he delivered it, he could not get paid, and, therefore, neither could Grady and Woods.[10] Grady reassured Eastham in March 1894 that he and Woods were "quite willing that you would have the control of our interests at Davis," and extended the date to April 1895 for Eastham to clear all the pulpwood from their tract. "We are both glad to have you make a profit out of the transaction as well as ourselves. And I know no one that I would be willing to put our interests in the hands of but yourself."[11] Eastham's grievances with the Thompsons had been festering for several years, but they were about to get much worse.

Nevertheless, business is business, and Grady and Woods had been hoping to sell their land for a long time. Albert Thompson gave them the opportunity. "I had a call from Mr. Thompson a short time since. Have you any dispute or trouble with him or his company?" Woods wrote to Eastham somewhat disingenuously.[12] Late that year, Woods wrote again and the news was ominous: "You have doubtless been informed by Mr. Grady of the sale to Albert Thompson of the Woods-Grady land." The cash offer was impossible to resist, Woods wrote, but "I hope the sale will in no way operate against your interest which both Mr. Grady and myself wish to promote. We had the assurance from Mr. Thompson that his desire in purchasing the land was that he might be in position to adjust amicably all questions of difference between you and the Boom Company."[13] Worse for Eastham, the agreement contained a potential threat to him as indicated in a letter from Grady to Woods in October 1895 and forwarded to Eastham: "I regret very much that the clause giving right to sue for damages previously committed was inserted. We did not stipulate for any such deed: and, I would suggest that you think it over before delivering it. I do not know that it gives Thompson any special advantage over Eastham that he did not have before for the Co. had full authority and privilege of constructing their dam on our property, and he would be as fully entitled to sue for damages to said dam as if they owned the land; but it would seem to make us parties favoring the boom company and against Eastham and I wanted to keep out of the whole thing."[14] Eastham was increasingly being pressed into a corner.

R. W. Eastham v. Blackwater Lumber Company

The seeds of conflict between the Thompsons and Robert Eastham had been sown and all too quickly began to bear rancid fruit. The most immediate complaints emanated from Eastham's inability to deliver his wood to the mill at Davis because the Blackwater River was choked with the company's logs, and the splash dam erected on the upper river, which flooded Eastham's property when filled, was absolutely necessary for the driving of logs. On a number of occasions Eastham expressed his conviction that the Thompsons intended to force him out of business, and blocking the river and taking him to court were tactics to that end.

Eastham had about 800 cords of pulpwood, for which he had paid Grady & Woods $400, and three valuable logs in the Blackwater River destined for the mill at Davis. To make matters worse, there was some disagreement between the parties over the rates (or boomage) the company charged for handling logs at the mill boom in Davis. Eastham's counsel, Wilson B. Maxwell, served notice to the company on March 5, 1894, that he intended to petition the court to appoint a commission to revise the rates of boomage for pulpwood charged by Blackwater Lumber Company, which he did on March 12.[15] Accordingly, a three-man commission was established, and in September it set the rate at twenty-five cents per cord, rather than the fifty cents a cord the company demanded as just compensation for the use of the company's capital and the labor costs to process the lumber accepted from independent contractors like Eastham. This benefited the individual loggers along the river, but cut in half the company's revenue from this source. The Blackwater Lumber Company filed official exceptions to the new rates and, flexing its political muscle, succeeded in replacing the three commissioners with friendly ones who then restored the old rate of fifty cents per cord.[16] The company's actions offered further evidence to Eastham and other independent loggers that the Thompsons were exercising their political power to drive them out of business, giving them a monopoly over the Blackwater's timber supply.

The conflict was formally entered when Eastham brought suit against the Blackwater Lumber Company for taking one cherry log and two ash logs without Eastham's permission. A summons was issued by Justice of the Peace J. M. Talbot on June 18, 1895, for a company official to appear before him. In the civil action, Eastham demanded judgment for the sum of $125 for damages, interest, and court costs. A week later, evidence was presented by both parties in the dispute, and the JP concluded that the company should pay restitution to Eastham in the sum of $71.50. Blackwater disagreed with the judgment, however, and appealed the decision to the Tucker County Circuit Court. The circuit court jury seemed to agree that Eastham had been wronged; nevertheless, the judge reduced the JP's award for damages to $32.50—$8.00 for the logs, and $24.50 for the work of Eastham's men breaking log jams in an attempt to free the logs that were stuck behind the company's logs choking the Blackwater River. Eastham regarded the verdict as inadequate and moved the court to reconsider. Unfortunately for him, the Tucker County Circuit Court jury sustained the amount set in the June verdict, and ordered that BLC recover its court costs from Eastham.[17]

Evidence presented during the June 1895 trial revealed the points of conflict between Eastham and the Thompsons, which subsequent actions would only compound. Testimony also made it very clear that more than a few logs were at the heart of the matter. Residents were taking sides according to their own perceived interests in the changes taking place in the local economy and whether the company was using its power to "bully" locals out of their traditional rights.

Under contract with the Blackwater Boom & Lumber Company, signed on March 1, 1892, Eastham had purchased the timber on several tracts of land in the upper Blackwater country that included pulpwood, spruce, and the aforementioned cherry and ash logs. He sold the pulpwood and spruce saw logs to the Blackwater Boom & Lumber Company, but not the cherry and ash, and the company agreed to purchase and remove the timber. Shortly thereafter, when the BB&L Co. went into receivership, Eastham entered an agreement with the receiver, Fairfax S. Landstreet, assigning to the BB&L Co. his contractual rights for the purchase of the timber in the Canaan Valley as well as "all the logs or pulp wood now skidded on the Grady and Woods tract of 444 acres." BB&L Co. agreed to pay Eastham $1,060, the amount he had agreed to pay the owner for the timber. He also agreed "to give to the Blackwater Lumber Company or their representatives free right of way to remove the timber and pulp wood now skidded on the Grady and Woods tract."[18]

Asked to explain the expenses he was suing the Blackwater Lumber Company to recover, Eastham claimed that nine men worked for him skidding the logs to the river and breaking up jams of BLC logs. He paid each of them $2.50 a day plus board, which totaled $49. Eastham estimated the cherry log was worth $30, and the two ash logs were valued at $44. He also sought $93 in damages from BLC. He testified that he left the cherry and ash logs between the skidway and the road about fifty yards from the river, because they would have to be hauled by team or rolled a good distance. Nevertheless, the logs were taken up by Thompson's crew and put into the river with the rest of the company's logs. The cherry log, about 18 to 20 inches in diameter and 16 feet long, contained 400 or 500 feet of lumber. It was cut into three logs, but two were missing and unaccounted for. Eastham was claiming damages for the "butt log," the largest one at the base of the tree. It was marked with Eastham's name in blue keel and his four ax marks. Three of Eastham's men had caught up with the logs and tied them to a big tree just below the upper splash dam, but again the logs got loose and were in the river somewhere. The pulpwood was broken into the river in March 1894, and Eastham's men drove it down the river until they came up against Blackwater's logs and could go no further. Eastham's men broke the log jam in the spring of 1895 as the water rose, but Thompson logs were being put in the river at the same time, and they rose ten feet high across the river so that nothing could pass. Eastham's pulpwood was lost among Thompson's logs, so he felt compelled to serve notice on the Blackwater Lumber Company to allow his logs to pass through.

Eastham's problem was that the cherry and ash he had cut were not paid for. He had promised the landowner, a man named

Idleman, that he would pay for them when he sold the logs to the BLC. When the logs went missing, therefore, Eastham had neither the logs nor the money he owed Idleman.

The Blackwater Boom and Lumber Company had built the upper splash dam on the Grady and Woods tract, but according to the sale agreement, the Blackwater Lumber Company now claimed they owned the rights to the dam. The BLC argued that it had used the dam since buying out BB&L Co.—with Eastham's permission. With payment of a fee, one of Eastham's men would open the dam for the company as necessary. Although Blackwater's lawyers, C. Wood Dailey and A. Jay Valentine, implied that Eastham was trying to control the dam so he could charge whatever he wanted to open it, this was probably not the case because Eastham allowed his men to keep the fees for opening the dam gates. The men who worked for Eastham lived close to Eastham's farm, and, like their Appalachian counterparts during the timber boom, they worked on farms in the summer, cut timber in the winter, and drove logs down river on the spring tides.

Blackwater lawyers also tried to undermine Eastham's claims by demonstrating that Eastham did not do much work: "Didn't you do most of your work riding the horse along the bank," they asked. "No, sir, you cannot work on a log with a horse," Eastham replied, and testimony supported his claim that he "worked as much as any of them." Counsel for the defense also attempted to establish that Eastham's men were inexperienced and therefore their work was not worth the wage proffered. They also attempted to show that there was not enough water to drive logs, again undercutting the claims of Eastham and his rivermen. Furthermore, they argued, Eastham worked harder at moving his own logs than moving BLC logs out of the way.

Plaintiff's counsel charged that Eastham's logs were clearly marked but that Sumner Thompson, who was responsible for supplying the mill with logs, willfully and knowingly broke the law by ordering Eastham's cherry and ash logs to be rolled into the river against Eastham's wishes. Harrison Cosner, who was driving logs for the Thompsons, explained: "We was driving these company logs . . . and Mr. Eastham came up the river bank, and I and John Nine, and a parcel of us was along there, and Eastham says to us, 'I don't want those cherry and ash logs rolled in,' or something to that amount, and the next day Mr. [Sumner] Thompson came along, and we said to him that Mr. Eastham didn't want us to roll those logs in, and he went to the butt end of the cherry log and says, 'this log has the company's mark on it, branded with a K, and we will roll that log in.'"

Asked if he knew anything about the ash logs, Cosner said yes,

> Mr. Eastham came up to us, while we was driving for the company, and said there was two ash logs and . . . they were branded by four ax marks, and a little E on them, and he said he wanted us to catch them up, or raft them rather, and he gave me a pair of wedges about that long, with little chains to it, and a rope, and I took it on my shoulder, and went up the stream, and Freel Cosner, and my son, rather, had found these two logs, and run them out to the shore, and gave them these little wedges, and they drove them in the logs, and Freel drove them above the dam somewhere about 150 or 200 yards, and tied them up to a birch tree.

Harrison Cosner saw the logs again only briefly in the spring of 1893. They still had the wedges in them, "but me and a whole lot of us was rolling the shore, and we had orders to take everything as it came, cleaning the shores, and this log come up, and a rope floated up in the water, and I got the rope, and Mr. Bourgault said, 'there is one of Mr. Eastham's logs. Let's knock the wedge out, and let her go,' and I took them out, and threw them in the camp, on an old stump, and told Bob where he could get the wedges.... Went on down with the balance of the logs. Of course, when we had orders to roll in everything, we had a right to put in everything." Asked during cross-examination whether, in driving the banks clean of logs, they drove any pulp wood belonging to Eastham, Cosner replied: "We drove everything," he responded, "there was pulp wood branded with E as well as other logs. It was our orders to roll in everything, and drive everything."

It was understandable that Eastham would lose track of his logs once they were rolled into the river, which was filled with logs nearly its entire length. Silas Brackman, a witness called by Eastham, testified regarding the condition of the river. "The river for several miles was full of logs. We walked for a good many miles, on the logs right down the river, most of the way from the bridge that crosses the Blackwater in the Canaan, the biggest part of the way, I think, the river was full of logs. There was one place down where they were putting logs, where they had the logs piled in the river lengthways, up and down, and there was four or five tiers of logs there, that were up a great deal higher than the banks of the stream."

Sumner W. Thompson, Frank's uncle who had managed the driving for the Blackwater Lumber Company during the five years that he had been in Davis, verified this account. Asked why he rolled in Eastham's cherry log, he replied simply that it had the company's circle "K" brand on it. The log was still in the river. In fact, he had seen it a week earlier, and went so far as to saw off the butt end and brought it to court where he pointed out the

Blackwater mark. The ash logs were still in the water very near the cherry log. On cross-examination, Sumner Thompson asserted that he had never seen the brand Eastham claimed was his in use since the Blackwater Boom and Lumber Company went out of business. And, yes, he knew that Eastham claimed it was his log, but as far as he was concerned, "the log belonged to the Blackwater folks, or the 'K' would not have been on it. That is the only way I had of knowing the log." Under questioning from Eastham's attorney, Thompson said that the ends of the cherry log were cut off by order of "the Blackwater people."[19]

Opening the Boom

After he put his pulpwood into the river and drove it downstream to where the BLC's skidways blocked the entire width of the river with logs, Eastham notified the company to open the river, but they ignored him and made no effort to open a channel for his logs to pass through. His logs remained trapped there through the summer and fall of 1894 as the company put logs in ahead of Eastham's. In spring 1895 Eastham hired some men to help him break the skidway landings and drive his logs down to where the Thompsons were putting logs into the river near the logging railroad. Eastham served another notice on the company to open the river; again it was ignored. Then he paid a visit to his lawyer, Wilson B. Maxwell. He was informed that the company had a legal right to use only half of the river, Eastham declared, and it "would have to give way so I could come through." Eastham then went to see Sumner Thompson and asked him why they did not "open up and let the logs come on out of the dam." In reply, the woods boss told him that "he had been after them [BLC] for some time to let him sluice some logs through and they wouldn't do it.

He had mentioned it to Frank Thompson and he wouldn't consent to it." For Eastham, this was further evidence that the Thompsons, general manager Frank E. in particular, were determined to drive him and the other independent contractors out of business.

Highly agitated after visiting with Sumner Thompson, Eastham walked upriver from Davis to the company's boom two miles above the mill. There he found two men fishing, and Eastham stopped to talk to them. They asked if he was driving to which he replied that he had been upriver to the splash dam at the mouth of the Little Blackwater (a tributary) to mark some of his logs but BLC "had damned the water back so I couldn't get to them." According to Eastham's account, one of the men asked if he intended to sluice through there, at the dam, but Eastham said he had not brought his "pike pole" with him to run the logs through. "One of them got up and walked out on the boom and said that he could open it if his arm was not sore." The other man, William Bumgardner, then walked out on the boom and after some effort pulled a pin, opened the boom and "threw the chain in the water." Eastham then walked out onto the boom and "pushed out what I could with the peevy and my feet. I suppose there were 75 or 80 logs."

While at Davis, Bumgardner had first worked in the woods, but a month or so after the boom was opened he left Davis, entered the oil business, and currently was living in Bays, Ohio. However, Frank Thompson discovered his whereabouts and paid him two dollars per day plus his expenses to return and testify. "I believe that Eastham will deny that he opened the boom and threw it on to you," Thompson wrote to Bumgardner, "as he thinks we do not know where you are. Should he do this, we want you to come here and testify to the facts in the case and put the blame where it belongs."[20]

The company was convinced that Eastham could be found guilty of opening the boom, whereas the defense sought to demonstrate that Eastham had every right to open the boom because the Thompsons illegally refused to give him access to a public waterway. Frank Thompson's willingness to pay Bumgardner to return to Davis and to testify in the case further reinforced Eastham's conviction that Thompson was determined to ruin him. Bumgardner's version of events differed from Eastham's: "Charles Dority [a woodsman for the local Beaver Creek Lumber Company] and I went up Blackwater fishing, and when we reached the dam Robert Eastham was there. He told us he was trying to open the boom and asked us to help him open it as he could not do it alone. Charles Dority, having a lame shoulder, could not help. I volunteered to help. We two, Eastham and myself, went out on the pier, he slacked the chain and I pulled the steeple. The boom opened of course and the logs started out." Eastham then went around to the other side "got on the boom and started logs out with his cant hook. By pushing on the logs of course the boom opened wider." Eastham left before the other two men, stating that he was going to Davis to get a pike pole. On the stand, Charles Dority gave essentially the same story as Bumgardner.[21]

The plaintiff also sought to prove that opening the boom was a flagrant act of disregard for the property of the Blackwater Lumber Company. Therefore, counsel attempted to demonstrate that the consequences of opening the boom, which backed up millions of feet of timber, risked destroying the mill, and hence the livelihood of the hundreds of workers who relied on it for employment. At least eight witnesses, including company officials Albert, Frank, and Sumner Thompson, testified to this effect for the company. General Manager Frank Thompson stated the company's position very clearly. Opening the dam and leaving it open was dangerous: "At that time there was yet a large body of ice and snow in the woods and as we were sure to get a very high water should we have but an hour or two of warm rain or a few warm nights, I had a notice posted on this dam and on the post to which the boom is fastened in the pier forbidding anyone to turn out logs without orders from us. This was intended for the river drivers employed by S. W. Thompson as we didn't suppose anybody else would open the boom," he testified on November 7, 1895.

Describing what could occur to the logs in the river, the mill dam, and the lumber yard if the boom was open and there had been a heavy rise, Frank Thompson contended that "at least eight or ten million feet of logs belonging to both the plaintiff and defendant in this case come on down the river to the boom at Davis and would, I have no doubt, have broken the boom, destroyed the piers and carried out both dams [a second one a mile below the mill] of the Blackwater Lumber Company and the two railroad bridges. The logs would then all have gone down the river and have been a total loss to the company of about sixty thousand dollars." Moreover, if the mill boom at Davis had held, these logs would have "packed the natural channel of the river solid full and thus have diverted the water from its natural course to that side of the river on which the mills and the principal part of the lumber yard are situated." The river banks on that side of the river were the lowest and, therefore, the rising waters would have carried away the one million feet of timber the company kept in stock. The flooding river would also have damaged the newly constructed storage dam for logs owned by the public, located downriver about one mile from the mill, and would have also washed out and undermined the saw mill, boiler houses, and dry-kilns "thus damaging them greatly if not entirely ruining them" and resulting in a loss of about $50,000.

One reason Thompson was not motivated to drive the logs downriver to the mill was that the company supplied the milling operation with logs by railroad during the winter when the river was frozen solid or in dry periods when there was insufficient water for river driving. These were the only occasions when the railroad, or "dinky line," was used to supply the mill with logs because it was much cheaper to bring them in by water. At the time of his testimony, the company had skidded to the railroad more than two million feet of logs to supply the mill because the river was frozen over. Frank Thompson did not consider it profitable to operate the mill with logs supplied by the logging railroad alone. In fact, damming the river to use the spring rises was crucial, for "at least 90 percent of the driving" was accomplished "with the spring waters and the aid furnished by the splash dams at that time."[22]

Blackwater Lumber Company's Injunction

Eastham was in serious financial straits by now. All of his money was tied up in about a million feet of pulpwood, the passage of which was blocked by the Blackwater Lumber Company's logs that, according to his lawyer, illegally jammed the river for miles above the mill. He had contracts for the mill to cut the logs in four-foot sections and deliver them onto a railroad car for shipment to a buyer. Since there was a chance that the buyer would back out if the wood was not delivered in a reasonable period of time, Eastham was under pressure to do something, and under pressure Eastham always became a man of action.

On advice of his counsel, Eastham sent several notices to Frank E. Thompson as general manager and vice president of the

Blackwater Lumber Company. In October 1894, one notice informed Thompson that his logs were obstructing the river, and since he did not seem to be "making any apparent effort" to move the logs, Eastham's pulpwood was "becoming greatly damaged by your said inaction." Therefore, "you are notified that I intend to hold you accountable for all damages occasioned to my said pulp wood by reason of your having obstructed the said stream and thereby kept it from floating into your said boom." In January 1895, Eastham sent another notice to Thompson to open and break the blockade or jam of logs which the company also ignored.[23] Finally, Eastham served the mill operator with another notice that if he, Thompson, did not open a channel for Eastham's logs, he would put men on the river to drive his logs "through to their destination on the spring waters & you are hereby further notified that after July you cannot under any circumstances use the upper dam for splashing as I am going to clearing & ditching to drain my land and will not permit you to back water on my land after that date."[24]

At this point, Frank Thompson finally decided he must make a countermove. In Tucker County, Circuit Court Judge Joseph T. Hoke was more than receptive to the industrialist's request for an injunction to prevent Eastham from interfering with company operations. The company's primary concern was what Eastham might do to its boom across the river two miles above the Davis mill, but the splash dam on the upper reaches of the river near Eastham's farm was also vital to the company's operation. Thompson's lawyers argued that the company had every right to continue using the splash dam to collect enough water to make a rise for floating logs down river during low water stages. The dam was erected on the 300-acre tract on which the Blackwater Boom & Lumber Company had purchased the timber from W. B. Maxwell and John J. Adams in August 1888, a tract that abutted

Eastham's farm. The agreement gave BB&L Co. the right to construct a splash dam across the river on the land. Acting for the company, Eastham himself selected the location of this dam. Even though Eastham subsequently purchased the Maxwell and Adams land, the company contended that Eastham was, nevertheless, bound by the agreement initiated between BB&L Co. and Maxwell and Adams, rights BLC claimed it had acquired with its purchase of BB&L Co.[25]

In formal rebuttal to Eastham's charges, the Blackwater Lumber Company countered that it did not block passage of other logs, only those held in the boom above the mill. These had not been moved because the water levels had not been sufficient to bring more logs down to the mill, and not because of some arbitrary and capricious act of the company. In summary, the company's bill of complaint contended that Eastham knew that the river was filled with logs when he cut and put his logs into the water. If he were permitted to damage BLC operations, many others would suffer, namely, the company's 150 mill employees, and another 100 men employed in logging and driving. Therefore, "the prayer of this bill is that the said Eastham, his agents or employees, and all other persons acting with or for him, be restrained from interfering with any of the booms of this company, or with any of its dams; that he be enjoined and restrained, especially, from interfering with the boom about two miles above the mill, . . . and that he be enjoined and restrained, especially, from interfering with the splash dam heretofore spoken of and referred to in the said notice from Eastham as the 'Upper Dam for splashing.'" Upon posting a $3,000 bond, the company was granted the injunction by Circuit Court Judge Joseph T. Hoke.[26]

Robert W. Eastham obviously held very different views, which he expressed through his attorneys, W. B. Maxwell and J. H.

Woods, in his response filed with Tucker County Circuit Court judge Joseph T. Hoke on July 2, 1895. Eastham claimed that he never opened or threatened to open the boom across the river and that the upper splash dam mentioned by the company was not located on the Maxwell & Adams land, or any other land either owned or controlled by the company. Eastham denied having "anything whatever" to do with the location of the splash dam, or that the dam was located pursuant to the company's agreement fashioned by BB&L Co.'s, dated August 30, 1888, rights which BLC now claimed. In fact, Eastham argued, a recent survey revealed that the splash dam was actually located on the Grady and Wood tract, rather than on the Maxwell-Adams tract. This news caused a stir among the plaintiffs for it undermined the company's claim that it controlled the dam. This tract fell under Eastham's management, as agent for Grady and Wood, and Eastham asserted that the dam presented "a constant menace, nuisance and injury" to him by "constantly flooding" seventy-five to one hundred acres of his best farmland.

Contrary to the company's claim that it had tried to move as many of the logs to the mill as water levels would permit, Eastham averred, there was more water for driving in the spring of 1895 than for many previous years. The BLC "systematically and purposely kept the said river full of its own logs" making it impossible for Eastham's logs to reach the mill. Eastham was under contract to deliver those logs to a third party, and if the contract was not met, he would suffer financial injury of at least $5,000. In fact, Eastham asserted, the company placed logs across the river specifically for "the purpose of obstructing the passage" of his logs with the intent to injure him. The company's motives were even more malevolent, he charged, for the Thompsons' ultimate goal was to gain "a monopoly in logs and lumber at its said mill to the exclusion of respondent and other persons who have the same and equal rights with plaintiff to the use of said river as a highway." This would not be the last time Eastham gave voice to the common belief among many locals that the Blackwater Lumber Company was creating a monopoly that would drive them out of business and off their own land.

Eastham acknowledged that he had served notice on the company of his intention to open the boom above the mill on the following spring rise if the company did not cease obstructing the passage of his logs. However, Eastham denied that he had "any intention or purpose of injuring in any way the property or premises of the plaintiff." Nevertheless, under the contract between Eastham and the Blackwater Lumber Company, dated January 31, 1895, the company had bound itself to take all of Eastham's pulpwood, which he was to drive to the mill at his own expense. The company's failure to open the river, therefore, would "cause him to suffer great loss and injury." He denied that the Blackwater Lumber Company had legal authority to construct dams on the Blackwater River. He insisted that the Blackwater River was a small stream which "is not and never was a navigable river"; therefore, it belonged to "the adjoining and abutting land owners, and that the title to the same has never been derived by the plaintiff or its predecessor the Blackwater Boom and Lumber Company from them."[27]

Eastham's protestations notwithstanding, on May 9, 1895, Tucker County Circuit Court judge Joseph T. Hoke awarded the injunction requested by the company, and bond was posted by Frank Thompson's father, Albert. The injunction restrained "R. W. Eastham his agents or employees and all other persons acting with or for him, from interfering with any of the booms or dams of said company and especially from interfering with the boom across the Blackwater River in Tucker County about two miles above the mill of said company, and from interfering in any way with the logs, property or operations of the plaintiff."[28] Now Eastham would escalate the contest into guerrilla warfare.

7

THE STRUGGLE FOR CONTROL

Blackwater Lumber Company v. R. W. Eastham

Charges and Countercharges

By late fall 1895, the Blackwater Lumber Company was ready for an all-out legal battle to crush R. W. Eastham in the courts. The Thompsons felt compelled to prosecute Eastham after a sequence of events that challenged their authority to use the river in accordance with their economic interests and the company's interpretation of its legal rights. To bring their erstwhile opponent to justice for violating the injunction barring him from interfering with the company's operations, the Thompsons filed a bill in chancery requesting that Circuit Court Judge Joseph Hoke order Eastham to show cause why he should not be charged with contempt for breaking the injunction served on him on May 17, 1895. The court readily complied with the company's petition and ordered Eastham to appear on the first day of the next term of court "to show, if he can, why he should not be fined and attached for his said contempt."[1]

While Blackwater's legal maneuvers were intended to eliminate Eastham's interference by breaking him financially and miring him in legal proceedings, Eastham's rejoinder elevated the issue by questioning the very meaning of riparian law in West Virginia. Citing several precedents, Eastham's counsel, J. Hopkins Woods, challenged the company's right to control the

Blackwater River on the grounds that it was "a natural highway and no exclusive use of any waters in it is or can be conferred by law or its charter upon it." In short, the stream belonged to the riparian land owners; Eastham's opening of the boom was in accordance with settled law, and undertaken to conserve his own interest in the stream rather than to injure the company. Conversely, he asserted, the evidence showed that the Blackwater Lumber Company "arrogantly" violated the law in "both its letter and its spirit" through "an exclusive and continuous appropriation of the stream for a distance of 16 miles." Woods asserted that the company's actions were only "remediable by a forfeiture of its charter." The brief filed by Eastham's attorney in March 1896 submitted that the Boom Law, which the company claimed gave it that right, "divests vested rights, creates monopoly, appropriates without first condemning, the natural property rights in water highways of the riparian owners, is the exercise by a corporation of the sovereign right of eminent domain, and infringes the 9th Sec. of Art. 3 of the Constitution of West Virginia." Therefore, the injunction was not only destructive of his timber interests, it was also unconstitutional.[2]

In a subsequent brief filed on April 14, 1896, Eastham's new counsel, Wilson B. Maxwell, leveled much broader allegations against the company, which most independent farmer-loggers in West Virginia experienced when confronted with corporate power: monopolistic tactics intended to drive smaller competitors out of business. The Blackwater Lumber Company obtained permission to build a splash dam on the site from the former owners, the Blackwater Boom and Lumber Company, but the dam was constructed on land not actually owned by Adams-Maxwell, but rather Grady-Woods for whom Eastham was serving in the capacity of caretaker. The water from this dam backed onto eighty acres of Eastham's most valuable land, his attorney asserted, without paying for damages to the land as required in the agreement. In effect, the company had "taken private property for its use without paying a just compensation therefore as required by the law in such cases."[3]

Eastham had more pragmatic grievances as well. In the spring of 1894 he put 1,028 cords of pulpwood into the Blackwater River. The logs were contracted to a pulp mill in Davis, but the Blackwater Lumber Company "by every means in its power sought to obstruct its passage down the river to its destination in Davis." In order to obstruct Eastham's pulpwood, the company "caused logs, or booms, to be placed across the river and worst of all used the main channel as a landing for logs from its narrow gauge railroad and piled its logs into the river ten or twelve feet high, extending across the river and up and down the river 300 or 400 feet so that it has since been an impossibility for Eastham to get his pulp wood past that particular place."

Moreover, the Thompsons resorted to "every artifice in its power to obstruct and injure Eastham in his operations." Hoping to placate the company, Eastham entered a contract with the BLC in which he agreed "to pay it the enormous and outrageous price of seventy five cents per cord for taking his pulp wood out of the river and loading it on the cars for him." However, this agreement only further emboldened the company, Eastham asserted, and it subsequently "took possession of some of his pulp wood and used it for skids," pulled a large part of it out on the river bank "to bleach and rot in the sun," and sent some of it to the pulp mill as its own timber. Worst of all, the company obtained the injunction restraining Eastham from "even touching his own property." If the Thompsons succeeded with this tactic, it would have made an example of Eastham and demonstrated "to others who might venture the brazen hardihood of attempting to engage in the lumber business on that river of what they may expect." The company's victory would then be complete, and "it will be absolute master of that river." If that were the case, Eastham argued, "all the many valuable parcels of timber tributary to that river will belong to it on such terms as its will or caprice may please to dictate, or else the timber will be permitted to remain in its virgin forest and the owner not permitted to reap its true value as he would be enabled to do if one of the public rivers of the state, one of nature's highways, was open to that public use for which it was intended by nature."

The public right to use "floatable" streams in West Virginia is no longer an open question, Eastham's counsel asserted. The courts have concluded that "the rights of a riparian owner having a mill dam across a 'floatable' stream must give way to the rights of the public to market the timber tributary to the stream. This is unquestionably the settled law of the state, and the company has no legal right "to array to itself the absolute dominion and control of this stream." Under its charter the company only had the power "to charge tolls, or boomage, on logs properly caught by it." West Virginia's laws of incorporation, Maxwell asserted, clearly established its "imperative duty to pass the logs of others through its boom within a reasonable time." The same statute provided that, if the boom company does "unreasonably delay" the logs of others, "the person so delayed may break any jam etc etc and the person responsible for such a delay shall be responsible for such expense etc."[4]

His attorney, Wilson B. Maxwell, argued that Eastham's pulpwood had been delayed in the water for so long that its value was greatly depreciated from decay. Realizing that "he was being willfully and intentionally delayed and damaged" by the company, Eastham opened the company's storage boom on two different occasions after the spring flood of 1895 had subsided, releasing "a couple hundred cords of his pulp wood along with several hundred of the company's saw logs. Although keeping the boom shut "tight as a clam" might have been detrimental to the company's short-term financial interest, Eastham's attorney asserted, the damages were "inconsiderable when compared with the 'object lesson' it was designed to teach Eastham and other operators who might have the effrontery to venture to do business on that stream; If Eastham and other operators could be 'taught' not to infringe upon the 'supreme dominion' of the plaintiff on that river it would very soon recoup any temporary damage it might sustain by shutting down its storage boom."

It was to prevent monopolistic practices such as these, Eastham insisted, that the legislature wrote the statutes protecting the rights of all persons with timber to use a "floatable" stream. Therefore, the Blackwater Lumber Company did not, and could not, have exclusive right on the river for it was prohibited in the West Virginia code. Contrary to the law, the company in effect had taken full and "absolute control and dominion over the entire stream as fully, effectually and completely as if the river was its own private property." In fact, Eastham argued, the Blackwater Lumber Company "carries its pretentions so far as to appeal to the court, by this proceeding, to restrain Eastham from doing the very things he legally has a right to do under the statute."

Maxwell concluded that this case could be summed up in a few words: "Eastham has just as much right to use the river for driving his pulp wood to the boom in Davis as the plaintiff has to use it for driving their saw logs to the boom in Davis." Nevertheless, the plaintiff illegally obstructed the river so that Eastham could not successfully drive his pulpwood and, under the statute, he had every right "to remove any obstruction which was in the river which prevented his pulp wood from floating to its destination." The fact that some of the plaintiff's saw logs came out of the storage dam and onto the boom in Davis when the dam was opened showed "conclusively that if that dam had not been closed by the plaintiff, . . . Eastham's pulp wood would have come on to its destination."[5]

Eastham's Land Flooded

Once it was determined that the upper splash dam was actually on the Grady-Woods tract, and that Albert Thompson had then purchased the land, Eastham served notice on the Thompsons barring them from using the splash dam because, when in use, it backed up water on his low-lying land and rendered it unfit for crops. Eastham took it on himself to document the amount of land affected by the backed-up water by surveying the land and producing a map which he submitted into evidence. According to his calculations, 83½ acres were directly affected. However, he argued that every acre of his land was affected in the long run, because he could not get to his land on the other side of the river, and the only woods he owned, without going through the adjoining property belonging to Henry Cooper. Moreover, the soil was a limestone loam 1½ feet deep and soaked up the water "from one end to the other," making it "mirey so that it is impossible to get through it." Without the dam, however, the land was "all dry land, as fine land as there is in the state of W.Va."

Blackwater Boom and Lumber Company had obtained permission from the previous owners of his land, Adams and Maxwell, to build a dam on this three hundred acres on the condition that "if any real or permanent damage was done to the land the actual damage sustained by them should be paid" by the company. However, neither Blackwater Boom and Lumber Company nor Blackwater Lumber Company had ever paid damages for flooding the land. Prior to purchasing the tract Eastham informed

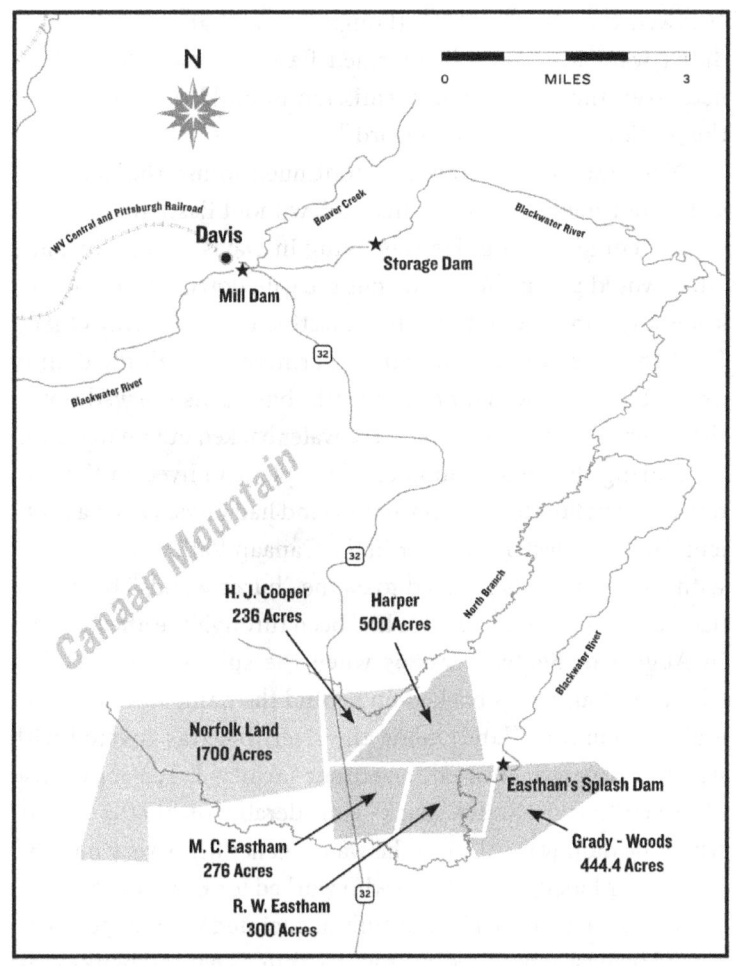

Canaan Valley and Eastham lands. Map by Than Saffel / WVU Press.

Maxwell that "if they [the Thompsons] had any rights here, I didn't want it." Maxwell informed Eastham that, although he had given the Thompsons permission to build the splash dam, the parties "never put it to record."

Nevertheless, the company continued to use the dam, and water continued to overflow his land, without Eastham's permission or compensation. He was living in Davis at the time, and "they would go up there and shut the gate down and I wouldn't know anything about it," Eastham testified. In the spring of 1895, Eastham gave Sumner Thompson permission to fill the dam in order to "get his logs off of my land," but he also served notice that after July 1 he "didn't want the water backed out on my land."

During the trial, a number of people who lived in the area testified that flooding on Eastham's land had indeed been a problem. H. L. Chidester, a farmer in the Canaan Valley, was familiar with the land locals referred to as the "burnt woods" because it had been damaged by fire. He had been through the affected area in August or September 1895 when the splash dam was full. Chidester found logs backed up behind the dam, and "a considerable amount of [land] along the river that was covered with water and partly covered." Another farmer, J. P. Propst, also observed that the water "backs considerably on that low land" when the dam was full, and the water "generally is very muddy."

W. K. Mauck, a farmhand who worked for Eastham, took the stand and testified that he was fully acquainted with the 300 acres owned by Eastham. If the river was within its natural banks most of the land would drain itself, he said, but claimed that 250 of those acres were affected by the backwater when the dam was full, and some 75 to 80 acres were covered by backwater. He believed that about 100 to 150 acres of Eastham's land would not be passable on horseback if the dam was full. Mauck had an interest in protecting his employer, and friend, but he did have specific knowledge of the issue because he had helped Eastham to survey the affected area. In addition to witnessing the high-water mark personally, he noted that, on a number of occasions when the high water drained, it carried logs that left marks around the outer edges, mashed the grass down, and then the ground baked in the sun.

H. J. Cooper, an old friend and neighbor of Eastham who lived on the adjoining farm, attested that the backwater made the land "marshy" even beyond where the water extended. Eastham could not get across the river to his land on the other side when the water was backed up "unless he would go up to Mr. Cosner's bridge." E. A. Harper, another farmer from Cortland, affirmed his belief that "the overflow of water from the dam when there is a bracket" would cover nearly fifty acres. On one occasion in the spring of 1895, he noticed the overflow when hunting cattle. "I started to go through the burnt woods and my horse came very near miring and I had to turn and go back out of there." His brother, C. S. Harper, also a local farmer, confirmed his brother's testimony on the effect of the damned up water on Eastham's property. He estimated the water had been backed up one and a half to two miles above the dam, but after the dam was put out of operation the land was dry and "one can ride over it now while you could not when the splash was on."[6]

The prosecution called its own witnesses to support the company's case. Whereas witnesses for the defense tended to be neighbors and friends, Blackwater Lumber Company called expert witnesses or those in its employ. "Qualified experts" was the signature of modern companies who encountered traditional resistance to their incursions, whereas locals relied more on experience and the traditional forms of knowledge. In this case, the experience of local farmers was trumped by expert "science" to determine the "real" answer.

Thomas Dailey fell into the "expert" category. An engineer and surveyor who had been engaged in his profession since 1881, Dailey was hired by Frank Thompson to ascertain how much land was "overflowed when a full head was on the dam." Dailey conducted a new survey, which determined that the dam was actually located on the Grady-Woods tract rather than the Adams-Maxwell land. Predictably, Dailey's calculations of backed-up water were much lower than Eastham's, estimating that twenty-one and three-tenths acres of Eastham's land were affected. The ground was dry at the time, but apparently Dailey followed a similar method used by Eastham of tracing the water marks left by the receding water. To reinforce his qualifications, and at the company's urging, the engineer recited his experience building railroads along streams in West Virginia and elsewhere in the nation by "ascertaining the high-water mark in order to lay our grades."[7]

Dam Dynamited

Early Sunday morning on June 23, 1895, the splash dam at the center of the dispute was blown up by dynamite. Because the splash dam was in a secluded area, there were no witnesses although some local residents heard the explosion. There were numerous rumors, however, and most people thought someone was dynamiting fish.

During the trial Eastham was asked to account for his whereabouts that weekend, and how he learned that the dam was blown. According to his own account, Eastham was standing on the street corner in Davis around that time waiting for Jonah M. Smith, the proprietor of the furniture and hardware store. The two men had arranged to go up to Eastham's place to do some

Sumner W. Thompson standing on the repaired splash dam destroyed by Robert Eastham. Courtesy of Sarah Thompson Fletcher.

fishing, so they met the next morning around 6:00 A.M., and rode together up to Jim Carico's farm where they spent the night. When the farmer's son informed them that the fish were not biting, Eastham and Smith decided to return to Davis early the next morning in time for Eastham to catch the train for Parsons to attend court. He stayed in Parsons overnight, and the next morning, Tuesday, he met Pete Harper and Frank Tolbard on the way to the station. Eastham testified that Tolbard informed him that "there was somebody dynamiting fish up yonder at the dam Sunday morning and I asked him how he knew, and he said he laid on the river there close to the dam about five or six o'clock he heard a blast go off." Shortly afterward, his neighbor Jack Cooper informed him that "lightning had struck the dam."

Asked how he knew, Cooper replied that he was fishing close by. He went to look at the dam and saw that "the post was split from the top to the bottom and a hole was knocked in down pretty near to the bottom of it." According to Eastham, that was his first knowledge of the dam explosion.[8]

Thompson's lawyer attempted to point the finger of suspicion at Eastham. Thomas Wheeler, a laborer who lived in Davis, testified to a conversation between himself and H. M. Hughes in June 1895 with Robert Eastham also present. Wheeler "was only joking" when he asked Hughes "what he would charge me for a hundred acres." During that conversation Hughes remarked that, "when there was a bracket on the dam," the land would be "overflowed." The company lawyer asked Wheeler if Eastham replied that "it wouldn't be overflowed any more as there wouldn't be any more brackets as he had put a stop to it." The defense's objection to leading the witness was sustained, but Wheeler declared: "I did not hear that." Eastham spoke about something, but he was certain it was about fishing.[9]

The notion that the dam had been struck by lightning or someone was dynamiting fish was put to rest by Peter Fernando, a Blackwater Lumber Company employee. He was sent to repair the dam, and asserted that "it looked to me like it had been blown to pieces with dynamite. A big hole was blown in the bottom. The middle post was split and one gate was blown to pieces. In the bottom we found a piece of water proof fuse about 3 or 4 feet long. The fuse had been burned out."[10]

David Keplinger, a woodsman employed by the Thompsons who resided in Davis, accompanied Fernando. He testified that he "found a piece of fuse sticking between two boards that were split." The fuse had been burned out. "What did Mr. Eastham ever say to you in reference to this damage to the dam and who it had been done by," Keplinger was asked. He replied: "Why he said that the lightning must have struck the dam. I told him that I did not think that there was fuse went with lightning," to which Eastham made no reply.[11]

After inspection, Sumner W. Thompson also confirmed that the upper dam gates were blown out because the bottoms of the gates were broken. Thompson did not hear the explosion, "but I know from the time that the head of water that was in the dam got to where I was that it was done very early in the morning."

Frank A. Tolbard, a lumberman and saloon keeper in Harmon, testified that he and a friend were fishing about a half mile above the upper dam when the dam was blown. At about "four o'clock in the morning" he heard a dynamite explosion which he thought a "pretty heavy one" just down river toward the dam. Asked if it could have been someone dynamiting fish, Tolbard stated: "Well I wouldn't think it was, it was too loud. Too much dynamite . . . unless they wanted to blow them all out on the shore."[12]

Shooting at the Dam

Between July 18 and 21, 1895, after the dam had been dynamited, Frank Thompson sent men to repair the dam. They were prevented from completing the task, however, when an unknown person commenced shooting at them from the thick forest cover.

Questioned at the trial about when he first heard of this shooting, Eastham claimed that "Sumner Thompson was the first and only man that I heard say anything about it, and the witnesses here on the stand." Eastham said he had been away from home at the time surveying on Backbone Mountain. Upon returning to Davis, he was sitting with Sam Turner and Dave Lambie on the doorstep of the Hill and Shobe meat market when John Nine approached and asked Eastham "what was doing up at the dam." Nine asked if hunters were responsible, but Eastham did not know.

His curiosity aroused, Eastham stated that "after dinner I got on my horse and rode up, went in to the dam and found Sumner Thompson there. I asked him what he was doing. He said that he was trying to raise a head of water and that somebody had shot at him that morning. I told him I didn't know anything about that; but that he was a 'damn' fool whoever he was, that the law didn't excuse him anymore for shooting at him than it did for killing him. I told him that Powell Grady and Hiram Woods had both written me not to let anyone trespass on their lands, and Hiram Wood told me not to let them use the water way in any unauthorized way whatever, and I notified Sumner Thompson and he said if that be the case he would do nothing more and he would quit and I went away." The next morning Eastham returned to Davis, and that, he said, "is all I know about it."

W. K. Mauck, a farmhand who had been living and working at Eastham's farm for about fifteen months, also had worked for Eastham as a cook in the camp near the dam during the winter of 1893–1894, and "helped to drive some." Prior to coming to Tucker County, Mauck lived in Front Royal, Virginia. According to the witness, Eastham had built a house in Front Royal in 1881 but was only a resident for "a short while, a summer or something like that. I don't know exactly how long he was there." Eastham offered him a job, and a month or so after Eastham returned to Tucker County, Mauck came to work on Eastham's logging crews and then as a farmhand. He remembered the day someone shot at Sumner Thompson's men while they worked on the dam and verified Eastham's version of his whereabouts, claiming to have seen Eastham in Davis about 11:00 A.M. on the corner in front of the butcher shop. Mauck had come to Davis to inform his employer that one of his horses was sick, and that he should check the animal's condition himself. Shortly afterward, Eastham left for his farm on horseback. The farmhand was apprised of the shooting that evening when he returned to the farm and Eastham told him.[13]

Dave Lambie, who operated the locomotive on Blackwater Lumber Company's narrow gauge railroad, also confirmed Eastham's testimony. "We met Mr. Eastham on top of the mountain travelling toward Davis. . . . I had been with Mr. Eastham all the forenoon of the day before here in Davis." Then "Mr. Eastham got on his horse some time about two o'clock to go to his farm."[14]

Sumner Thompson was also called by Blackwater's attorneys to give a statement. Two weeks after the dam had been dynamited, Thompson sent two men to repair it. While the men were at work, "someone come into the woods just below the dam in the forenoon and commenced shooting." Whoever it was fired eight or ten shots, "and one ball struck within a few feet of where one of the men was at work. This was two weeks at least after the dam was blown up."

(Q) *You say that this shooting was in the forenoon, please state whether you continued there at work and whether the defendant Eastham came to where you were at work on the same day after the shooting and said anything to you, if so, what did he say?*

(A) We kept on at work on the dam. Mr. Eastham came there while we were at work about five o'clock in the afternoon of the same day. He asked me by whose

> authority I was there at work repairing the dam. I told Mr. Eastham that I didn't need any authority from anyone to repair it, that by my contract with the company for driving logs, I was to keep the dams in repair. Then Mr. Eastham says to me, don't you know that I notified the Blackwater Lumber Co. that they couldn't use this dam after the first of July. I told him that I didn't, that I had nothing to do with his affairs and the Blackwater Lumber Co., that he and they could settle their own affairs, that it was my business to repair the dam and I was going to do it. He says to me then that he was determined that the dam shouldn't be repaired, that he had commenced to clear some land along the river there, that he wasn't going to have them gates shut down and his land covered with water. Then he says that he be damned if he was going to have this Blackwater Lumber Co. run over him and destroy his property unless they done it over his dead body, that there would certainly be trouble if I insisted in going on repairing the dam and shutting the gates. Then he went on to say that the Blackwater Lumber Co. had no rights to put the dam there nor never had. I told Mr. Eastham if that was the facts of the case that I didn't think I would do any more work on it at present.

Thompson's men finished up what they were doing with a temporary repair so they could at least get a small head of water on the dam of about three to four feet. The dam itself was still useable, because the water went under it through the hole caused by the explosion. Under cross-examination by Wilson B. Maxwell for the defendant, Sumner Thompson testified that he was not positive of the date of the shooting, "but I think it was somewhere from the middle to the last of July."

- (Q) *As near as you could tell, how far was the party away from you who was doing the shooting?*
- (A) It is pretty hard to tell how far he was away as I could not see any smoke, but I should judge from the report of the gun that he was 25 or 30 rods [137 to 165 yards]—something like that.
- (Q) *Was there more than one ball struck near where you was at work, so far as you know?*
- (A) I don't know that there was.
- (Q) *Did you or any of your men go to investigate who it was that was doing the shooting?*
- (A) No, we did not, for the reason that the woods and laurel was very thick where the shooting was done and I knew we could not get there without him seeing us and getting away.
- (Q) *Did you or any of your men 'hollow' or make noise as to attract the attention of the party who was shooting after the bullet struck near you?*
- (A) No, we didn't hollow, nor did we make any more noise than we had been making driving spikes and so on about the work. We kept on about our work.
- (Q) *How long was it after the shooting until you seen Eastham to have a talk with him?*
- (A) I think it was seven hours or more. I think the shooting was done between nine and ten o'clock in the forenoon and he came there to the dam in the afternoon of the same day.
- (Q) *Did you say anything to him relative to the shooting?*

(A) Some time while he was there talking I told him about the shooting that was done there in the forenoon. I think he said he didn't do it because he was in town all the forenoon.[15]

Only two of Thompson's employees, Peter Fernando and David Keplinger, were working on the dam. Fernando had worked in the woods for S. W. Thompson for two years, and was one of the men repairing the dam when the shooting occurred. He gave his deposition in February 1896, about six months after the shooting episode. Consequently, like others who testified, he was not certain of the exact date, yet he clearly recalled what happened:

The first day we got there about 9 o'clock and was cleaning up things and shut out the water. The next day we were working on the dam. I was up on the top and got the block and tackle, and tried to get up the middle post on the dam, and I heard two or three shots fired. I didn't take any notice of it, I thought it was some boys or hunters firing at squirrels or something. They fired four or five more as fast as they could and I looked around. I could not see anybody. Dave Keplinger was working down below he called up to Mr. Thompson he said they fired a bullet down into the dam. Mr. Thompson says, "Oh no, I don't believe that!" He says "yes, they made dirt fly around." We went down and found a place where the bullet struck and glanced off. In all they fired between ten and fifteen shots. That was all for that time.

Afterwards I was working down below and heard some heavy words and went up. I saw a strange man there, a big man. After he went away I asked who he was and they told me it was Mr. Eastham. Mr. Thompson told him if he think [*sic*] the Blackwater Company had no right to use the dam why didn't he take it by the law. He told Mr. Thompson he could fight him and any two men he had there. Mr. Thompson told him that he didn't have to do that. Let the law settle it would be the best way.

David Keplinger, another S. W. Thompson employee working on the repair with Fernando, also offered his recollection of what transpired that day:

(A) Yes sir, I was there. I was down in the sluice way calking the cracks and somebody got to shooting at us. They shot 8 or 10 shots. There was a ball struck on the floor about a foot and a half from me and throwed the chips up against me. Then in the evening R. W. Eastham came there and asked Sumner who gave him leave to come in and trespass on him. I didn't understand what Sumner said to him. Then Sumner told him that someone had been shooting at us out of the brush thicket. He told him that whoever done it wasn't as good as a dog, not half as good. Eastham said it was not him. He said if it had been him he would have come there and done it. Then he offered to give Sumner and me and Pete Fernando the three of us a gun apiece, and he would go out and fight us all.

(Q) *Did you after that on any occasion when you wanted to use the dam for a splash ask Eastham's permission?*

(A) Yes sir. I came down here and I seen him over here and I asked him because I did not like to go about the place because I had been shot at there. There was not any of them give me permission to ask him. I just did it entirely of my own accord.[16]

After the shooting incident, Thompson sent Alfred Mick and George Carr to fill up the hole in the bottom of the dam gate that the water had washed out with gravel. "They went there about the middle of September and commenced work, and they worked on till the 21st day of September" and then went home after Eastham ordered them away. Thompson claimed that the dam had not been used since that time.[17]

Eastham's version of this encounter was a bit more nuanced. It began when a neighbor, Fred Cooper, was down in the field gathering his cows and came by the house. "Cooper asked me who those men were going across the bottom from the Ruffin house. I told him I didn't know who they were. He said they were two hard looking customers. One of them had a gun and the other a blanket on his back and they went over towards the dam. I had several notices up on the place, warning people not to trespass on it, fish, hunt, or range through it in any way." Eastham went to the dam to investigate and found

> somebody had built a little camp out of some loose planks that was there and had a fire built in a stump right in front of it. I looked in the camp and saw a gun and some bed clothes laying in there. I looked down towards the dam and saw a smoke about 15 or 20 feet from the dam, and I went down and found Alf Mick and Ans Carr a digging away the bank and asked them what they were doing there. They said that Sumner Thompson had got them to go there to fill up a hole that had blowed in the dam. I asked them if they didn't know that I had posted that land and they said they didn't know anything about it, if they had they wouldn't have come down there. . . . They would leave, but asked me if they might stay there till Sumner Thompson came up as he had promised to come that

day.... I told them that I didn't blame them for it, that they didn't know anything about it. That Sumner Thompson and the Blackwater Lumber Co. were the ones I held responsible for it.[18]

Alfred Mick, a farmer from Red Creek, Randolph County, worked in the woods for S. W. Thompson. His deposition for the plaintiffs was calculated to plant the idea in the jury's mind that Eastham was a violent man who had announced his intention to hurt Sumner and Frank Thompson, and was, in fact, capable of shooting them. The men were working on the dam when Eastham came by and nailed up a no-trespassing notice and told the men to stop what they were doing. As Mick recalled, Eastham declared that "if I catch Sumner Thompson and Frank Thompson here I will hurt them and I will hurt them bad." He couldn't remember the exact words, but claimed that Eastham "told us to come out of there and quick; and he said if there was any more men put there he was going to commence as soon as he got in sight pouring lead in on them. He said when he went to leave that he didn't expect it to end with anything only trouble."

Mick's working partner, George A. Carr, also a farmer from Randolph County, echoed Mick's statement. Eastham ordered them to stop work, and tacked up a no-trespassing notice.

"He told us to get out from there and not to come back any more. Said he didn't want to do anything to us as we were sent there to work. He said that we didn't know there was any trouble about the dam. He was telling us about some man being shot at there, or that there was some shooting done there at the dam." According to Carr, Eastham told them that if it had been him pulling the trigger " 'there would have been some better shooting done' or something to that amount. He said more, but I don't recollect. He said 'that Sumner Thompson and Jack Thompson

(I think it was Jack Thompson he said) was the men he wanted to catch there.'" Prompted by counsel if he meant Frank Thompson, Carr said yes, "Frank Thompson, that's the name."

> (Q) *Did Eastham say what he would do if he caught Sumner Thompson or Frank Thompson there?*
> (A) He said he would hurt them and would hurt them bad, if he caught them at work at that dam.
> (Q) *Did Mr. Eastham go away and leave you there?*
> (A) Yes sir, he went away and left us there. We told him we were going though shortly, as soon as we got our things fixed up, but he went off before we did.

Asked what reason Eastham gave for wanting to hurt the Thompsons if he caught them at the dam, Carr replied: "He said that it [the dam] made back water on him. He said that he was just getting his land so that it was worth something and he was not going to have the water backed on it."

After that, Mick and Carr stopped work. It was Saturday near noon, and they went home without finishing the repairs. Asked if he had been back since, Carr replied: "No sir, I 'haint' been back since."

Mick's and Carr's testimonies both conflicted with Eastham's deposition. Also, it must be noted that there were mutually hostile feelings between Eastham and Mick because Eastham had previously accused Mick of theft, and ordered him to stay off his property. Eastham's attorney, Wilson B. Maxwell, challenged the veracity of Mick and Carr when he questioned J. P. Probst.

> (Q) *Are you acquainted with the character and reputation of said Alfred Mick and George A. Carr, for their truth, veracity, and honesty among those who know them?*

(A) Well their character and reputation generally there in that neighborhood is mighty bad.
(Q) *From that reputation would you believe them or either of them on oath?*
(A) I wouldn't like to.[19]

Burning the Splash Dam

Fire was a perennial danger in the woods. George B. Thompson, Frank's nephew, recalled years later that Blackwater Lumber Company owned a water tank railroad car, "the first fire-fighting equipment ever used for combating forest fires" in Tucker County. The year 1894 was remembered for its fires. The fires commenced in early May after the woods dried out. One fire broke out on the Canaan slope of Cooper Mountain and continued to burn until July until it was finally contained to one spruce stub near the railroad. After the fire was put out a red hot shell remained, and when the men cut down the damaged timber in order to spray water on it from the tank car, the embers scattered fire in all directions. The two streams of water from the tank car were too weak to control the fire, and "soon the slash was a roaring HELL." The skidways burned hot and fast. "The ground under them was composed of scurf and would burn to the rocks." In spite of constant vigilance to prevent fire in the slashings, "one dry, windy day a fire started and by noon the next day it reached into the old slashings near Davis. This fire burned a hole in the sky.... The fire followed the new railroad and burned the camp and the large crew had to work like beavers to cut trails into the green laurel to save themselves and the horses."[20]

Shortly after Mick and Carr attempted to repair the hole blown in the dam, and Eastham ordered them not to come back, the splash dam was set afire and burned to the waterline sometime between Saturday, September 21, and Monday, September 23, 1895. Eastham testified that the dam had been burned once before "some four or five years ago" during one of the frequent forest fires. Asked when he first heard about the dam being burned the second time, Eastham replied that the first time he was aware that the dam had been burned was on Sunday, September 22, 1895, when two passing neighbors informed him.

The following year, 1895, was also a bad year for forest fires. Eastham's attorney steered his questioning to establish that the presence of fires in the woods were an alternative explanation to the suspicion that his client had intentionally set fire to the dam. In fact, fires had erupted in several locations near Eastham's property in 1895. There was a serious fire near Sam Collins's place, and another between the bridge and John Nine's land which burned for about a month. There was another fire on "Buck" Rogers's place just west of Eastham's farm that began to spread, and Eastham "fired the grass around the lot there at the house to keep it from the barn. It was coming in every direction. I fired against [it]. It was a general fire for several days there" and it burned "a considerable distance below the dam along the river."

H. H. Anderson, one of Eastham's farmhands, stopped to visit with Eastham when he observed smoke coming from the location of the dam. Ed Johnson and Frank Cooper were also present.

(Q) *State whether you observed any forest fires burning upon that Sunday, and if so in what directions were they from the Eastham house where you were?*

(A) Well there was a good many fires and one was northeast, one was south or southeast. I don't remember exactly, one was southwest, and one was west.

Anderson asserted there was a fire that seemed to be a fresh one, or a restart, when he, Johnson, and Cooper were at Eastham's. They first saw the smoke at around four o'clock in the afternoon. Eastham's attorney prompted his witness to establish that his client was not near the dam:

- (Q) *If you know state where Mr. Eastham had been all day up until the time you observed this smoke raising.*
- (A) At his residence on his farm.

Under cross-examination, Anderson testified that he had arisen on Sunday morning around eight o'clock. Eastham had been at his farm for about a week, and remained three or four days after that Sunday. It was during the three or four days that he heard Cooper say the dam was burned.

- (Q) *Did you and Mr. Eastham sit at the house all day until four o'clock in the afternoon?*
- (A) The largest portion.
- (Q) *Weren't you away from Mr. Eastham during all that time?*
- (A) No sir. None of any consequence.
- (Q) *How long have you lived on the Eastham place in Canaan Valley?*
- (A) I came there last August [1895].

Anderson was still a resident when his deposition was taken in 1896.[21]

Frank Cooper, the son of Eastham's friend and neighbor Henry Cooper, also was on Eastham's porch visiting on Sunday when the smoke was spotted. Asked how he remembered that occasion, Cooper stated that he and Ed Johnson had ridden up to Eastham's place and were visiting with him on the porch. "We observed smoke, what I thought to be near the location of the dam."

> (Q) *State whether or not you observed any other fires burning in that vicinity at that time?*
> (A) Yes sir. I saw fire near the river near a man's house by the name of Collins. Also there was fire on the mountain to the right of where the country road crosses, which could be seen from that place.
> (Q) *Where were you at and who was with you at this time you seen these three fires?*
> (A) We were sitting on the porch at Mr. Eastham's house.[22]

The Thompsons resorted to the courts to achieve their aim of controlling their mill's timber supply in the same manner taken by natural resource incorporators throughout America during this era. West Virginia legislators modified the state's law and its court system to encourage and protect capital investment. Consequently, when Eastham challenged the Blackwater Lumber Company's right to control the Blackwater River, the Thompsons sought a sympathetic judge to issue an injunction prohibiting Eastham from interfering with company operations. Convinced that Eastham was responsible for dynamiting the splash dam, shooting at the men sent to repair it, and ultimately burning it to the waterline, the circuit judge complied with a company request by ordering Eastham to demonstrate in court why he should not be fined and his property attached for breaking the injunction. Proving Eastham responsible for these acts of resistance was another matter entirely. Not for the first time, company officials misjudged both Eastham's resolve and resourcefulness. By now Frank Thompson and Robert Eastham had become implacable enemies, and their friends feared the worst.

8

THE SHOOT-OUT AND "LAWYERS BY THE DOZEN"

The relationship between Frank Thompson and Robert Eastham had hardened into an implacable hostility, with each making threatening remarks and accusations against the other. For Thompson, Eastham's uncooperative behavior seemed an irrational determination to sabotage his business. Eastham, on the other hand, believed it was clear that the mill operator intended to control the Blackwater River and the Canaan Valley virgin forest. To accomplish his goal, Eastham was convinced that Thompson planned to drive the independent timber operators out of business and shackle small landowners to the company's will. Not only did Thompson's actions deprive Eastham and his neighbors of their ability to control and benefit from the use of their own land and resources, but they also represented an affront to traditional community standards of civil behavior and his sense of personal honor. What was economically rational for twentieth-century businessmen was an abuse of power to nineteenth-century notions of individual freedom and the right to a sustainable life.

The fatal showdown between Thompson and Eastham was sealed when the two antagonists were brought together at the county seat for a totally unrelated court case on March 18, 1897. Alice Williams of Parsons had sued Karl Degler, the twenty-two-year-old son of a restaurant owner in Davis, for fathering her child. He refused to marry her or to pay for the child's care.

Ms. Williams was represented by William G. Conley, Absalom M. Cunningham, and Alston G. Dayton, prominent lawyers about whom we will hear much more below. Mr. Degler was represented by Adonijah B. Parsons, Lloyd Hansford, and L. S. Auvil. It was a hotly contested trial, but on March 11, 1897, the court sided with Alice Williams. The defense appealed for dismissal, but the judge denied the motion and ordered Carl Degler to pay child support, deposit $1,000 in security with the court, and pay court costs.[1]

According to county historian Homer Fansler, "The people of Davis resented the decision against Degler," a resentment which was "spurred on by agitation generated by Eastham." Degler's attorneys prepared a petition, subsequently signed by sixty-three citizens of Davis, to grant Degler a new trial, and presented it to the presiding judge, John Homer Holt. Judge Holt considered the petition an attempt to intimidate the court, and he promptly subpoenaed the sixty-three signers to appear on March 18, 1897, to answer to charges of contempt of court. Acting as their spokesman, Eastham argued that the right of petition was protected by the constitution and could not be denied. Ignoring Eastham, the judge fined defense attorneys A. B. Parsons and Lloyd Hansford twenty-five dollars each; H. J. Wagoner, prosecuting attorney, twenty dollars, and Robert W. Eastham and Max Blass five dollars each. Those who merely signed the petition were discharged upon payment of costs.[2]

Gunfight at the Parsons Depot

A special train was chartered to carry the petitioners to Parsons on the Thursday morning of March 18, 1897, and to convey them back to Davis that evening after the contempt hearing.

West Virginia Central and Pittsburgh Railroad depot in Parsons where the Eastham-Thompson shoot-out occurred in 1897. Courtesy of the West Virginia and Regional History Center.

Dr. William A. Brown, a Davis physician, had sent a telegram to C. L. Bretz, who managed the railroad, to reserve a car for the purpose and gave his personal obligation for fifty dollars and all people returning would pay a dollar for a ticket and "the more the merrier."[3]

After leaving the courthouse, and before the petitioners boarded, Eastham attached a placard to the railway car that his Republican enemies characterized as insulting. The words were taken from "Her Bright Smile Haunts Me Still," a song popular among Confederate cavalrymen during the Civil War. Everybody understood the inference that Judge Holt was "haunted by the bright smile of Alice Williams." Frank E. Thompson was in Parsons on business, and as the 7:30 P.M. special was the last train for Davis, he boarded with a companion, H. D. Cole. Robert W. Eastham entered the train car several minutes before departure, and almost everybody agreed on the outlines of what happened next. Seeing Thompson taking a seat, Eastham approached his enemy, called him a "perjurer" (referring to his lying in the court cases they had against each other) and a "S.O.B.," and slapped him hard across the face. Eastham then turned to continue up the aisle to his seat, and Thompson followed him with a drawn pistol. When he was within a few feet of Eastham, someone yelled "look out," and Eastham turned just as Thompson fired two shots. By then Eastham was struggling to draw his pistol which was caught on the lining of his coat pocket. Thompson fired four shots at Eastham: one missed and went into the roof, two glanced off Eastham's forehead, and the other grazed his left chest. Within that instant, Eastham returned three pistol shots: one striking Thompson in the left arm, one in the left thigh, and another in the abdomen. According to local folklore and the testimony of bystanders, Eastham shot through his coat pocket. He was heard to comment from time to time that it was best to "shoot 'em in the belly with a gun in your pocket; they don't get over it and nobody sees you shooting." This was mentioned time and again by the prosecutors during Eastham's trial as proof of his predisposition to violence. The public also embraced the story that Thompson fired an "owl-head" pistol, an inferior make with low compression and a short barrel without rifling. Had Thompson's pistol been a good one, many believed Eastham would have died on the spot.[4]

Dr. Benjamin M. Smith, a physician in Davis, entered the passenger car between twenty and fifteen minutes before 7:00 P.M. and took the third seat back on the right side next to the window. When he rose to open the window he heard gunshots. He turned facing the aisle and saw two men shooting. The two men were within arms' reach, and, although he recognized them as Eastham and Thompson, the incident happened so fast that he could not determine who shot first or how many shots were fired. Dr. Smith stepped into the aisle and separated the two antagonists after the last shot. He and Eastham "were not friendly," and had not spoken to each other for more than three years. Therefore, Dr. Smith addressed his words to Frank Thompson when separating the men. "Mr. Thompson replied to me. 'You dam son of a bitch, what in the hell have you got to do with this Dr. Smith.' Now I can't exactly remember my words. I said, don't you know the lives of these men are in danger from this shooting." Dr. Smith had pushed Eastham back in a seat, spoken to Thompson, turned back to Eastham and for a second time pushed him back into a seat. Then he called to the rest of the passengers to keep the men apart. "I saw Mr. Eastham bleeding profusely from a wound as I thought in the head. The second time that I spoke to Mr. Eastham I told him that he must sit down and stay in the seat. He replied, looking up at me and said, 'Dr. Smith, Dr. Smith,' said it twice, and that was all he said." The third time the physician called for help from the passengers, he remarked to Eastham: "You are badly hurt," and he responded, "Yes Dr. If I die give me a decent burial."[5]

According to Dr. Smith, Eastham had "two wounds, one shot, on the right side of the frontal bone, what we would call a deep flesh wound, tearing off the covering or plowing up the periosteum and injuring the outer table of the skull. It also cut two branches of the temporal artery. He lost from one pint to a pint and a half of blood." The second was a superficial wound on the right side over the ninth or tenth rib. Both of these shots were so close that the powder was blown onto Eastham's face. The ball from the second shot was discovered in his shirt by one of the deputies and Rev. Mr. Hollis at Eastham's house in Davis. It had perforated his vest and two shirts, Dr. Smith testified. "That ball was turned over to the proper authorities."[6]

The fatally wounded Thompson walked with assistance from the passenger coach at the depot to the Helmick Hotel as passengers and onlookers watched in stunned silence. Local physicians W. A. Brown of Davis and a Dr. Miller were quickly in attendance at Thompson's bedside; two other local physicians arrived shortly thereafter, Dr. Joseph Johnston of Parsons and Dr. C. R. Foutch. The latter, a surgeon, examined Thompson and found three wounds. One was "simply a flesh wound" in the left arm. A second wound in the thigh was in the center of the thigh. Dr. Foutch believed that the ball had struck the bone for it could not be located for extraction. The third wound in the abdomen, which penetrated the body "about one and a half inches to the left and one inch straight above the navel," was the most serious. "A ball entering where this did and passing through the body and lodging around to the left of the spinal column in the muscles of the back would have to pass through or by organs that to injure would in itself [be] almost fatal."[7]

Doctors Johnston and Foutch determined that to save Thompson's life surgery was necessary, and he would have to be moved to the hospital in Cumberland. They departed Parsons on the train for Cumberland at about 1:00 A.M. with the wounded man, and arrived at the Western Maryland Hospital at 6:00 A.M., September 19. Doctors Johnston and Foutch immediately performed an operation known as laparotomy. "After opening the abdomen we found it filled with blood and blood clot and after removing them we removed the intestines [and] found the intestines injured in two places," one only slightly and the other a partial perforation of the two "outer coats" caused by being grazed by the bullet. The mesentery and blood vessels that carried the blood supply to the intestines were perforated in three or four places causing severe internal hemorrhage. Dr. Foutch saw Thompson for the last time that afternoon at about 2:00 P.M. after which he and Dr. Johnston returned to Parsons by train.[8] At 1:30 A.M., March 20, 1897, the thirty-five-year-old lumberman died; his body was returned to the family's hometown of Norway, Maine, for burial. Dr. Johnston opined that Thompson died from the "extreme shock" resulting from the abdomen wound, and Dr. Foutch concurred.[9]

Thompson's cousin, George Benjamin Thompson, was with his uncle Albert and aunt Mary in Cumberland when Frank died. On March 18, 1930, thirty-three years to the day later, he recorded his memory of that tragic moment:

> 33 years ago today Frank died at the Western Maryland Hospital in Cumberland, Md. I was boarding with Joseph P. Dunwoody's at 916 South 46th Street in west Philadelphia and while at breakfast in the morning read in the paper of the shooting by Eastham.
>
> Soon after reaching the office at 915 Betz Building messages began to come in and one from Frank asked to have Dr. Montgomery sent at once.
>
> Mr. [Fairfax S.] Landstreet came in to get the facts concerning the affair but I could give him little information.
>
> A[lbert] Thompson and wife [Mary] was on their way to Davis but was going to stop a few days in Washington. I wired him in care of Congressman A. G. Dayton. Also in care of several lumber dealers whom he usually called, and succeeded in locating them just in time for them to secure a train for Cumberland on the B. & O. that would reach there about 4 P.M.
>
> I left Phila at noon and reached Cumberland at 8 P.M. Went up to the hospital and found Uncle Albert and Aunt Mary

there. Mr. D[ayton] was with them. They had operated on Frank and while he was still alive he was unconscious and remained so until about 2 A.M. when he died.

I was at the Queen City [hotel] when Uncle Albert came and told me. He was deeply grieved, but would not come into the room and continued to walk in a dazed condition until sunrise. Aunt Mary was prostrate by his death and alone except [for] Uncle Albert, Dayton and myself.

At sunrise we went to Butlers undertaker rooms and they selected a coffin and arranged to take the remains to Norway, M[aine] for burial. It required about all of my time sending and receiving messages.

At one time Uncle Albert decided I should go to Davis, but reconsidered and I went East with them about noon. At Washington D.C. Mrs. Dayton met the train with some clothes for A. G. [Dayton] and her presence even for the short while was a great help and comfort to Aunt Mary.

The Judge [Dayton was appointed to the U.S. District Court for the Northern District of West Virginia in 1905] was of great help to them virtually taking charge of all arrangements, and the friendship continued to the end. They are all gone now. The Judge died first [on July 30, 1920] and Mrs. Dayton outlived the others.

I shall always remember that night. The last time I saw Frank alive I went with him to board the train for Davis at 24th and Chestnut St. [Philadelphia]. He had come in from New York and was in excellent spirits. We went into a small saloon near the station and had a glass of beer. He joked me about maintaining my residence in Davis and insisted I continue to do so and keep the shotgun oiled and clean. I always have felt if I had been there it would not have happened.[10]

Eastham, it turned out, was only slightly wounded, and immediately returned to his home in Davis. Tucker County Sheriff Riley Harper arrested him on March 25, 1897, on a warrant issued by Justice of the Peace William F. Lipscomb charging that Robert W. Eastham "feloniously, willfully, maliciously, deliberately, and unlawfully did slay, kill and murder one Frank E. Thompson, against the peace and dignity of the state."[11] The defendant's lawyers filed an appeal of habeas corpus on March 31 with John Homer Holt, judge of the three-county Third Judicial Circuit, in Grafton, Taylor County. Three of Eastham's friends, George H. Johnson, Lemuel W. Parsons, and Silas R. Blackman, cosigned the bond of $3,000 to secure Eastham's release from jail. Bail was denied, however, and the court ordered Sheriff Harper to present Eastham at the courthouse in Grafton, on Monday, April 5, 1897, at 5:00 P.M. to be formally arraigned.[12] Throughout the proceedings that followed, and until his trial began on the morning of November 23, 1897, Eastham remained in the county jail in Parsons.

"Lawyers by the Dozen"

The trial of Robert Eastham for the murder of Frank Thompson became a cause célèbre in the partisan struggle between the Democrats who stood for traditional local republican values, individual personal property, and weak government, versus the Republicans who favored protecting the property of the corporations, market-oriented business, and the concentration of power in a strong government. Tucker County traditionally was

R. W. Eastham "Bob Ridley." From Williamson, *Mosby's Rangers*, 242.

evenly divided between Democrats and Republicans. By the end of the nineteenth century, the Republican campaign to control the county mirrored the party's resurgence in state government. For the first time since 1869, behind the leadership of Stanley B. Elkins, who faced no resistance from his father-in-law, Henry G. Davis, who headed the Democratic Party, the Republicans finally regained power in the state in the election of 1896. That same year, William McKinley was elected president, and George W. Atkinson, a Republican from Ohio County, was elected governor. Both houses of the state legislature fell under Republican rule, excepting a few brief interludes, for the next thirty-six years. Elkins had been chosen U.S. senator from West Virginia in 1895 and served until his death in 1911.

The West Virginia Republican Party was united behind the project of incorporating West Virginia into the national market

The Tucker County sheriff's residence was in the front and the jail was in the rear of this building. Structurally the building remains the same as it was in 1897 when Eastham was incarcerated in a second-floor cell. Photograph by Ronald Lewis.

system, but they had to fight for control county by county against the Democrats. In 1894 Davis refused to support the reelection of Democrat William L. Wilson to Congress from the Second District, which included Tucker County, because Wilson had opposed tariffs on coal and lumber. Meanwhile, Elkins openly supported the Republican candidate, Alston G. Dayton, and he succeeded in sliding the district into the Republican column.[13] The election aroused bitter feelings in the district, but county Republicans lost no time in exerting their newly acquired power while the Democrats redoubled their resistance. The shooting death of Frank Thompson in 1897 was widely viewed as a tragic result of this political struggle, with Thompson representing the

Republican resurgence that threatened to monopolize the county's most valuable natural resources. This conviction among independent farmers was asserted time and again by Eastham and his supporters, and it seemed clear in the political context of the time that the small landowners of the Blackwater River and Canaan Valley were losing control of their own resources to a company with the economic and political muscle to monopolize the county's wealth.

The Eastham-Thompson feud reveals how those forces came into play, and the actors responded according to their received cultures. The attorneys who represented the contesting parties in court were more than "hired guns"; they were local field commanders in the ideological war for the hearts and minds, and more important, natural resources of Tucker County. Locals felt even more threatened because the presiding judge in the Eastham murder trial was on the side of the resurgent Republicans.

Circuit Court Judge John Homer Holt was born in Gilmer County on June 19, 1857. He attended the local schools, the Preston Academy at Kingwood, and taught school for five years before he began the study of law in the office of George H. McGrew in Kingwood. He was admitted to the Kingwood bar in 1878, then moved his office to Grafton in 1881, but he served much of his time as counselor and lobbyist in the nation's capital. Holt quickly rose to prominence in the Republican Party and was "stanchly identified with the protection principle for American industry." He entered politics early, was elected to the West Virginia House of Delegates in 1878, and served as a delegate to many of the state party conventions. He was chairman of the 1892 state convention that tapped Thomas E. Davis of Grafton as the party's gubernatorial candidate. He also played a major role in the convention of 1894 that nominated Alston G. Dayton for Congress, the attorney who now pleaded the state's case against

Eastham before him. He also chaired the Republican state convention that nominated George W. Atkinson who became the state's first Republican governor since the 1860s. Holt was elected judge of the Third Circuit in 1896 and was reelected in 1904.[14] From the foregoing it is easy to see why the defense attorneys, and perhaps the jurors, believed that the defense confronted a hostile political judge with serious conflicts of interest. One of the more riveting features of the Eastham murder trial is the large number of high-profile attorneys who were engaged on both sides. Collectively, the Washington, DC, *Evening Times* described them as an "unusual array of legal talent," and the *Alexandria Gazette* declared that "the ablest lawyers have been employed" to try the case.[15]

Prosecuting Attorneys

At least five of the eight attorneys prosecuting the state's case against Eastham were active Republicans. Alston Gordon Dayton was born on October 18, 1857, in Philippi, West Virginia. His father, Spencer Dayton, was born in Connecticut where he practiced law before moving to what is now Barbour County, West Virginia, in 1847. During the Civil War Spencer Dayton was a staunch supporter of the Union cause. After completing public school, his son Alston enrolled at West Virginia University where he earned the AB degree in 1878, and the MA in 1880. He was admitted to the bar in 1878 and entered partnership with his father in the firm Dayton and Dayton. In 1879 he was appointed to fill an unexpired term as prosecuting attorney for Upshur County, and in 1884 was elected prosecuting attorney of Barbour County. Even more than his father, he was a strong adherent to the Republican Party, which led to his election to Congress from the Second District in 1894, a seat he held for the next ten years. In 1905 Dayton was appointed as federal judge to the U.S. District Court for the Northern District of West Virginia with the help of his friend U.S. Senator Stephen B. Elkins, and continued his work on the federal bench until shortly before his death in 1920. Since Frank Thompson was a prominent Republican in his district, it comes as no surprise that Dayton was, as one newspaper reported, "Thompson's personal friend."[16]

Unlike Alston Dayton, who was born into an upper-middle-class family and found his path into the legal profession unobstructed, William G. Conley's road to success was quite the opposite. Only after working as a farm laborer and mule driver on railroad construction, as a coal miner, coke drawer, quarryman, and sawmill man to help his widowed mother and sisters did he acquire an education. Conley was born near Kingwood, West Virginia, in 1866, where he attended and then taught in the local schools from 1886 to 1891, when he was elected Superintendent of Free Schools for Preston County. Subsequently he attended West Virginia University and graduated with a law degree in 1893, and established his practice in Parsons, in neighboring Tucker County. Conley was soon elected to town council, in 1896 elected Tucker County prosecuting attorney, and in 1897, the year of Eastham's trial, he was elected mayor. During his residence in Parsons, Conley also found time to found and edit the *Parsons Advocate*, a strong local newspaper that adhered to the Republican line politically, and has survived to the present day. Conley was a rising star in his party who was subsequently appointed to the office of attorney general of West Virginia, and in the general election that fall won a full term. By the time his term ended in 1913, Conley was one of the prominent voices in the state Republican Party. He moved his practice to Charleston, and

Alston G. Dayton, Republican congressman and future federal judge, was the lead attorney for the prosecution in the case against Robert Eastham. Courtesy of the West Virginia and Regional History Center.

William G. Conley, prosecutor for Tucker County in the case against Robert Eastham and future Republican governor of West Virginia. Courtesy of the West Virginia and Regional History Center.

his connections within the Republican Party grew accordingly. In 1928 Conley was elected governor.[17]

Absalom M. Cunningham was born in Buckhannon, Upshur County, in 1864. Like Conley, he attended local schools and prepared himself to be a teacher, a vocation he followed for twelve years. During this time, he followed the familiar route of reading the law while earning a living in the classroom and was admitted to the bar in 1892. Cunningham established his first office in the lumber town of Hendricks, Tucker County, where he remained for the next sixteen years. Cunningham developed a very successful practice in Tucker County. A staunch Republican, he served as prosecuting attorney from 1893 to 1897 and was elected to the state legislature in 1903 and 1904. George W. Atkinson, the biographer of the West Virginia Bar, described him as "a man of large stature, of splendid address and of commanding personal appearance," a "naturally sociable" man, and an "orator of force and power" who commands people's attention. All were ingredients that served to make him "an unusually successful trial lawyer." Cunningham devoted himself primarily to his practice, but he also interested himself in business. He organized the Miners and Mechanics Bank at Thomas, near Davis, and like most businessmen of his day, he took "a lively interest in every movement for the development of the internal affairs of this section of the state." In 1909, he moved his office to the much larger town of Elkins, in neighboring Randolph County, where his opportunities were expanded considerably.[18]

Little is known about John Andrew Howard of Wheeling. From 1888 to 1896 he was the prosecuting attorney of Ohio County and became a "renowned corporation lawyer and public utility organizer and executive." By the 1920s his son William C. Howard joined him in the firm of Howard & Howard, Wheeling.[19] John

Howard was experienced in presenting cases before the Supreme Court of Appeals and was chosen to make the state's rebuttal in *Eastham v. Holt* (discussed in chapter 9) brought before the high court on appeal by Eastham's lawyers.

Two Democrats also joined the legal team of prosecutors, one of whom, John James Davis, was a distinguished lawyer with a statewide reputation. John Davis, his father, was born in Shenandoah County, Virginia, but moved to Clarksburg, Harrison County, western Virginia in 1825 where he became a prominent businessman and held the offices of sheriff and justice of the peace. During the Civil War John Davis was "a strong Southern sympathizer." John J. Davis was born in Clarksburg in 1835, spent his entire life in that city, and died there in 1916. He attended the local academy and at seventeen began studying in a local law office. John J. completed his studies at the Brockenbrough School of Law in Lexington, Virginia, which became the law school at Washington and Lee University, and at the youthful age of twenty entered practice in his hometown.

Before long, John J. Davis was engaged in politics, and according to historian James Morton Callahan, performed "a historic service in the formation of the State of West Virginia." A stanch Democrat, he was elected to the Virginia Legislature in 1861, and that year was a member of the Second Wheeling Convention which approved the establishment and organization of the new state of West Virginia. As a "conservative unionist," he opposed statehood if it meant the abolition of slavery—northern abolitionists called them "copperheads." He also was a ready ally of those former Confederates who joined together in 1872 to replace the Republicans with Democrats and write a new state constitution more acceptable to southern sensibilities. John J. became one of the most prominent leaders in the state's Democratic Party. He was elected to the West Virginia legislature in 1870, was active in several national campaigns, and served two terms in Congress from 1871 to 1875.[20]

John J. Davis was an archconservative who adhered to the values of the Old South even though he supported industrialization. In addition to his status as a prominent attorney, therefore, it is likely that he was added to the prosecution team because of his archconservative stance on property rights (and race). Another factor in his favor was his opposition to the Henry G. Davis faction of his party, the Regulars, making him someone who could appeal to the sizeable Redeemer segment of Confederate sympathizers in Tucker County who supported Eastham and undoubtedly would be represented on the jury.

Another Democrat who joined the state's team was Adonijah B. Parsons who was born in 1845 on a farm near St. George, the original county seat of Tucker County. He was a farmer, and, like so many country lawyers, also a school teacher. In 1870 he began reading law and was admitted to the bar at St. George in 1872. He played a key role in establishing the Democratic Party in Tucker County, was elected prosecuting attorney on the Democratic ticket in 1876, and then elected to the West Virginia House of Delegates in 1882. Parsons also held several other local posts, such as county surveyor and mayor of St. George. Although he raised cattle and horses on his farm, Parsons devoted most of his energy to the successful practice of land and criminal law. Regarded as very persuasive with a jury, he was one of the busiest lawyers in Tucker and adjoining counties. For this reason, "scarcely a case comes before the Court in which he is not a counsel for one side or the other," according to one contemporary.[21] In addition to being an effective trial lawyer in the local courts, and apparently quite comfortable serving as either plaintiff or defense counsel, it is likely that he too was someone well known and trusted by county residents.

Two state's attorneys did not play a prominent role in the trial, although they were officially on the team. Edward P. Durkin (one newspaper referred to him as "Durkey") was a thirty-year-old, single lawyer living in a boarding house in Thomas during the trial. His parents were natives of Ireland, but Durkin was born in West Virginia. According to a county historian, he served as mayor of Thomas in 1900–1901, but his political affiliation is unknown.[22]

Another state's attorney who did not play a major role in the trial was James Porter Scott. In 1880 he moved to St. George from Taylor County and brought his newspaper, the *New Era*, with him, but renamed it the *Tucker Democrat*. He sold the paper in 1881 and its new owner, William M. Cayton, moved it to Parsons after that community became the county seat in 1893. Scott had been among the "army" that removed the court records from St. George to Parsons. As newspaper editor in 1880, Scott obviously was a Democrat, and he must have remained loyal to that party; he was a Democrat when he served as prosecuting attorney for Tucker County from 1921 to 1925. As vice president and then president of the National Bank of Parsons, he also became a prominent local businessman who undoubtedly strongly supported industrialization and incorporation and, therefore, was categorized as a "safe" Democrat. During his career, Scott also served several terms as mayor of Parsons.[23]

Defense Attorneys

Even more so than the state's team, the eleven attorneys for the defense were drawn from one party, the Democratic Party, with a single exception. Nevertheless, because the party itself was

St. George Courthouse and several court officials (ca. 1893). Several of these men played a role in Eastham's trial. Adonijah B. Parsons (second from left) was an attorney for the prosecution; Wilson B. Maxwell (third from left) was one of the lead defense attorneys; Lloyd Hansford (sixth from right) was also an attorney for the defense; William M. Cayton (third from right), a lieutenant in the county Democratic organization, served as county clerk.

composed of a coalition of factions, defense attorneys represented a more diverse group. As the leader of West Virginia's Democratic Party, Henry G. Davis was forced to take into consideration all of the party factions relevant to a particular situation in order to maintain the coalition. Each county's political circumstances were unique. There were no "Agrarian" or "Kanawha Ring" factions to figure into the political mix of Tucker County, leaving the balancing act between the "Regular" and "Redeemer" factions. Political parties were expected to provide patronage to their leadership, which included supporting them in a partisan fight. The Eastham trial was shaping up as political retribution, forcing Davis to exert his influence by sending his personal and company attorneys to lead in defending one of his lieutenants.

C. Wood Dailey, a "Regular," was the chief attorney for Davis and Elkins's West Virginia Central & Pittsburgh Railroad, a line that linked Davis, Parsons, and points west with the east coast. He was born in Romney, Hampshire County, in 1849, educated in private schools in Cumberland, Maryland, and read law, which allowed him to pass the Hampshire County Bar in 1870. For twenty years he served as the county's prosecuting attorney, until 1892 when he was appointed judge of the Thirteenth Circuit Court. After moving to Elkins he became mayor of that city and one of the original stockholders of the Davis Trust Company. Dailey served as a political operative for Davis as early as 1884, when Grover Cleveland defeated George Blaine for the presidency. Davis lost out in the patronage scramble for a major appointment, however, because the president channeled these through West Virginia senator Johnson N. Camden. Nevertheless, Dailey remained a major ally of Davis and traveled to Charleston as the chief lobbyist for the Davis and Elkins interests until his death in 1908.[24]

Another Davis man, and member of the "Regular" faction of the Democratic Party, Cyrus Oscar Strieby, handled local matters for H. G. Davis. A state historian described Strieby as "easily one of the leading attorneys" practicing at the bar of Tucker and Randolph counties. He was born in Williamsport, Pennsylvania, March 13, 1866. His father moved from Lycoming County to a farm in Hampshire County, West Virginia, in 1880 when Cyrus was fourteen. At sixteen Strieby secured a teaching certificate and taught in a Hampshire County school for four years. With his earnings he enrolled in Susquehanna University and completed his degree in 1889, and subsequently earned the MA degree as well. After graduation he taught for another year, and then began the study of law at St. George, Tucker County, in the preceptorship of Wilson B. Maxwell. Strieby received his license to practice law in December 1890 and became an associate of W. B. Maxwell for the next three years before moving to Davis to establish his own practice. In 1911 Strieby relocated to Elkins, the county seat of neighboring Randolph County, and built up a substantial practice.[25] As Davis's attorney on the ground, he was a leading figure in the armed removal of the courthouse from St. George to Parsons along with Robert Eastham and others of the Redeemer faction.

John Thomas McGraw, a Regular Democrat loyal to both H. G. Davis and Johnson N. Camden, often served as a liaison between the two Democratic allies. A tycoon in his own right, McGraw was born in 1856 at Grafton. McGraw was educated in the Catholic schools of Grafton, St. Vincent Academy in Wheeling, and graduated from Yale University law school in 1876. He was admitted to the Taylor County Bar that same year and appointed one of the West Virginia counselors for the Baltimore & Ohio Railway, a position he held for many years.

McGraw became a prominent leader in the state Democratic Party as a young man. From 1880 through 1885 he served as prosecuting attorney for Taylor County, and in 1882 was appointed an aide-de-camp at the rank of colonel to the staff of Governor Jacob B. Jackson. Thereafter, he was appointed to several important patronage jobs when the Democrats held the presidency. President Grover Cleveland appointed him Collector of Internal Revenue for the state of West Virginia, and then to the post of U.S. disbursing agent for the public buildings in Clarksburg, Charleston, and Wheeling.[26] He also served as a member of the Democratic National Committee from 1896 to 1916. This might explain why William W. Arnett (discussed later in this chapter) replaced McGraw early in the Eastham trial. McGraw was an archconservative and more useful to the larger corporate interests of Davis and Elkins, devoting his time as their watchdog on the Democratic National Committee. He did remain on the legal team, however, and assisted from time to time.

McGraw's rise to wealth and political influence was furthered by the dominant men in the state's Democratic Party, U.S. senators Davis and Camden, and he assiduously cultivated their favor. He emulated their careers as industrial developers, creating the Pocahontas Development Corporation to speculate in timber lands in Pocahontas County, and to establish its county seat-town of Marlinton. His success was assured when the Chesapeake & Ohio Railroad extended a branch up the Greenbrier River, arriving in Marlinton in 1900. He was involved in innumerable other businesses, but in later years suffered financial reversals that left him reliant on his family.[27]

It is not clear whether Wilson Bonnifield Maxwell was a Davis man, or to which faction of the party he belonged. It is likely that he was chosen because he was Eastham's personal friend and counselor who represented him in earlier cases involving the Blackwater Lumber Company, making him familiar with the background of the case. A well-respected and trusted figure in the county, he played a major role in the courtroom during the Eastham trial.

Maxwell was born in Randolph County in 1853 to parents from pioneering families in western Virginia. His father, Rufus Maxwell, was an attorney who established his office in St. George, and in 1857, one year after the county was founded, became the first prosecuting attorney for Tucker County. Wilson grew up in St. George, received an education in the public schools, and then attended West Virginia University prior to studying law under his uncle, attorney Edwin Maxwell of Weston, Lewis County.

Wilson was admitted to the bar in 1874, and for twenty-five years practiced in Tucker County from his office in St. George. In 1899 he moved to Elkins, Randolph County, where the opportunities were greater for a lawyer of his accomplishments. Although he was not active in politics, Wilson B. Maxwell was well-known as a strong supporter of the Democratic Party.[28]

Five attorneys represented what might be called the Virginia-Confederate-Redeemer contingent on Eastham's defense team. All of them were truly distinguished attorneys who practiced in Eastham's home district, the Virginia counties of Rappahannock, Warren, Clarke, and Fauquier. Undoubtedly they all knew each other, as former Confederate soldiers identified with Eastham, and/or friends of the Eastham family; one was an Eastham cousin. No doubt they were present to help prevent what they perceived as the likely political lynching of one of their own.

The most distinguished of this group was Holmes Conrad. He was born in Winchester, Virginia, in 1840, the son of Robert Young Conrad, a prominent lawyer of that city who served as Virginia attorney general from 1857 to 1862. Holmes Conrad attended Virginia Military Institute and the University of Virginia. When the Civil War broke out, he enlisted with the 1st Virginia Cavalry and saw action throughout the war. He was commissioned lieutenant, in 1862 was appointed adjutant, and elevated to the rank of major in Thomas Rosser's cavalry division.

After the war, he began the study of law in his father's office, was admitted to the Virginia bar in 1866, and joined his father's practice. He was elected to the Virginia legislature in 1878 and served until 1882. His influence rose in the Democratic Party, and in 1893 President Grover Cleveland appointed him assistant attorney general of the United States, becoming solicitor general in 1895. He left that office in 1897, the same year as Eastham's trial, which probably explains how he would have the time to join Eastham's defense team even in an advisory capacity. In 1901 Conrad joined the law faculty of Georgetown University. Conrad was retained by the McKinley administration as government counsel on several important cases argued before the Supreme Court, a venue for much of his practice in his later years. His most successful case was probably his last, when he represented Virginia and the bond holders in *Commonwealth of Virginia v. State of West Virginia*, in which was decided the amount West Virginia should pay to Virginia as its part of the public debt precipitated by the formation of the new state when it split away during the Civil War.[29]

Another of the Confederate-Redeemer contingent defending Eastham, William Willey Arnett, was practicing in Wheeling at the time. The biographer of the West Virginia Bar described Arnett as a consummate professional who was "in the front rank of criminal lawyers at the Wheeling Bar probably unequaled in his knowledge of criminal law, certainly unexcelled in its presentation to the jury." He claimed that Arnett defended "some of the most noted *causa celebre* in West Virginia" and attributed his success to his shrewd handling of testimony. "It is universally conceded that Colonel Arnett was one of the greatest natural lawyers that West Virginia ever produced."[30]

William W. Arnett was born in 1843 in Marion County, West Virginia. He attended Fairmont Academy and then Allegheny College at Meadville, Pennsylvania, graduating in 1860. He studied law with Alpheus F. Haymond, who became a judge on the West Virginia Supreme Court of Appeals. Arnett was admitted to the bar in 1860 and established an office in Fairmont. When the Civil War broke out he enlisted with the 31st Virginia Infantry. He enlisted as a private, but was quickly appointed by Virginia Governor Letcher to the rank of lieutenant colonel of what became the 25th Virginia. Arnett resigned his commission, however, and returned to his old company whereupon he was elected captain. Arnett served in that role until 1863 when he was elected colonel of the 20th Virginia Cavalry, a post he held until the end of the war. He distinguished himself in extensive action during his military career and was wounded at Cross Keys and at Bristoe Station. Arnett served with Stonewall Jackson's Shenandoah campaign and participated in engagements in his home state, including the Battle of Droop Mountain in 1861.[31]

Because the new state of West Virginia required a "test oath" of officeholders swearing they had never been in rebellion against the government, Arnett opened his law practice in Berryville, Clarke County, Virginia, after Appomattox. In 1868 he was elected to the Virginia legislature from Clarke County, and reelected to a second term. Giving up a promising political career, in 1872 he relocated to St. Louis, Missouri, where he rose to wealth and prominence as a criminal lawyer. Arnett returned to his native state in 1875, after all of the restrictions against former Confederates had been lifted, and located in Wheeling. Immediately he became one of the leading attorneys in the state by triumphing in a number of high-profile cases, such as the litigation over removal of the state capital from Wheeling to Charleston. According to Atkinson, "After his resumption of practice in West Virginia he was retained on the defense or prosecution of almost every important criminal case before the courts in his region."[32]

Much less is known about the other counselors in the Virginia contingent. James Marshall McCormick was born in 1849, graduated from the University of Virginia, and established his practice in Berryville, Clarke County. He served three terms as mayor of Berryville and as commonwealth attorney for nine years, and served in the state senate. McCormick was prominent in the state Democratic Party and was a member of the Democratic National

Convention that nominated Grover Cleveland for president. He was also a large landowner in Clarke County and owned a home in nearby Battletown.[33] A newspaper covering the Eastham trial referred to him as "the renown" lawyer from Virginia.

Similarly, only the barest facts are known of Horatio Gates Moffett. At the time of Eastham's trial he was commonwealth's attorney for Rappahannock County. Moffett would have known the Easthams, including Robert, very well. After the trial, according to Eastham's great nephew and namesake, "as far as the Easthams were concerned, any Moffett had the job of commonwealth's attorney [for Rappahannock County] if he wanted it." Henry Hawkins Downing, who was born in Fauquier County in 1853 and practiced law in Front Royal, Warren County, also knew the Easthams. An unconfirmed newspaper report identified Downing as Eastham's cousin. Downing was a member of the Virginia House of Delegates for Clarke and Warren counties, 1885–1887, 1889–1891, and 1893–1895. Later in life he also served in the Virginia Senate representing Clarke, Page, and Warren counties from 1916 to 1919.[34]

Howard J. Wagoner's role on the defense team was indicated by an entry in his diary for May 23, 1897: "Going back and forth all month to Parsons, court in session Eastham trial for murder of Frank Thompson." Wagoner was another local Regular Democrat loyal to Henry G. Davis. He trained under Wilson B. Maxwell, a leading lawyer in the Eastham trial, and knew most of the parties personally. For example, in another diary entry for April 16, 1896, he recorded that "Joe Strieby and I rode horseback to St. George and attended wedding of Cyrus O. Strieby [H. G. Davis's lawyer] and Miss Addie Adams."[35] Like several of the Regular Davis Democrats on the defense team, Wagoner was born in Mineral County, Davis's home county. After graduating from Fairmont State College, he became a school teacher in

Mineral County and then in the town of Davis where he moved in 1887. He too read law in the office of Wilson B. Maxwell, was admitted to the bar in 1895, and practiced law in Davis, in addition to owning a store and serving as the town's postmaster—a political appointment he received as one of H. G. Davis's lieutenants. He also served as Tucker County commissioner from 1893 to 1895 and in the House of Delegates during the 1899–1901 term.[36]

William C. Clayton was another Mineral County lawyer and close confidant of Henry G. Davis who assisted with the Eastham trial. As early as 1879 he prepared a last will and testament for Davis in his law offices at Keyser. His association with Davis grew over the years with the latter's rise as an industrialist and politician, and he became a corporate counselor for Davis's West Virginia & Pittsburgh Railroad. He often was in Charleston lobbying for the West Virginia and Pittsburgh Railroad and in 1898 carried Eastham's manslaughter conviction appeal to the Supreme Court of Appeals. Like McGraw, he was an influential leader in the West Virginia Democratic Party in his own right.[37]

The lone Republican on Eastham's defense team appointed by H. G. Davis was Francis Marion Reynolds, another Mineral County connection. Born in Taylor County, West Virginia, in 1843, he attended local schools, the academy in Morgantown, and then studied in the Morgantown law offices of Bunker and Brown. Reynolds was certified to practice law in 1865 and opened an office in the small village of New Creek, the county seat of the recently established Mineral County. The town was renamed Keyser in 1873 in honor of William Keyser, vice president of the Baltimore & Ohio Railway.

Reynolds practiced alone for a number of years, but eventually joined forces with Joseph T. Hoke, who preceded Circuit Judge John Homer Holt on the same bench before which Eastham was tried. Reynolds became a leader in the state Republican

Party. He served two terms as prosecuting attorney of Mineral County, 1872–1876 and 1888–1892. Moreover, he served a total of twelve years as prosecuting attorney of Grant County and was elected to the House of Delegates in 1894 and again in 1900 and 1902, where he served as floor leader for the controlling Republican Party. He twice cast his vote for Stephen B. Elkins for U.S. senator. In 1904 he was elected judge of the newly created Sixteenth Judicial Circuit, which was formed of Mineral, Tucker, and Grant counties, and reelected in 1912. Judge Reynolds was also a prominent Keyser businessman, was also involved in the development of the local coal industry, and owned an operating farm. Even though he belonged to the opposing party, therefore, Reynolds was an old and trusted Davis confidant.[38]

Although traditional standards of behavior in the backcountry were more accepting of physical violence under certain circumstances such as self-protection, Tucker County residents were shocked that the bad blood between Eastham and Thompson would come to such a tragic culmination. Both men were popular and respected among their respective constituencies, and the shoot-out exposed the chasm that had opened within their midst between the traditionalists and the modernizers. They expected a spectacular trial but were utterly bewildered as to why such an "array of legal talent" converged on Parsons to try the case. Few residents appreciated the stakes involved in what, for them, was an unfortunate incident resulting in a tragic death. Only a few leaders in the "war of incorporation" to link West Virginia's back counties into the national markets comprehended that the outcome of Eastham's trial might determine the terms of that transition in the county, and which political faction would guide it.

9

JURY SELECTION AND THE APPEAL

Selecting a Grand Jury

During the June term of the Tucker County circuit court, the grand jury convened to hear the charges against Eastham. After investigating the circumstances the grand jury decided that murder was not the appropriate charge and instead returned an indictment for involuntary manslaughter, a misdemeanor. The prosecuting attorney, William Conley, insisted that the prisoner should be indicted for the greater offense of murder and dismissed this indictment. Eastham's attorneys immediately moved that the defendant either be dismissed or released on bail, but Judge Homer Holt overruled both motions. Instead, he ordered that another grand jury be drawn to consider the indictment and adjourned until August 2 when the second grand jury would be impaneled. Because homicide was admitted by the defendant but he claimed it was justifiable, Judge Holt charged the second grand jury to return an indictment for murder, and leave the degree of the offense to the determination of a petit jury. Before the grand jury had reached a conclusion, however, the foreman reported that the jurists were hopelessly split in their opinions between murder and involuntary manslaughter, probably because of the judge's charge. Instead of correcting course, on August 4 Judge Holt discharged them as a "disagreeing jury."

Judge Holt then summoned a special grand jury to consider the Eastham case. William M. Cayton, clerk of the Tucker County

Court, was ordered to draw sixteen grand jurors to be summoned from the panel for the special grand jury to meet on August 5, 1897. The court dismissed five as unqualified, and so the next day the judge ordered William B. Haller, even though he was not a sworn deputy as the law required, to assist in summoning six qualified replacements from the bystanders. One of the six new selectees was excused as unqualified, and again Haller was ordered to choose a replacement. After the five bystanders were seated it was ascertained that one of them, P. W. Lipscomb, was a constable, and therefore ineligible. Again, Judge Holt ordered Haller to choose another qualified grand juryman. Subsequently, the judge's selection of Haller, who was never sworn in as a deputy sheriff, became a matter of contention between the opposing sides.

Judge Holt's method of jury selection was not in accordance with Section 2, Chapter 157, of the Code of West Virginia. According to the code, the county court at its regular term was required to prepare a list of no less than 100 and no more than 150 "freeholders" chosen from the county's magisterial districts. The state code specifically excluded constables, keepers of hotels or taverns, surveyors of roads, or owners or occupiers of steam or water grist mills. The names of potential jurors were to be written on slips of paper, or ballots, which were to be folded or rolled so the names were not readable, deposited in a box, and delivered to the clerk of the circuit court for safekeeping.

Instead of adhering to state code, the county commissioners met in the jury rooms at the courthouse while the county clerk was not present, and created a list of names from which grand jurors should be drawn for the ensuing year. The potential jurors' names were then written on slips of paper and deposited unfolded into a box. Not surprisingly, defense counsel argued that this grand jury was selected illegally, and in a manner that was prejudicial to Eastham receiving a fair trial. So, too, was the judge's selection of a private individual to act in the capacity of the sheriff who then chose jurors from bystanders rather than drawing them from the box.

After the third grand jury was duly sworn in, Judge Holt proceeded to deliver another lengthy, and even more insistent, charge; since homicide was established by the evidence it was the duty of the grand jury to return a verdict of murder, without hearing further witnesses, and let the petit jury determine the degree of the offense committed. Should they choose not to perform according to his instructions, the judge threatened to charge them with contempt of court. The special grand jury was then sent to its room under the charge of the sheriff. They were not permitted to separate and were kept together until 7:30 P.M. when they returned to court without a decision. Again they were sent back to the jury room and kept there until nearly 11:00 P.M. when they finally found the indictment for murder that Judge Holt had demanded.

Even more irregular, upon the recommendation of prosecuting attorney William G. Conley, the circuit court appointed outgoing prosecuting attorney Absalom M. Cunningham as assistant prosecuting attorney for the adjourned term of the court, which began on August 2, 1897, and continued until after the indictment. At the same time, and with the full knowledge of the court, Cunningham was also being paid by Albert Thompson, father of the deceased, to assist the state prosecutors. As the prosecuting attorney's assistant, he questioned witnesses and read affidavits in the case against Eastham. Moreover, Cunningham was in the grand jury room during the entire period when evidence was being presented and discussed against Eastham, the same evidence on which the indictment was found. Defendant's counsel rightly took exception, claiming that his actions improperly influenced the grand jury and trammeled the defendant's rights.[1]

The Appeal: *Eastham v. Holt*

Judge Holt's insistence on an indictment for murder prompted a chorus of criticism from Tucker County citizens friendly to Eastham, and a vigorous defense from those who supported Judge Holt and the Thompsons.[2] By the time the special grand jury indicted Eastham for murder, his attorneys had already petitioned the West Virginia Supreme Court of Appeals on a writ of prohibition to "dismiss the rule in this case as having been improvidently awarded," and for a writ of habeas corpus to release the defendant from jail. The petitions were accepted by one of the judges, probably Marmaduke Dent, and immediately brought before the court. Arguments were presented on August 3 and 4, 1897, by Wilson B. Maxwell and Marshall McCormick representing Eastham, and John A. Howard representing the state.[3]

The Supreme Court of Appeals for West Virginia had convened in Charles Town where the attorneys presented their cases for most of Wednesday and Thursday morning, September 2 and 3, 1897, with a "large crowd" in attendance. Ten days later, on September 14, 1897, the high court made its decision. The main question before the jurists was whether the facts justified writs of prohibition and error. At this time only four judges sat on the Supreme Court of Appeals, which presented a problem in cases of a tie. And in the Eastham case the high court was evenly divided 2–2, with judges Marmaduke H. Dent and John English for and Henry Brannon and Henry C. McWhorter against. Consequently, without a majority, the writ of prohibition was denied, the case was not dismissed, and the court's action let the indictment against Eastham stand. In the habeas corpus proceedings, the court again split 2–2 and, therefore, refused to order Eastham's release. While the high court considered his case, Eastham was confined to a jail in Charles Town. Following the court's decision, he was remanded back to the Tucker County jail in Parsons to await his trial on charges of murder.[4]

Upon denial of the writ of prohibition, Eastham's counsel moved for a rehearing, and once again the appeal was rejected by the same divided court. Judges Dent and English favored a reargument of the case. Judge Dent observed that "the result of a divided court is simply null. It determines nothing, but leaves the controversy as though there had been none. The court owes it as a duty to the public to reach an agreement and decide the case if possible. Both divisions may be wrong, but both cannot be right."[5] As with the original case, the opposition of Judges Henry Brannon and Henry C. McWhorter overruled the rehearing by a split court.

The struggle for dominance between the agrarian and industrial worlds during the 1890s was personified in the lives and decisions of two judges on the West Virginia Supreme Court of Appeals, Marmaduke H. Dent and Henry Brannon. The legal historian John Phillip Reid has observed that the state's highest court was shaped by neither a strong chief nor an outstanding scholar, but rather came of age during the industrial transition while Judges Dent and Brannon debated "the important legal questions of their day and, by debating them, defined them." Representing two competing economic and legal philosophies, they made the law "reflect the sociological attitudes of the West Virginia in which they lived." Strong and opinionated judges, Dent defended the natural rights–common law Virginia tradition imbedded in the philosophy of the receding old order, while

Brannon was one of the principal architects of the legal positivism embraced by the emerging new order. Their struggle can be read in their opinions, usually with one dissenting from the other, in cases where "competing traditions struggled to control the future direction of West Virginia law."[6]

Both Brannon and Dent favored industrial development for the benefits it would bring to the state, but Dent was inclined to protect the "common man" from corporation abuses. Brannon, on the other hand, leaned toward allowing corporations a free hand to compete, and if a few individuals were damaged in the process they were the unfortunate casualties of progress for the many. Both judges also came to criminal law from strikingly different perspectives. According to his legal biographer, Dent was "one of the last expounders of pure, undistilled classicism," that stressed free will and moral accountability in human behavior. He believed that our law was rooted in the Mosaic law of the Ten Commandments, and Dent's literal interpretation of the Old Testament, as engrained within the English common law, grounded his theory of criminal law.[7]

During the 1890s there was a trend in penology to shift away from an emphasis on retribution to reformation, and a focus on the character of criminals rather than the nature of the crime. Dent rejected this approach out of hand. In his view, the law made no excuses for crimes that were occasioned by either "inherited or acquired depravity." He believed that the crime, not society, must be judged, but never forgot that justice itself must be objective. Thus the law cut both ways: if the defendant was "to be held to an exacting standard of guilt," the state was "bound by an equally exacting standard of proof... for the protection of innocency from unmerited condemnation through the imperfection of human justice." In other words, in case of doubt, always err on the side of caution.[8]

Therefore, Judge Dent gave defendants the benefit of the doubt on every criminal-law technicality. Two of Dent's colleagues, John English and Henry C. McWhorter, more or less agreed with Dent's classical criminal-law theory, but they were less inclined "to require that the prosecution observe every technicality of the law." When they determined that a defendant represented "a discernible menace to society," they readily abandoned procedural safeguards in favor of an approach "somewhat akin to social-defense criminology." Thus Dent was often in the minority.[9]

Henry Brannon was Dent's most frequent opponent. He and the other two judges who usually concurred with his judgment were "more concerned with the potential danger than with the past or present guilt of an accused." Brannon's attitude toward crime in West Virginia was based on a "danger-to-society" argument, rather than on moral or religious grounds. Brannon was "reluctant to disturb murder convictions obtained under traditional common-law definitions, and usually could be counted on to uphold a jury verdict." He often disagreed with the findings of juries, especially in railroad cases that went against corporations, but did not tamper with verdicts in criminal-law cases. On the other hand, Dent "usually opposed any invasion of the jury's function by the Supreme Court," but on the question of granting new trials for procedural errors or technicalities in criminal cases the two judges clashed sharply.[10]

Therefore, Dent, and on this occasion, Judge English, favored Eastham's petitions based on procedural flaws, even though there was no question that Eastham had fired the shots that killed Frank Thompson.

The defendant's counsel claimed that the process of selecting a grand jury had been tainted and that Judge Holt had usurped his authority, thus jeopardizing Eastham's chance of getting a fair trial. Judge Holt confirmed that, once the third grand jury was seated, he did indeed instruct jurors to return a murder indictment and to allow the petit jury to determine the degree of the offense committed. And, yes, he did place the grand jury in charge of the sheriff who was ordered to prevent them from separating or communicating with anyone until they returned said indictment. The judge justified his actions on the ground that "it was necessary to obtain an impartial grand jury and prevent it from being unduly influenced by outside pressure." Based on Holt's admissions, Judge Dent favored dismissing the case on the writ of prohibition, declaring "an impartial grand jury meant one that would find an indictment for murder, in accordance with the evident desire of the judge, as shown by his several instructions to the successive grand juries."[11]

The fundamental question raised by the judge's actions was "whether the judge was guilty of such usurpation or abuse of power as renders the indictment void, and therefore no indictment, but a nullity." West Virginia Code, section 1, chapter 110, Dent asserted, declared unequivocally that, in cases of judicial usurpation of authority, the writ of prohibition was the "ordinary and proper remedy to restrain inferior tribunals within the scope of their legitimate powers. Rightly so, for it ... prevents the abusive, oppressive, or tyrannous use of judicial power in response to partisan passion or private malice." In such cases the Supreme Court must determine what is right, he continued, "for it would be monstrous to refuse to allow the most ignorant criminal to plead ignorance of law, and yet accord a high judicial functionary, presumed to be learned in the law, such a privilege, in justification of his assumption of illegal powers or authority." It is the duty of the courts, Judge Dent further stated, "to obey, uphold and enforce all legislative enactments within constitutional limitations, and not ... to usurp for itself the constitution and statute." Reflecting his strict constructionist approach, Dent asserted that to do so "is not to adjudicate, but to legislate. Judicial legislation is entirely too common, and is a very unwise, dangerous, and unnecessary experiment, to say the least.... The plain letter of the statute... has narrowed the inquiry in this and all similar cases to the mere question of usurpation or abuse of power."[12]

Legislation made clear the process of summoning and impaneling grand juries, Dent opined, and mandated that the courts "conform strictly to the law." Therefore, the grand jury must be selected as prescribed by the law for "there is no security to the citizen but in a rigid adherence to the legislative will as expressed in the statutes for our general guidance." Grand juries were recognized as a means to protect citizens from "unfounded accusation or unjust prosecution." Under the law, a grand jury is defined as a judicial court of inquiry and, therefore, must be "summoned and impaneled strictly in accordance with the provisions of the general law enacted for the purpose by the legislature."[13]

Judge Holt "purposely and materially departed from the method provided by the legislature for the selection of grand juries," Judge Dent asserted, and justified his actions by appealing to the common law. However, the common law was trumped by the state's constitution and statute (section 10, chapter 157, W.Va. Code), neither of which authorized "the discharge of one grand jury because it refuses to be governed by the illegal instructions of the judge, and the summoning of another who will quietly submit to such instructions." Permitting a judge to discharge and summon grand juries until he found one agreeable to the judge was not the intention of the legislature, "and such abuse of power should not be tolerated." It was "judicial usurpation or abuse of power to place the grand jury in custody of the sheriff. Such excessive power, though honest in purpose, should be denied because in unscrupulous hands it might be used to further dishonest ends."[14]

The "most glaring innovation and usurpation of power," Dent charged, occurred when Judge Holt "assumed authority to examine the regularly summoned and duly qualified (according to legislative requirement) grand jurors of their voir dire [competency]," and then to "reject some and accept others according to the mere whim and caprice of the judge." He then proceeded to fill the vacancies on the jury thus "clothing himself with absolute power to determine arbitrarily of what person the grand jury should consist." Partisan "prejudice and passion" pervaded the entire political system, and protecting citizens from "partisan passion, and private enmity under color of the discharge of official duty," was the "great object" in view when the legislature defined the procedure for summoning and impaneling grand juries. "Because such power is dangerous in the hands of the unscrupulous or malicious, it is denied to all."[15]

Dent was convinced that Judge Holt had completely overstepped his bounds. Judges were given no power in the selection of grand jurors; their duty was to insure that the law was enforced, and that included protecting the rights of the accused as guaranteed in the selection of the grand jury "in accordance with the law as written." Just because two grand juries, "composed of thirty-two upright citizens, duly qualified and chosen in the manner provided by general legislative enactment, refused to indict," Dent declared, did not mean that Judge Holt "was justified in adopting extra-legislative means to obtain an impartial grand jury that would indict the prisoner." For the grand jury to be "impartial," in Judge Holt's view, it must agree with the opinion of the judge. "If this is not the exercise of despotic judicial power, such a thing is impossible, and *Magna Charta* is the monumental mistake of the ages."[16]

Judge Dent concluded, therefore, that Circuit Judge Holt "exceeded his legitimate powers and jurisdiction" in summoning, impaneling, charging, and controlling the third grand jury, in violation of the constitution and the state's code. Consequently, the indictment obtained by such illegal methods was void, and the trial of the defendant, Robert Eastham, should be prohibited. An indictment obtained in the "highhanded manner" employed by Judge Holt was "undoubtedly sufficient to raise the presumption that the possibility of convicting the prisoner on a charge of murder, if fair trial in accordance with the law be afforded him, is but slight."[17]

Judges Henry Brannon and Henry C. McWhorter did not concur with the opinion of Judges Dent and English on the writ of prohibition, the petition for habeas corpus, or rearguing the case. They represented the trend toward legal positivism, which took more notice of pragmatic issues arising out of the new conditions created by industrialization and modernity.

Judge Brannon was not persuaded that Circuit Court Judge John Holt had abused his power in seating a grand jury acceptable to the court. In his opinion, it was within the common-law power of the court to dismiss a grand jury (Code 1891, s. 10, c. 157). For Brannon, the fundamental question was whether "the work of the later grand jury [was] a valid indictment?" Judge Holt ordered a new list of grand jurors to be compiled when "he learned reliably that the county clerk, whose duty it was to draw the second grand jury, was openly and avowedly in sympathy with the accused, and that the names in the box from which grand juries were to be drawn, and from which the last one had been drawn, were on slips of paper not folded so as to conceal the names, but open, so that the clerk, if he desired, could select particular ones." The county clerk sympathetic to Eastham was William M. Cayton, a Democrat. Although he had not advocated the removal of the county seat from St. George to Parsons in 1893, as did Eastham, Cayton was a brother-in-law by marriage to Eastham's attorney Cyrus O. Strieby. It is likely Cayton's close relationship with Strieby and Henry G. Davis caused Republican prosecutors to suspect his reliability. Judge Holt considered it his duty to open the box "in the presence of the prosecuting attorney and clerk of the circuit court," when he was "reliably informed" that the clerk was likely to "draw an unfair and partial grand jury" if he had the chance. After finding the slips of paper unfolded and the names unconcealed," therefore, he ordered a new list to be drawn according to Section 2, chapter 157 of the code.[18]

The heart of the case, however, concerned the third grand jury, Brannon asserted: "I view all antecedent circumstances as immaterial, and this grand jury and its indictment must stand or fall on their own strength or weakness." Eastham's counsel argued that this was the third grand jury summoned for the same term, and that the code allowed no more than two. "Why not? This ought not to be the law, if it is," Brannon declared. The plaintiff objected on the basis that the court had illegally excluded certain individuals by asking prospective jurors whether they had formed an opinion. However, Brannon reasoned, this "cannot have been meant that the court, which has the duty of impaneling, is powerless to carry out this legislative intention" by inquiring into their qualifications; "this was a ministerial rather than a judicial act." The jurist agreed that the court did improperly exclude five individuals and selected five others when the law allows for replacing only two. Defense counsel argued that this was a violation of the accused's rights and that the jury was not fair, Brannon continued, but Judge Holt swore that "grand jurors had been approached and tampered with by friends of the accused," and he deemed it his duty, under the circumstances, to put these questions to rest in the effort to get an impartial grand jury.[19]

Both judges agreed on the facts, but Brannon came to a very different conclusion than Dent regarding Judge Holt's action: "Does it nullify the indictment? I think not." There was no claim that the jurors substituted were less qualified than those unseated; if the case was tried by a fair, qualified jury, "that is all the party can ask." Moreover, he continued, a grand jury is "merely an accusing body," and the most important consideration was whether "the prisoner has been justly accused or not."[20]

Eastham's counsel also took exception to the fact that the jurors chosen from bystanders were summoned by an unauthorized person. The county court approved the sheriff's request that William B. Haller and William F. Lipscomb, both Republicans, be appointed as special deputies for the purpose of serving summons on the special grand jury, when the defense contended that their authority extended only to those on the list and did not include summoning the bystanders. "This is drawing a very refined point," Brannon opined. Even though the special deputies were unauthorized to issue a summons, Brannon continued, "is it possible this can destroy totally the legality of the grand jury, and make its work void? To say so would be a travesty on justice."[21]

On the critical question of whether Judge Holt abused his authority, the opinions of Judges Brannon and Dent reflected the chasm between their legal philosophies. Brannon saw no error in Judge Holt's charge to the grand jury that if the evidence was sufficient to make a case of "willful, deliberate, and premeditated killing, then you should find an indictment for murder," and allow the defendant to plead any legal defense before the petit jury. "Is the complaint that this constructively tells the jury that all homicide is *prima facie* murder, and ought to be so indicted?"

In fact, this was the usual and proper action in such cases. "The judge did not tell this jury it could find an indictment for manslaughter, as clearly it could, under chapter 144, West Virginia Code. But who will say it is error to omit it from a charge?" Once a "true bill" had been returned, it was "immaterial whether the court erred in charging or omitting to charge, as the question then is to try the case, and learn whether the accused is guilty."[22]

Brannon also rejected the charge that Judge Holt demonstrated prejudice against the accused. Even though the second grand jury found for manslaughter rather than murder as instructed by Judge Holt, and the circuit judge used language that was "uncalled for and useless," his comments did not show prejudice toward the accused. He simply insisted that under the circumstances there should be an indictment for murder, and a petit jury should then pass on the true grade of the offense if the accused was found guilty. Brannon saw nothing unreasonable about this action "on the part of a public functionary charged in large measure with the administration of criminal law." The ill-feeling generated between the court and defense counsel was unfortunate but was it sufficient to demonstrate a "corrupt prejudice by the judge against the accused" that justified the high court in "excusing the accused from answering before a jury?"[23] Brannon concluded that it was not.

The petition for a writ of prohibition also stated that, when the indictment for involuntary manslaughter was dismissed, the court refused to discharge the accused. Instead, the state's attorney called another grand jury. Just because the prosecution did not want to pursue a misdemeanor charge of involuntary manslaughter did not mean that Eastham should have been released from jail as the petitioners contended. "I understand it to be in the power of the court, and common practice, to hold the prisoner at the State's motion," as sanctioned by the West Virginia

Code, section 12, c. 158, Brannon countered, even though a lesser crime was found by the grand jury. It was also clear that there was no abuse of power of Eastham's continued incarceration, which "is in the undeniable discretion of the court."[24]

The petitioner complained of irregularities, but they "affect none of his substantial rights, and are merely technical" in nature. None of the grand jurors who found indictment were unqualified to serve, nor was it "complained that the jury actually impaneled was not a good one, but that other persons equally good had a right to be placed on it." Brannon declared that there was "no law that gave an accused person the right to have grand jurors accepted by the court who have formed and expressed unqualified opinion that he is innocent."[25] Judge Brannon concluded, therefore, that there were no grounds for voiding the indictment or supporting the writ of prohibition.

And so, because the four-member court was equally divided, the motion to dismiss the case and Eastham's application for a writ of prohibition failed. To bring further attention to their long-standing recommendation to legislators that a fifth judge should be placed on the bench, the judges editorialized in a note appended to the judgment: "This is another notable instance of the evil of the Court's being composed of an even number of judges."[26]

Selecting a Petit Jury

With the legal challenges to the grand jury selection process unresolved by the Supreme Court of Appeals, the accused was returned to his jail cell in Parsons, and the trial of Robert W. Eastham began. The state expected to prove him guilty of murder, and the defense hoped to show that Frank E. Thompson's death resulted from an act of self-defense.

From the beginning the trial was a highly contentious affair, and the selection of a petit jury proved to be every bit as charged as the selection of a grand jury. Denied bail, Eastham remained in close confinement in the county jail in Parsons as his trial proceedings commenced on November 23, 1897. The trial took place in the Knights of Pythias Hall on Main Street since a courthouse had not yet been constructed. The jail and sheriff's residence had been completed, however, and Eastham was held in the otherwise unoccupied women's section on the second floor presumably to make his long confinement more comfortable, and probably not inconsequentially, the sheriff was a friend of the prisoner.[27]

The trial was, in the words of a local newspaper, "one of the most sensational legal battles in the history of the state."[28] The case became a cause célèbre because of the prominence of the two men, the "stupendous array of legal satellites from Virginia and West Virginia" serving as counsel for each side in the contest, and the widespread public interest in, and newspaper coverage of, the trial. Circuit Judge John Homer Holt presided from the bench.[29]

On Tuesday, November 16, Eastham appeared before the court and twelve pleas of abatement were filed by his attorneys. The state objected to the filing on the grounds that none of the pleas constituted a legal defense, and the court adjourned until the next day. The following morning, Wednesday, November 17, "attorneys for the defendant moved to quash the indictment. This motion was overruled and a bill of exceptions taken to the ruling of the court." The state's objection was sustained by Judge Holt. The defense's twelve pleas of abatement also were objected to once again by the state and sustained by the judge. "The prisoner was then called to stand up at the bar of the court while the clerk read the indictment charging him with the murder of Frank E. Thompson. When asked by the court to plead to the indictment a plea of not guilty was entered by the prisoner." The rest of the day was taken up with the selection of jurors. Thursday, November 18, saw "several lively tilts" between opposing attorneys over the admissibility of certain questions asked the jurors, but otherwise little was accomplished.[30]

Big city newspaper reporters descended on the small town of Parsons to cover the trial and filed their reports with eastern newspapers in Boston; New York; Philadelphia; Baltimore; Washington, DC; and Pittsburgh. They also came from innumerable smaller regional towns. No doubt the "city slickers" made fun of the rural "hicks," but the country boys also had their fun at the expense of the city boys. Tucker County historian, Homer F. Fansler, whose family was among the first settlers in the county, related one such city/country encounter involving a family member: "Bill Fansler was in Parsons during the trial with a wagon-load of pumpkins for sale. A reporter from New York, who had never seen a pumpkin, wanted to know what they were. Bill told him that they were Horseshoe Run oranges that had been developed over long years of plant breeding. The reporter purchased the wagon-load, and had them crated and shipped to New York."[31] The multitude of newspaper reporters was outnumbered by the far larger crowds of curious spectators who came to Parsons to witness the event. "New arrivals are coming in on every train, and the crowds in attendance are enormous," many of them ladies, one reporter wrote.[32]

Split evenly between Republicans and Democrats, Tucker County citizens immediately took sides, but they were not necessarily comfortable about it. Reporters noted the ambivalence among those who did not have a stake in the affair. Both Eastham and Thompson were "genial, pleasant men," one local reporter observed, and it was "difficult to see how either would have such an enmity that it resulted fatally."[33] Divisions and loyalties, accentuated by the legal tactics used by the lawyers on both sides to ensure that the jurors chosen served their clients' best interest, led to a bitterly contentious process of jury selection. Forty-one of the forty-six jurors on the regular panel were examined on their competency to serve by November 25, but only six had been found qualified and accepted. And yet, "every man with but one or two exceptions, declared himself free from prejudice, bias or previously formed opinions, and stoutly maintained his qualification until the probe of persistent inquiry and the testimony of witnesses summoned for the purpose, exposed the juror's utter unfitness and incompetency." By the following day, November 26, the entire panel of jurors summoned for the term had been exhausted, and still a jury had not been secured.[34]

One newspaper lamented that "what promised to be a sensational trial" had become "tiresome through the extended fight over the jurors. A man to be one of the twelve who will act upon Col. R. W. Eastham's future existence has to undergo an extremely rigid examination." The reason for the "tiresome" vetting process was that "there is such an atmosphere of suspicion and fraud that neither side will accept a man until he is sounded thoroughly as to his acquaintance with either one of the principals in the late lamented affair, for nearly everyone in Tucker County seems to have known Thompson and Eastham, and to be warm friends of one of the two or both of them." The case attracted so much attention, and the individuals involved were so well known, that it was difficult to find a juror without an opinion. Republicans worried about Eastham's popularity, and believed that his supporters would try to stack the jury in his favor. "It seems like the woodsmen in the back part of the county have announced their intention of getting Eastham off by hook or crook, and the prosecution are on their guard," reported one paper. "A number of these foresters have been summoned, and attempted to qualify as jurors, exhibiting a most unheard of desire to get on the jury. Everyone has been challenged, and witnesses have been secured to impeach their qualifications."[35]

Two challenges illustrate the prosecutor's fears that Eastham's friends would pack the jury. One involved Christopher Columbus Cosner, "a woodsman, hunter and lumberman, who swore that he had no opinion, didn't read any newspaper accounts of the homicide, didn't take any newspapers, never saw one in a month's time, and had no conscientious scruples against hanging." However, witnesses testified that upon being shown a picture of Frank Thompson, Cosner had commented: "He'll never shoot two more shots. He's gone where all infidels go." Another episode involved J. J. Long. The prosecuting attorney charged that the jurymen had been "tampered with," claiming that after being selected as a juror Long had visited the rooms of "attorney Lipscomb," probably Camden Lipscomb who was a friend of Eastham, in the Occidental Hotel where they drank whiskey together. At first Long denied that the incident happened, but, when challenged by a witness's testimony, he rediscovered his memory and recanted his denial. Long insisted that the trial was never discussed, but the state's attorney was unconvinced.[36]

Just thirty-five when his life ended, Thompson was a relative newcomer to Tucker County. Although he was described as "one of the wealthiest young men in the State," who owned "large lumber interests in the town of Davis," was deeply involved in the business life of the county, and closely allied with the Republican Party, he was viewed as an outsider who lived among the people but was not one of them.[37] Eastham, on the other hand, was nevertheless accepted and admired by ordinary people, especially the "old pioneers and woodsmen," even though he was not descended from one of the early families. In fact, the Grafton paper reported, "He was a sort of king among them in the early days." Eastham came to the Canaan Valley when it was still a wilderness. He arrived with little more than "a dog and gun and camped in the woods. In those days the community was more or less lawless, but Eastham was a man of courage and soon established himself as a terror of evil doers as well as a man whom it was best to leave alone." Nevertheless, Eastham's "simple unconsciousness of manner won him friends all over the county," particularly among the woodsmen. Their outrage with the prosecution for bringing murder charges against Eastham was "terrific," it was reported, and Judge Holt's life was said to have been "in danger at first because he wouldn't submit to their desires and demands. This feeling has now quieted down somewhat."[38]

However, Judge Holt also had his supporters, particularly among the Republican newspaper editors. Prompted by Judge Dent's negative commentary in the appeals that defense counsel brought before the Supreme Court of Appeals, one Republican newspaper editorial declared that "the friends of Judge Holt claim he has been much misrepresented in this case." Contrary to his detractors, Republicans agreed with one editor who claimed that the judge "has presided with undoubted fairness and impartiality, and the consensus of opinion among members of the bar, irrespective of their views in this case, is that he has always acted in accordance with the dignity of his office and with great circumspection, in view of the disturbed condition of the county at the time of the homicide when wild threats of throttling juries were heard at every hand." When the ruling of the Supreme Court of Appeals split 2–2, the editor thought it necessary to point out that "Judge Dent, who scored Judge Holt, was formerly, when practicing with the latter, his bitter enemy. They scarcely spoke, and it is hinted that Judge Dent has carried with him to the supreme bench the old ill feeling. As for Judge English, who concurred in the opinion of Judge Dent, it is said he is a relative of Eastham." The latter statement was false, either based on pure fabrication or unsubstantiated rumor.[39]

On Wednesday, December 1, it appeared that the "eager crowds who have thronged Parsons for a fortnight to hear this famous trial" would soon get their wishes. The attorneys had been "engaged in a battle royal from this morning til evening in the examination of talesmen, today, closed the conflict tonight in an extraordinary debate, and their eloquence and oratory thrilled and entertained one of the largest audiences that ever listened to a trial in Parsons," a Wheeling newspaper reported. The following day, however, Francis M. Reynolds, counsel for the defense, challenged the entire panel of jurors and filed a motion to quash the panel, alleging that they had been illegally drawn. Judge Holt overruled the motion, which Reynolds undoubtedly had expected, and testimony commenced. A southern-Democratic newspaper sympathetic to Eastham issued a terse, indicative statement: "A jury has been secured in the Eastham case, and the trial will proceed. It is believed Eastham will be acquitted, as he ought to be."[40]

10

ON TRIAL FOR MURDER

State v. R. W. Eastham

The Trial

The jury was finally selected from a panel of ninety-two qualified residents, and on Thursday morning, December 2, 1897, Robert W. Eastham went on trial for his life. Calling numerous witnesses, the state presented its case during the first week. Whereas the Republican press was quick to declare the testimony "very damaging" in demonstrating that Eastham had long intended to kill Thompson, the Democratic press confidently predicted that Eastham would be exonerated.

Henry J. Cooper was called by the state on Friday, December 3. One of Eastham's best friends and nearest neighbor in the Canaan Valley, he was an "old veteran of the Confederate army, and served in the war with Eastham." Prosecutors claimed Cooper as a witness before the defense, so it was reluctantly that he admitted to dashing off to Virginia "to see Eastham's brothers and friends about trying to get him out of jail and take him away from here before the trial." Under cross-examination by the defense's Horatio Moffett, Cooper denied that he was trying to stir up mob violence by removing the prisoner from the county jail. He claimed that he fled from Tucker County to Rappahannock County, Virginia, "at his own expense, and took refuge with the brothers of Eastham there, to avoid being a witness against the accused." A Republican paper reported that Cooper had "urged the raising of a mob to rescue Eastham from the jail in Parsons," but ignored the fact that Cooper vehemently denied the allegation.[1] On the stand, Cooper described his visit to Eastham in jail earlier in June 1897 when he brought the defendant a pint of whiskey. Cooper acknowledged that Eastham had related how he entered the train car, "brushed down" Thompson, proceeded two steps up the aisle before Thompson fired two shots at him, and he fired the fatal shots from his coat pocket.[2]

W. K. Mauck accompanied Cooper on his flight to Virginia and recounted the same story from the stand on Monday, December 6. Mauck was a native of Front Royal, Virginia, near Eastham's old home place, and was a tenant on Eastham's farm in the Canaan. Mauck testified further that Eastham had declared many times his intention "to either break up the Thompsons or kill both father and son." Mauck then dropped a bombshell in the courtroom when he admitted that Eastham had hired him "to blow up the Thompsons' dam in the Blackwater" and even "furnished the dynamite" to do it. Mauck also caused a stir when he confessed that it was on Eastham's behest that he shot at the workers trying to repair the dam to scare them off the job. In fact, he had used Eastham's own Winchester and smokeless powder. The Republican press gloated that "the evidence created a sensation and rather rattled the defense. Mauck was on the stand all afternoon."[3] Undoubtedly, it pained both Cooper and Mauck when they were forced to testify for the state and gave information that tarnished their friend's reputation and undermined his defense.

The most potentially damaging testimony was given by Fairfax S. Landstreet, the general manager of the Davis Coal and Coke Company, who lived in Davis and knew both Eastham and Thompson. By order of the court he served as receiver for the sale of the Blackwater Boom and Lumber Company to the Blackwater

Lumber Company, and attended the bidding that was said to have started the trouble between Frank Thompson and Robert Eastham. Landstreet testified that he had met Eastham on the street in late summer or early fall of 1895, and Eastham asked him to come to his house. "I went there and he told me that he had been having some dispute with the Thompsons" and he implied that "he was going to settle it by means of some bodily harm." After considerable discussion, Eastham declared that "he had studied the matter over, knew about what he was doing, and come to that conclusion, and I found it wasn't much use to argue the question further with him, and I left him." Mrs. Eastham was not present when these discussions were going on, but entered the room as they came to a close. "I remarked to the Col. that he ought to consider his wife in the matter . . . and she remarked that she was prepared for any consequence that might come." After he left Eastham's house, Landstreet paid a visit to Albert and Frank Thompson, informed them of the conversation he had with Eastham, and communicated the threat made against the Thompsons. "The matter was discussed some little time between us and it was suggested that I make some arrangement to see if I could not purchase for Mr. Thompson Mr. Eastham's property. I consented to make the effort, and had a talk with Col. Eastham a short time afterwards, and told him I thought it was a good idea for him to sell his property to the Thompsons, and in that way settle up all differences." Eastham's sense of honor was being challenged, however, and "he did not propose to be run out of the country." Landstreet asked Eastham how much he would take to sell his property, and he quoted a price "that I thought was very excessive, and the matter was dropped."[4] When Landstreet suggested that Eastham's friends would distance themselves from him if he committed violence against the Thompsons, Eastham replied that "his friends would stick with him, and said Tom Davis [H. G. Davis's brother] would stick with him too."[5]

Most of the state's witnesses swore under oath that Eastham made threatening statements against the Thompsons: Thomas Esley claimed that Eastham vowed he would not be satisfied until he had the Thompsons' blood; Charles M. Hebb heard Eastham say there would be "hell" on the train going back to Davis from Parsons; Simon Boyd heard Eastham assert that, if Thompson went on the train, "he would not go a live man"; and H. M. Warden testified that he was present when Eastham declared that the Thompsons had "about seen their last days in Davis."[6]

Congressman Alston G. Dayton, a leading attorney for the state, compiled a summary of statements from twenty-three individuals who would bear witness that they heard Eastham make statements about harming the Thompsons over a several year period. Included were the testimonies of Alfred Mick, George Carr, and David Keplinger which were taken from the Blackwater Lumber Company's injunction suit against Eastham. All three were present at the dam trying to repair it when Eastham threatened harm to the Thompsons if they persisted in those efforts. Several others testified that Eastham had declared that the only way to deal with the Thompsons was to "shoot it out with them." Eastham also told Henry J. Cooper that "he intended to shoot it out with them, and didn't care what the result was because he was getting old anyhow and [they] couldn't cheat him out of many years." Several other witnesses gave similar testimony to that of Simon Roy who claimed that the defendant vowed that if Frank Thompson boarded the train for Davis "he would go up a corpse."[7]

Thomas Daily talked with Eastham frequently, and on more than one occasion Eastham stated that he had attempted "to insult the damned Thompsons and get fusses out of them for the last two years, but they would never resent any of his insults, and tried to provoke an attack out of them" so he could "fill them full of lead." According to Daily, Eastham complained that he had posted around town a brand he was using to mark his logs which Frank subsequently claimed in court that he had never seen. Eastham wanted Thompson "to understand that he was accusing them of perjury," and that "he wanted to provoke him into resenting it, get a fuss out of him, but that Frank Thompson had not resented it because he was a damned coward." Moreover, Daily claimed that Eastham "met Frank Thompson against the mountain one day, and that he, Eastham, was carrying a scythe and that when he saw him coming he made up his mind to cut off the damn son of a bitch's head if he had not given him the road."[8] Former Third Circuit Court Judge Joseph T. Hoke returned from his post as U.S. Consul to Windsor, Nova Scotia, Canada, a distance of over 1,100 miles, to testify in the case. He had presided in two suits involving the defendant, *Eastham v. Blackwater Lumber Company* and the company's injunction suit against Eastham. Judge Hoke had advised Frank Thompson not to go to the dam because he might be killed by Eastham, but had also recommended that Thompson arm himself for self-protection.[9]

After a long period of incarceration, Eastham's first appearance in the courtroom since the trial began prompted a reporter to observe: "The long confinement does not seem to have visibly affected the prisoner. Since his incarceration he has grown a full beard and has become fleshy. This has changed his personal appearance to quite a degree. He attends the trial day by day and looks on with apparent indifference."

On Saturday, December 4, the defendant's wife and his sister Emma caused a flurry of excitement when they appeared in court for the first time, taking seats directly behind the defendant and his counsel. Their appearance was "the occasion of a war of words" between state's attorney Alston Dayton and defense counsel James Marshall McCormick, the former insisting that if Mrs. Eastham was to testify "she should be excluded like the other witnesses, and the latter contending that she ought to remain." In the end, Judge Holt permitted her to stay.[10] Thompson's father, Albert, took the stand on Wednesday, December 8, relating how the trouble with Eastham developed and culminated in the death of his only son. "The white-haired father" brought tears to the eyes of jurors and "expressions of sympathy from counsel for the defense, who declined to cross-examine him."[11]

The hearsay evidence submitted by the state certainly painted a picture of a man whose intention was to cause grievous bodily harm to the deceased and seemed to lead directly to Eastham pulling the trigger with intent to murder. Unfortunately for the state, even most of the witnesses called by the prosecution unequivocally testified that Thompson fired the first shots, although provoked by Eastham, and that the defendant returned fire in self-defense. A number of the state's witnesses, Lee Gum, Clarence Taylor, William Hennings, W. A. Baily, B. D. Wolford, Thomas Wheeler, and H. S. Hunter among them, did not actually see the shooting because it was over in a matter of seconds. Of the approximately twenty-five people in the passenger car at the time, most of them heard and/or saw Eastham swear at Thompson, some saw Eastham slap him, but few actually had their eyes fixed on the two men, or had an unobstructed view of them. They heard gun shots, saw the men react to them, but did not see who shot first.[12]

At least two witnesses intimated that Thompson did not shoot first, although their conclusions were temporized. D. A. McCrea said he observed Thompson take his seat, Eastham approach and slap him across the face, and then saw Thompson draw his revolver. McCrea swore that "two shots were fired by somebody before Thompson fired at all," but he could not swear that they were fired by Eastham whose back was toward the witness. S. W. Groghan was standing on the platform at the depot with a view inside the passenger car. He swore that the first two shots were fired from the Elkins end of the car and that returning fire came from the Davis end of the car. The witness only learned later that "Eastham stood in the Elkins end of the car." He did not hear Eastham make any threats to Thompson, and his view of the coach's interior was obscured by the failing light.[13]

H. D. Cole, a personal friend of Frank Thompson who accompanied him to Parsons, sat in the seat next to him during the shoot-out. He agreed with most witnesses in stating that when Thompson took his seat, Eastham approached, called him vile names, and struck him in the face. Cole departed from the standard story, however, when he claimed that Eastham took "two steps forward, turned and thrust his hand in his right coat pocket. Thompson then arose and drew a pistol from his hip pocket, holding it down at his side, hesitatingly, a moment, and then shifted it in front of his body, pressed it close to himself, and covered it with his other hand. Then the first two shots were fired, but not by Thompson, for the witness never took his eyes off the latter's revolver, and swears positively that Thompson did not fire those first two shots."[14] Cole's testimony was undoubtedly clouded by his close personal association with the deceased, perhaps a desire for retribution for his friend's death, and an attempt to gain some solace for the bereaved father. He helped to carry Thompson to the hotel, assisted in removing the bullet from his back and left arm, and was with Thompson "from the time he was shot until he was buried at Norway, Maine." Yet, he did not see Eastham's pistol, which was on Eastham's left side.[15]

Jurors undoubtedly dismissed his version of the encounter as biased testimony. The regional Republican press, particularly the *Parsons Advocate*, *Grafton Sentinel Weekly*, and the *Wheeling Daily Intelligencer*, gave ample coverage to the daily proceedings but their reporting was clearly slanted against Eastham. Commenting on the above evidence, the *Grafton Sentinel Weekly* asserted that "the testimony so far against Eastham is of the most overwhelming and damaging character. It shows that the killing of Thompson was one of the most cold blooded and premeditated ever perpetrated in the State. It does not seem possible that the defense can counteract the testimony adduced by the State."[16]

Fortunately, murder cases are adjudicated in the courtroom rather than in the newspapers. Three of the state's own key witnesses swore that they had seen the entire incident from a position that gave them a close and unobstructed view of the exchange, and their version of events was decidedly favorable to Eastham's case. John W. Hockman, who knew both the defendant and the deceased, took the stand and related the now familiar sequence that led to the shooting. He entered the passenger car and took an aisle seat within three rows of the rear of the car next to Dr. Benjamin Smith. Eastham entered the car and came up the aisle. When he reached the seat where Frank Thompson was sitting (four or five seats in front of Hockman toward the front of the car) he said that he did not want "you dam traitors in this car" and then struck Thompson in the face. Hockman was not sure if it was with an open hand or his fist, but he heard the blow. "Mr. Eastham then came on up to right opposite where I was sitting and turned to his right and facing the front of the car, and Mr. Thompson got out of his seat and turned facing towards Eastham and myself and probably made one step, drew a pistol and they commenced firing right by my side. I hallowed at them, and said what in the hell are you fools doing stop that shooting, you will shoot some of us." Hockman claimed there was a total of between six and nine shots fired, but it was over in an instant. "They just quit. . . . They both stood there for a second or two, just gazing at each other, Mr. Eastham sat down on a seat, on the opposite side of the aisle from me." Dr. Smith saw blood running down over Eastham's face before he sat down and remained in his seat while several men carried Thompson out of the car to the hotel.

Defense attorneys Wilson B. Maxwell and Cyrus O. Strieby cross-examined the witness:

(Q) *When did you first see Frank Thompson have a revolver, how long before he fired?*
(A) When he arose from the seat and got up facing Mr. Eastham. When his hand came up I saw the blaze from the revolver. [Asked how far past Thompson Eastham was when the first shot was fired, Hockman said not over four seats.]
(Q) *How many shots did Thompson fire before Eastham commenced shooting at your side?*
(A) I think there were two.
(Q) *Could you tell the difference between the report of Eastham's revolver and Thompson's?*
(A) I thought I noticed the difference. One was right by my side and the other was 4 or 5 seats in front of me.
(Q) *In what position did Eastham have his revolver while he was shooting?*
(A) It was in his pocket. Right hand pocket next to me. In his coat pocket at his right hand side. When the firing was over I noticed by his side the pistol slipped through the pocket, that is the barrel of it.
(Q) *[By the state] What time in the evening was this?*

(A) Between 6 & 7 o'clock to best of my knowledge. The car was lit up.[17]

J. A. Houston, another witness called by the state, testified that he was only "slightly acquainted" with either Thompson or Eastham. Houston sat down just behind Eastham, who was at the time standing in the aisle. His version of the verbal exchange between the two antagonists varied slightly from Hockman's but added to the description of who shot first.

> I heard him ask Mr. Thompson what business he had on this car. And at the same time he slapped him and says, "God dam you get out of here" and Mr. Thompson walked out from between the seats, he had his hand dropped down behind him as I supposed and after he got in the aisle he drawed out a revolver. Mr. Eastham stepped back a step or two. Mr. Thompson took a step or two forward, followed him, and raised his revolver and fired. Mr. Thompson fired the second shot before Mr. Eastham fired. Mr. Eastham had his hand down in his pocket, and I thought he was trying to get out his revolver. I did not see a revolver, and then I saw, a blaze come out of Mr. Eastham's coat pocket. . . . They were both firing at the same time. After Eastham commenced firing, Thompson was still firing.

Houston estimated that about six or seven shots were fired in all. "I think there were several persons hallowed at them and said, 'for God's sake stop shooting,' I think Dr. Smith, but won't be sure." He did not hear Thompson speak before or after the shooting. On cross-examination, Houston responded, "yes sir," to the question whether he saw Thompson draw his revolver from his pocket. He did not know from which pocket because his right hand was hanging down. He had his hand on the seat when Eastham struck him. Defense counsel asked: "What motion did Eastham make which made you think he was trying to get out his revolver?" to which Houston replied, "He had his hand in his pocket and [I] saw him moving his hand up and down and thought his revolver was fast."

Houston was one of the signers of the petition involving the Degler paternity suit and, like Hockman, had come down on the train from Davis with the other petitioners to answer contempt of court charges in Judge Holt's court (see chapter 8). Houston did not know whether Thompson had an interest in the *Williams v. Degler* case, but he saw Thompson in "the court-room while the contempt proceedings were going on." Asked what Thompson was doing there, Houston replied that "he seemed to be enjoying, what I called our misfortune, and was laughing a good deal." Another witness verified this account. Asked by defense counsel whether he had seen Frank Thompson in the courtroom while the contempt proceedings were underway against the signers of the petition, J. M. Reed replied: "I saw him there. I was sitting on the bench behind him." Thompson had "a long paper there with a lot of names on, and looked them over as the witnesses were called out, and laughed over them." Reed did not know if Thompson was one of the petitioners, but he thought not.[18]

Called by the state, Reed related substantially the same story about the Eastham-Thompson confrontation as Hockman and Houston. He was acquainted with both men but could not say with certainty whether Eastham struck Thompson. He did hear Eastham ordering Thompson out of the car, but after the altercation

> Mr. Eastham stepped back and Mr. Thompson walked right out into the aisle and drew his revolver and shot twice. Then after he done the shooting Mr. Eastham fired. I don't know

how many shots were exchanged. Mr. Thompson's revolver was knocked out of his hand [and] fell on the floor by my feet and I kicked it right in under the seat. Mr. Thompson reached down to get it and then he asked me if I picked up his revolver and I said no sir, I kicked it under the bench. When Mr. Thompson left the car I reached down and got it. I stuck it in my pocket, carried it home to Davis. Mr. Harper [the Sheriff] came there on Saturday and got it. There was one load in the revolver. I had my umbrella laying by the side of me in the aisle and it was shot.

Reed was uncertain which hand Eastham used to strike Thompson, but his right hand was hanging by his side and "he had an umbrella under his arm." Reed did not see Eastham's revolver, but he saw him fire. Eastham "couldn't get it out of his pocket and he fired through his pocket." According to Reed, Eastham "was fussing around in his pocket and had his umbrella under his arm." But his testimony varied slightly when he claimed that Eastham pulled his revolver from his hip pocket.

(Q) *Did Eastham step back or did he go on in the same direction he was going after he made the motion as though he was going to strike him?*
(A) He stepped back.
(Q) *Did Eastham step back before or after he commenced shooting?*
(A) Eastham stepped back right after he made the motion with his arm.
(Q) *Did Thompson advance towards Eastham before shooting?*
(A) He did, he came right out in the aisle and stepped right up to Eastham and fired.

(Q) *How close were Eastham and Thompson together when they were shooting?*
(A) They were so close that the fire caught in Eastham's umbrella. It caught fire and somebody grabbed it out of his hand, I don't know who it was. They set it between the seats. I saw the umbrella burning, grabbed it up in my hands, and put the fire out.
(Q) *At what part of Eastham's body did Thompson aim the first shot?*
(A) I think it was the right side.
(Q) *At what part of Eastham's body did Thompson aim the second shot?*
(A) The head.[19]

The state rested its case against R. W. Eastham on Wednesday, December 8, 1897, and the next day his attorneys launched their defense. The Republican *Wheeling Daily Intelligencer* reported that defense witnesses swore that Thompson "fired first, exactly the opposite of the testimony of the prosecution." Since most of the witnesses for the state testified that they did not see who shot first, or asserted that Thompson fired the first shots, it is difficult to conclude that the newspaper's version was anything but a partisan, and less than accurate account of the evidence presented. Conversely, it was true that the defense found numerous witnesses who agreed with most of the prosecution's witnesses that Thompson fired first and Eastham fired in self-defense. Witnesses for both the state and the defense also were resolute in their contention that Eastham precipitated the fatal shoot-out when he confronted Thompson and slapped him across the face—still the ultimate challenge to masculine honor in the 1890s.

Thomas Burger, a prominent lumber dealer of Cumberland, Maryland, also witnessed the confrontation in the car. Since the incident, however, he had been paralyzed (probably by a stroke), so his deposition was taken by lawyers with Frank Thompson's father present. The substance of his deposition supported the details of the altercation, and confirmed the other witnesses' testimony that, after Eastham slapped Frank Thompson and began to walk away Thompson "started after him with a drawn revolver." Eastham turned around and seeing the revolver in Thompson's hand, "plunged his hand into his right hand coat pocket, where he kept his own pistol." However, Eastham's pistol apparently "caught fast in the pocket, and while he was trying to draw it Thompson fired." Mr. Burger insisted that "the first shot was fired by Thompson, and that Thompson had his gun drawn before Eastham shoved his hand in his pocket."[20]

In order to establish self-defense, West Virginia code required that defendants demonstrate that bodily harm was imminent and no avenue of retreat was available. Since the confined space of a railway coach met the requirement, Eastham's attorneys based their case on that principle. Two criteria were important to establishing that Eastham had acted in self-defense: first, that Thompson was the aggressor and Eastham had his "back to the wall," and secondly that he had no recourse other than to defend himself.[21]

Most testimony suggested that Thompson demonstrated aggression and Eastham acted in self-defense, and defense counsel successfully drew out both points from several witnesses. Another defense witness, J. F. Wilson, called to the stand on Thursday, December 9, described how "Thompson arose, with revolver in hand, stepped two steps out into the aisle and pointed his pistol at Eastham," whose back was turned away from Thompson as he walked away. Just as Eastham turned his head,

Thompson fired. Eastham then turned around, and Thompson fired again, then both men fired their pistols simultaneously. "Thompson fired the first two shots," according to Wilson's reported testimony. Another witness, William Silver, called to the stand by the defense attorneys related essentially the same story with additional nuances. According to a reporter, Silver stated that "Thompson arose, drew a revolver from his side coat pocket, stepped out of his seat and walked down the aisle until he came to Eastham, when he deliberately stretched his arm out full length, placed the pistol against Eastham's breast and fired. Then again placing the pistol to Eastham's forehead Thompson deliberately fired a second time. The shooting then became mutual, but Thompson fired the first two shots." Allen Hayes, also called by the defense, substantiated Wilson's and Silver's versions of the shooting in that Thompson placed the pistol to Eastham's body and fired twice. However, Hayes denied that either shot was directed at the head, claiming instead that both shots were fired full at the breast. Thompson did, however, fire the first two shots.[22]

The defense called another nine witnesses to the stand, seven of whom substantiated this version of events. A number of witnesses were called to contradict testimony presented by the state. Among them were Eastham's brother Philip and cousin George Eastham who contradicted the testimony of Henry J. Cooper who had visited them in Virginia and, according to the state's attorneys, urged Philip and George to break Eastham out of jail.[23]

Then, on Monday and Tuesday, December 13 and 14, Robert W. Eastham himself took the stand. His attorneys had obviously made the decision to allow him to testify with the expectation that his appearance would gain him a sympathetic advantage. Eastham related the sequence of events as he remembered them. After entering the passenger car, he walked down the aisle toward his seat at the back of the car. When he was opposite where Frank Thompson was sitting, Eastham stopped and called Thompson "a perjured s—of—a—b—and then slapped him in the face," and ordered him out of the car. Eastham reaffirmed that Thompson "followed him and shot him in the right side and forehead as he turned," and insisted that "he shot to save his own life."[24] As a reporter described the scene: "Donning the blood bedraggled and bullet rent garments he wore in the affray, he took up the fatal pistol, and dramatically gave his version of the encounter."[25]

On cross-examination Eastham avowed that he had no intention of killing Thompson, and only "shot to hit" him. Eastham finished his testimony on Tuesday, December 14, and both sides rested their cases at 3:30 P.M. Serious legal wrangling ensued between counsel regarding the nature of the instructions to be given to the jury; the state contended that the case should not be delayed for the preparation of instructions before final arguments began, while the defense insisted that even a day or two for preparation might be necessary. Again Judge Holt sided with the state ruling that there would be no delay to prepare for the closing arguments, and limited arguments to six hours for each side. At 4:00 P.M. on Tuesday evening, Alston Dayton opened with a lengthy speech; the Republican press described his one-and-a-half-hour-long presentation as one of "great force and power, not to say eloquent." Then William Arnett, representing the defense, spoke until 7:00 P.M. without a recess, a speech described as "learned and comprehensive."[26]

Court was adjourned until the following day, Wednesday, December 15, with arguments beginning with C. W. Dailey for the defense. His presentation took up most of the morning, and was followed by Marshall McCormick in the afternoon to close for the defense. The argument for the state was closed by John

J. Davis, John A. Howard, and prosecuting attorney William Conley. Waxing eloquent, a Republican newspaper described the Honorable John J. Davis's two-and-a-half-hour-long presentation a "full and fitting close" to a remarkable legal struggle: "The tall form of the 'old man eloquent' towered above the jury like an avenging spirit, while his silver locks and his silver voice charmed all who heard him. He closed with a beautiful peroration that was worthy of the effort and the occasion." This brought to a close "one of the most noted and sensational murder trials ever had in the history of the state," another Republican paper reported.[27]

On Thursday, December 16, court reconvened at 5:00 P.M. to hear the jury's verdict. Republican-oriented newspapers expected a conviction, and Democratic-leaning newspapers anticipated either acquittal or a hung jury. Both reported surprise and consternation when jury foreman T. W. Wilmoth arose and announced that "We the jury find the defendant guilty of involuntary manslaughter."[28] Jury deliberations had lasted merely three hours, with only two ballots taken. Reflecting the division of the county, the first ballot stood six for acquittal and six for murder in the first degree. Prior to the second ballot, however, the jury came to a compromise agreement on involuntary manslaughter; those who had voted for murder agreed so long as Eastham served jail time, and those for acquittal accepted that Eastham was more than an innocent bystander in the fatal confrontation. In the end, the state's argument for murder and the defense's plea of self-defense both failed because of the good judgment of the jurors. Settled law in West Virginia was that if, in such cases, the accused had initiated the situation that required the accused to kill his assailant in order to save his own life, then the killing was not excusable homicide, and the defendant could not take refuge in a plea of self-defense. On the other hand, it was also settled law that leveling insults, curses, and slaps at someone was never sufficient justification for assault with intent to kill. In short, Eastham provoked Thompson into shooting him, but Eastham was not completely innocent in the tragic event. The judge and the state might have done all in their power to make an example of Eastham for their own purposes, as many believed, but the jury rendered its verdict of involuntary manslaughter based on the evidence and their understanding of the law.[29]

When the verdict was announced Judge Holt ordered an immediate recess until 7:00 P.M. that evening. "Eastham was at once surrounded by his friends, who warmly congratulated him and grasped him cordially by his hands. His equanimity was not in the least disturbed by these demonstrations of friendship and, after thanking them, he retired with the sheriff to the jail to await the sentence of Court." People began to crowd into the courtroom just before 7:00 o'clock. For the culmination of such an extraordinary trial, with so many "legal luminaries" taking center stage, observers witnessed a surreal scene. The temporary courtroom had no electricity, and, according to a newspaper account, "one dim lamp furnished illumination for the dingy, close apartment, and the people arriving with lighted lanterns made the scene interesting and strange." Prior to the announcement of the verdict, and "fearing a demonstration on behalf of Col. Eastham," the mayor of Parsons ordered all of the saloons closed by 7:00 P.M. Judge Holt entered the courtroom at 7:30 P.M. "The crowd was breathless with expectation, waiting to hear the verdict, when the judge coolly ordered the prisoner remanded to the custody of the sheriff and court adjourned until 9 o'clock" the next morning.[30]

On Friday, December 17, 1897, court reconvened, and the room was "jammed with people" to hear Eastham's sentence. With Eastham standing before the bar, Judge Holt briefly reviewed the circumstances surrounding the death of Frank Thompson. In concluding, he declared: "You did not deny killing Frank Thompson. In their mercy the jury decided to give you a punishment of the lowest order. They decided that you had no right to the plea of self-defense. As to what the punishment shall be the statute is silent. I am compelled to look to other sources, and I find it is in the discretion of the court. The court may put you to jail for five years and still be within the law. The only bar is the statutory one that cruel and unusual punishment shall not be inflicted. The court, after going over all the authorities, has arrived at the conclusion that you be confined in the county jail for two years." After a consideration of his nine months already served, the judge sentenced Eastham to fifteen months of close confinement.[31]

The Defense Files Exceptions

Immediately after the judge announced his decision, the defense moved to set aside the verdict and to order a new trial. The state's attorneys objected, and the judge "promptly overruled" the motion. In response, defense attorney William Arnett objected to the penalty of two years in the county jail. The sentence was "without authority of law," he asserted, because there was "no punishment prescribed by statute whatever for involuntary manslaughter" in the West Virginia Code. Since Eastham could only be tried for involuntary manslaughter and not for murder, the case should be abandoned. On those grounds Arnett filed a writ of error and requested the Supreme Court to order a new trial.[32]

Defense attorneys immediately filed a total of fifteen bills of exception with the Supreme Court of Appeals. The challenges focused primarily on Judge Holt's refusal to admit into evidence testimony from witnesses who heard Thompson make threats against Eastham, even though the judge had accepted hearsay evidence from the state's attorneys. For example, the defense put Thomas Valley on the stand to prove that, prior to the shooting on March 18, 1897, the witness was passing through the Blackwater Lumber Company's lumber yard when he saw Frank Thompson and Eastham in conversation. Eastham stormed away, and Valley heard Thompson remark that "we will never get rid of that fellow ... unless we, or I, (the witness does not remember which) kill him, or words to that effect." The witness could not say if those words were ever communicated to Eastham, so the court sustained the state's objection and refused to allow the evidence to be presented. Similarly, Frank A. Parsons testified that Frank Thompson had hired him to survey certain tracts that Eastham had previously surveyed and found the lines did not align. When Eastham informed Parsons that he was wrong, Parsons communicated his statement to Thompson, prompting him to exclaim that the "damned son-of-a-bitch is always meddling in my business, and we will not get rid of him unless we put him out of the way ... or kill him, or words to that effect." But Parsons, like Valley, could not be certain that the statement had ever been communicated to the defendant, so the judge refused to allow it to be introduced as evidence.[33] George H. Johnson was also willing to testify that he was present and heard Frank E. Thompson declare in June 1896, that if Eastham "ever crossed his path, he would put a bullet through him, or words to similar import, but admitted that they could not show that this threat of said Thompson had ever been communicated to the defendant." Once again the state's objection was sustained by the judge and the testimony was not admitted into evidence.[34]

Conversely, the court did allow the state to introduce testimony intended to show that Eastham had made threats against the Thompsons on a number of occasions. Not all of these statements had been communicated to Thompson, nevertheless, they were admitted. J. E. Houston, for example, testified that, on the day of the shooting, when there was no time to communicate a threat, Eastham had announced to his friends Houston and Lee Gum that there were "some damned sons of bitches that will not go on that train." Houston responded, "Is that so, Colonel?" When Eastham responded in the affirmative Houston asked of the defendant "What are you going to do about it?" The defendant replied, "You will see." The defense moved to exclude Houston's testimony, but the court overruled the motion and allowed the evidence to go to the jury.[35] The other exceptions filed by the defense attorneys presented other examples to demonstrate that Judge Holt showed bias in the admission of evidence to the detriment to their client's receiving a fair trial. To make matters worse, a sympathetic newspaper reported, Eastham was prosecuted for murder, and this folly was exacerbated by the $3,000 in legal expenses charged to the state to achieve a decision that Eastham had admitted to at the beginning of the trial.[36]

Press Response

Predictably, the newspapers responded to the jury decision according to their political orientation. The southern Democratic *Parkersburg Sentinel* declared that the punishment imposed on Eastham by Judge Holt was "extremely excessive and the highest punishment ever inflicted in this State at any time before has been twelve months. He will not give up the ship."[37] There was some justification for the paper's assessment. Involuntary manslaughter was considered a misdemeanor, which, according to the West Virginia Code, was punishable by a fine not exceeding $500, or imprisonment for not less than six months and not more than one year, or both. Moreover, the *Sentinel* continued, the sentence was "an extraordinary one, and not at all befitting the offense proved." The judge stated that he found no authority in the statute for imposing such a penalty, and so he consulted the common law. "We believe that, as a rule, most anyone can justify anything they do, even if it be wrongful, by seeking unrecognized authority for their justification. The proper place for the penalty was within the state statutes, where the offense was defined and the punishment provided for. The conduct of the judge throughout the trial was not compatible with that impartiality and freedom from prejudice which has been the pride and boast of the American judiciary."[38]

Charges of bias against Judge Holt brought out the business-oriented Republican editorials in response. The *Grafton Sentinel Weekly* noted that, when the judge delivered his punishment, there was "considerable comment" on it in the press. The above-mentioned editorial published in the Democratic *Parkersburg Sentinel* was reprinted in the *Grafton Sentinel Weekly* along with a vigorous response:

> The malice and spleen behind the above is born of the fact that Eastham was a confederate soldier and his sympathizers had hoped that he would escape without any punishment whatever. Frank Thompson was a northern man who went into the wilds of Tucker County and did a great deal to develop its almost untrodden forests. He, in the pursuance of his large business interests, ran counter to the interests of Bob Eastham. Eastham vowed his intentions to kill Thompson.... Through the manipulations of corrupt court officials and the tactics of counsel for Eastham's defense the plans of the latter's friends to prevent even so much as a

legal investigation of the cases almost succeeded. That Eastham was guilty of cold blooded, premeditated murder was patent to every honest man in Tucker County.... Six of the men who composed the jury that tried Eastham declared in their jury room that they believed him guilty of murder in the first degree. The testimony of Mr. Landstreet, Mr. Daily and the man Moore [actually W. K. Mauck], who testified that he was the man who blew up the Thompson boom [splash dam], all three personal friends of Eastham and unwilling witnesses for the State, was sufficient alone to warrant such a finding as these six jurors said they believed ought to be the verdict. The finding returned is a disgrace to Tucker County, and the verdict a license to kill every "foreigner" who comes into the county to invest his money and develop its resources, provided he is not an ex-guerilla or a member of Gen. Mosby's free booters.[39]

Screaming for "law and order" to improve the business climate was common editorial policy for papers interested in boosting business investment. The Grafton paper also reproduced an article from the *Elkins Mountain Echo*, which proclaimed that the outcome of the Eastham trial was "even worse than we supposed possible." That within a few hours a twelve-member jury could bring in a verdict of involuntary manslaughter instead of murder "is a sad comment on the idea of trial by jury, and especially of the stuff of which Tucker County juries are composed." The trial proved beyond a doubt, the *Mountain Echo* opined, that Thompson's death was an act of premeditated murder. It seemed to the editor that Eastham "knew pretty well how far he could count upon a Tucker County jury. And the event shows that he did not 'reckon without his host.' We do not know the prisoner at all, and can have no personal feeling against him, but we are filled with sad forebodings for the future of the county when we see the ease with which the most dangerous criminals can commit crime and go practically unwhipped of justice."[40]

The *Wheeling Daily Intelligencer*, another influential Republican organ, refuted the charges of political bias in the proceedings:

> In view of the effort on the part of some papers to make it appear that political prejudice plays a part in the prosecution of Colonel Eastham, it may be interesting to state that the petit jury which is now trying him is composed of seven Democrats and five Republicans; the grand jury that indicted him stood nine Democrats and seven Republicans, and the counsel who are prosecuting him stand five Democrats and three Republicans; and a Democratic supreme court passed upon the proceedings and refused to prohibit them.[41]

The *Randolph Enterprise* of Elkins was more balanced and accurate: "It is said the jury did not sustain Colonel Eastham's plea of self-defense; it certainly did not sustain the State's plea of malicious killing even in the mildest form. The truth is Colonel Eastham and his counsel offered to plead guilty to involuntary manslaughter, but they were refused the privilege. It is perfectly plain that the jury intended by its finding to vindicate the return of the first grand jury, which indicted Eastham for involuntary manslaughter and which was [resisted] by Judge Holt."[42]

Comments from the West Virginia Bar were more introspective and closer to the truth of the matter:

> The prosecution proved a cold-blooded murder. The defense proved that it was surely a case of self-defense.

The jury struck the difference as near as possible and said manslaughter. The judge endeavored to make the manslaughter as odious as possible by straining the law in the penalty imposed. Thus we have one of those cases that divide a court and a community as to the degree of guilt involved. . . . In all cases tried by a court, and especially in all cases like this, it is just as important that justice should appear to be done as that justice should be actually done.[43]

The attention given by reporters covering the trial to Eastham's experience in the Civil War as a Mosby Ranger demonstrates that the bloody shirt might have been buried but was still exhumed as needed. What side you were on still held cultural and political significance as a statement about your identity and relationship to the body politic. Eastham was portrayed as a daring hero by newspapers identified with the conservative democracy, the Confederacy, and the traditional agrarian/southern values it was created to uphold. They never missed an opportunity to admire guerrillas like Eastham. Like the "Lost Cause" itself, the significance of which grew in magnitude with the passing years, Eastham's very real exploits as one of Mosby's Rangers were elevated to the stuff of legend. This explains why so many honored Robert W. Eastham, alias "Bob Ridley," with the respectful moniker of "Colonel" even though he neither rose to that rank nor sought rank above private, and never used the title himself.[44]

During the period when Eastham's trial was pending, the 43rd Virginia Battalion, Confederate Army, also known as Mosby's Rangers, held their fourth annual reunion and banquet at the Eutaw House in Baltimore, Maryland. Among the letters of regret received by the Baltimore committee was one from

"Col. Robert W. Eastham, of Davis, W. Va., one of Mosby's old men," an Alexandria, Virginia, newspaper reported. The paper reprinted the letter in full:

> My Dear Old Comrades: I received the invitation to meet our boys of the Forty-third Mosby Battalion, C.S.A., in Baltimore, but circumstances will prevent [me from attending], as I am held here without cause. I think all are familiar with and know the facts of the case by this time. I am right and will come out all right if I have half a show. I had set my heart upon being at the reunion in Baltimore, but I will be prevented, and do not know whether I will ever see the old boys again, but, be it as it may, they can rest assured that my whole soul is with them. I give you my best wishes and hope that you will all have a good time. P.S.—Tell the boys that I was shot twice before I fired a shot.[45]

The letter was distributed to the press by the reunion committee and appeared in Republican and Democratic papers alike.

On the motion of Frank Kennelly, of Clarke County, Virginia, the convention secretary was directed to send a letter of sympathy to "Col. Robert W. Eastham" of Davis, West Virginia, "assuring him of their belief in his innocence of any crime."[46] Colonel John S. Mosby, commander of the 43rd Virginia Battalion, was unable to attend the reunion because he was on the Pacific coast recuperating from a serious accident. Much earlier, less than a month after the shooting and death of Frank Thompson, and prior to his accident, Colonel Mosby sent a letter to Bob Eastham:

> Alexandria, Va.
>
> April 13, 1897

Mr. Robert Eastham

Dear Bob,

I have seen some notice in the newspapers of your unfortunate difficulty & that you were in prison. I hope that you are in no danger & that your deliverance will soon come. I wish it were in my power to help you, but be assured that you have the deep sympathy not only of myself but of all your old comrades. You were a good soldier—we are all hoping that you will soon be free.

Your Sincere Friend

John Mosby [signed][47]

Like Eastham's open letter to the fourth reunion of Mosby's Rangers, Colonel Mosby's letter to Bob Eastham was released to the press and widely reprinted. Both are reminders that men like Eastham whose identities were formed at a young age by the crucible of the Civil War carried that searing experience with them for the rest of their lives. Lacking that wartime experience, younger men like Frank Thompson ultimately could not understand men like Robert Eastham. Nor could the "new men" comprehend the resistance of the "old men" to the incorporation of the wilderness; they simply belonged to two different chronological and cultural worlds.

Eastham's Escape

On Sunday, January 31, it was reported that Eastham was "stricken with paralysis." He was "unable to move or speak," and the physicians and his friends were fearful of the outcome. The prisoner had been suffering from rheumatism for some time, but it was not known whether this affliction was the cause of his paralysis.⁴⁸ Then, in early May, six months after he was sentenced to two years' close confinement, the wire services hummed with reports of his escape:

> It is learned here that Col. Robert W. Eastham got out of jail at Parsons, W. Va. last Sunday night and that his absence was not discovered until the next morning. It is said he used wooden keys with which he unlocked two doors, got into the jail basement, and escaped to the outside through a window. It is reported that he was aided by a confederate, who had provided a horse, on which Eastham rode away. Recently Eastham claimed that he was paralyzed. It is believed that he was shamming. . . . It is believed that Eastham has made his way to his old home in [Rappahannock] County, Va. Eastham was a Confederate scout. He is a well-preserved man of about fifty-five years, and is a daring horseman. He is well acquainted with the country through which he traveled in effecting his escape.

An item in the Staunton, Virginia, newspaper reported that Eastham had escaped jail in Parsons and made his way through Romney, West Virginia, and was on his way to join General Fitzhugh Lee's corps.⁴⁹

When Eastham was sentenced to two years for involuntary manslaughter his lawyers had immediately appealed the judge's sentence to the Supreme Court of Appeals of West Virginia. Argument on a motion for a new trial was set for early in June. Even though Eastham had already made his escape, the application for a writ of error matured, and on June 8, 1898, the appeal came up on argument. "Very elaborate speeches" were made by Attorney John A. Howard for the state and Col. John T. McGraw for the defense. It was reported that the court would consider dismissal of the appeal because Eastham was a fugitive from justice. That same morning "an attache of the court stated that Eastham was with Gen. Lee's army, and in a short time would be with that corps engaged in an active campaign against the Spaniards. Should this be the case, it is not likely the Tucker County man will ever be again arraigned in the Thompson case." On September 15 the Supreme Court of Appeals of West Virginia took up the case of the *State v. Robert W. Eastham* pending on a writ of error and dismissed it because the witness was no longer in custody.[50]

How Eastham escaped remained a mystery, but one of the theories that gained favor among the residents of Rappahannock County, Virginia, claimed that "Bob Ridley's" cell was opened by a friendly insider, and a saddled horse waited for him in the alley to carry him home to Rappahannock County. This was a distance of more than one hundred miles, however, and seems unlikely in its impracticality. One thing is certain: a friendly insider with access to the keys either unlocked the doors or allowed wooden keys to be made. The wooden key theory is recited to this day in Flint Hill. Sheriff Riley Harper, a Democrat and former Confederate soldier who had joined Eastham in removing the county court records to Parsons, was known as a friend of the prisoner. He would have had custody of the keys and both the opportunity and incentive to leave the cell unlocked. Certainly Eastham's opponents suspected Harper. This theory is augmented by the fact that to escape through a basement window Eastham would have had to enter the sheriff's residence, which was a part of the jail building, to access the basement. It is possible that the county clerk, William M. Cayton, who served in that office from 1891 to 1903, assisted in some manner. He was a highly partisan H. G.

Davis Democrat, and brother-in-law of C. Wood Daily, Eastham's lead attorney and Davis's own counselor. In the most likely version, once out of his cell the prisoner descended the stairs into the basement and clamored out an open window presumably to avoid the possibility of being seen departing through the front door. Once in the street he climbed into his friend Silas Blackman's surrey and was whisked off to Rowlesburg, West Virginia. At the depot he likely boarded an eastbound Baltimore & Ohio passenger train, which would have conveyed him to a convenient station close to his home place. The theory that Silas Blackman, of nearby Bretz, conveyed Eastham to the railway station in Rowlesburg was confirmed by Blackman's son in an interview with Eastham's great nephew.[51]

A local legend circulates in Rappahannock County that, not long after Eastham's escape, a posse from West Virginia in search of the fugitive stopped a man on the road to ask how to get into Rappahannock County. Implying that they were looking for Eastham, according to the story, the Virginian responded that it was not difficult for posses to get into Rappahannock, but they had a poor record of ever getting out. There is a similar story passed down in the Eastham family of attempts by authorities in West Virginia to extradite Robert Eastham, but a family historian has found no documentary evidence to support the story. Nor has any evidence been found in the governor's papers in either state that a request for extradition was ever sent or denied. Back home, it appears Eastham lived out the rest of his life without being harassed by the law, and died in 1924 at the age of eighty-two without spending another day in jail.[52]

EPILOGUE

The lack of documentary records makes it impossible to reconstruct more of Robert Eastham's biography, but a fairly reasonable sketch of his character and temperament can be drawn from the fragmentary evidence that does exist. Eastham as a daring young man emerges in fleeting glimpses through reports of his exploits as one of Mosby's Rangers during the Civil War. His image then takes on a sharper focus during his more than twenty-year residency in Tucker County (1876 to 1898), and especially the mid- to late 1890s documented in the trial records. After he escaped from jail in May 1898 and fled back to his hometown of Flint Hill, Virginia, Robert "Bob Ridley" Eastham recedes into the shadows, only rarely to reemerge over the next twenty-six years. Even though he was a fugitive, it is unlikely that Eastham was in hiding from the authorities. It seems more likely that a tacit understanding existed whereby West Virginia would not pursue him if he did not return to the state. Undoubtedly the Virginia governor would have denied a request for extradition, but there is no evidence in the state archives that West Virginia governors made such a request. In Virginia Eastham became something of a folk hero, and his eccentricities were given wide latitude because of his record of service to "the cause."

To protect his property interests while incarcerated, Eastham took the wise precaution in March 1897 of selling the 300 acres he had purchased from W. B. Maxwell in October 1895 to his sister Emma for $975. The following year, Emma sold the land to their youngest brother, Charles B. Eastham, for one dollar. On July 8, 1903, Mary Eastham sold the 263½ adjoining acres that she owned to Frank Cooper, a son of Robert's friend and neighbor Henry J. Cooper, for $1,800.[1] Ironically, all of the land which had been owned by Robert and Mary Eastham eventually fell under the ownership of the Thompson Lumber Company after it bought out the Blackwater Lumber Company in 1905. George B. Thompson, Frank's cousin, managed the Thompson Lumber Company and continued on as general manager of the Babcock Lumber Company when it purchased the company in 1907. What had been the Eastham acreage became part of "The Willows," Ben Thompson's Canaan Valley farm.[2] Thus came to an end Eastham's presence in West Virginia.

Back in Rappahannock County, Virginia, if Robert Eastham was hiding from authorities, he was doing it in plain view. He and his wife operated a post office in Flint Hill for the first few years, and then in 1900 settled into life on a ninety-seven-acre farm between Flint Hill and Washington, Virginia. He continued to engage in entrepreneurial enterprises. For example, he was a stockholder in the Valley Turnpike Company and was elected to the board of directors at the company's annual meeting in 1908. The company owned the turnpike from Winchester to Staunton, a distance of about one hundred miles. A Richmond paper regarded the turnpike as "perhaps the most important road in the State."[3]

Robert Eastham also remained dedicated to his comrades in arms and to the ideals held dear by loyal ex-Confederates. A local couple, Mr. and Mrs. Joseph Reid, successfully raised money to construct Willis Chapel in honor of Albert Gallatin Willis, a twenty-year-old ministerial student who fought with Mosby's Rangers. In reprisal for the alleged murder of two federal soldiers by Mosby's men, U.S. soldiers decided that one of the two captured rangers should hang. Willis was offered a chaplain's exemption, but he refused in order to spare the life of his married companion. Willis reportedly prayed for his executioners before he was hanged. His remains were buried in a small cemetery behind the Flint Hill Baptist Church, and the Reids were also successful in acquiring a proper grave marker to replace the old sandstone slab. Mr. Reid and "Bob Ridley" set the new monument in place.[4]

Other aspects of his personality remained even after he left the wilderness of Tucker County, West Virginia. In 1985, Robert Eastham's great nephew related that older people who remembered the old ranger from their childhood "without exception adored him." His love of guns and hunting preoccupied him to the end of his life, and when he went into the woods he "always took a youthful companion with him."[5] The old Rebel's great great nephew Edwin I. "Butch" Eastham, who has always lived in the Flint Hill area, recounted local stories he had heard about "Bob Ridley" as he was growing up. He remembered hearing that he always wore a long coat like the dusters worn by cavalrymen and cowboys. Also in his coat pockets he always carried hard candy to pass out to the children who flocked to him. In that great coat that he wore, presumably when the weather was cool, his great nephew surmised that he probably still carried a revolver in one of those pockets. "I think he always carried a gun until the day he died." Butch recalled that an elderly man who had known Robert Eastham confirmed that "he always had a pistol on him." Another story involved his preference for the company of his dogs. He once went to the home of a wealthy friend to participate in a fox hunt. When invited to spend the night, he indicated that he would sleep outside with the dog if it was not welcome inside the house as well. The friend relented and allowed both man and dog to sleep inside.[6]

The legend of Robert "Bob Ridley" Eastham as a man who never "wore smooth" is further demonstrated in a story related by his namesake. "In later years, he was foreman of a jury at the Rappahannock courthouse in Washington. The sheriff reported to the judge that Eastham and his fellow jurors were drinking whiskey in the jury room to lubricate their deliberations. The judge had the foreman called out and questioned him. When Eastham tried to evade a bit, the judge ordered the clerk to put him under oath. Bob Ridley then admitted all, exclaiming, 'Hell, judge, I can't lie under oath!'" Expanding further on this theme, Edwin Eastham related a story he had heard a number of times as a youth. An armed desperado on the run from a posse was holding a hostage at gunpoint in the refuge of a local church. Eastham entered the church and convinced the man to release the hostage and give himself up. Given the choice Eastham offered him, which was to deal with the law or deal with him, the desperado delivered himself over to the posse.[7] It is obvious that Robert Eastham had attained folk hero status, making it difficult to distinguish between tall tale and oral history.

Robert's wife Mary gave birth to no other children after the death of her daughter Eliza at the age of three. "Mollie," as the family called her, died on April 3, 1922, and eight months later, on December 12, 1922, Eastham married Bessie Jordan. He was then eighty years old and Bessie was fifty-six. They moved into her home, "Mount Prospect," near Washington, Virginia, which she had inherited from her father. Two years later he suffered a stroke and fell from his horse into a cold stream. He died shortly thereafter on April 7, 1924, at the age of eighty-two. In retrospect, it seems an appropriate closing of the circle that death would claim "Bob Ridley" while still in the saddle, bringing an end to his long and colorful career. His time on earth certainly was full of adventure, but it brought little in the way of fortune. He owned

Robert "Bob Ridley" Eastham, a former Mosby Ranger, at the Confederate monument constructed on the Washington, Virginia, courthouse grounds in 1900. Courtesy of Rappahannock County Historical Society, Washington, Virginia.

no land, and the value of his personal effects was assessed at $7,342.08, most of which was in the form of notes for money owed to him, along with a Ford truck, and a colt.[8]

The premature death of Frank Thompson, who was unmarried and without children, meant that the industrialist left no significant legacy beyond a promising career tragically cut short. His parents and his sister Sarah Maude were despondent over his death and reportedly never fully recovered from his loss. Frank's remains were temporarily interred until Maude constructed a mausoleum in Norway Pine Grove Cemetery, just outside their hometown of Norway, Maine. Their father, Albert, survived his son by more than twenty years. A wealthy man, his mansion at 4045 Walnut Street in Philadelphia still stands, and over the years has served other purposes, including that of a fraternity house for neighboring University of Pennsylvania students. According to an obituary, he was "of an innovative mind" and a "tireless worker." Albert was one of the first lumbermen to use a Shay locomotive to stock his lumber mills in Pennsylvania and West Virginia, and was the first manufacturer of West Virginia spruce to successfully compete with northern manufacturers on the east coast. Even after retirement he remained "extensively interested in bituminous coal properties in West Virginia, and anthracite coal in Pennsylvania; but owing to ill health had not been actively engaged for the last two years." He was described as "an active, fearless man of strong convictions, a loyal friend and an able defender of his rights." Albert Thompson was also a man who was "greatly interested in public affairs," who had represented his town in the legislature of New Hampshire, and as town clerk and justice of the peace. He also supported the schools, churches, and other public institutions in his community. The first sales office Albert established in Philadelphia was in the Betz Building and for more than twenty years he maintained an office in the Lincoln Building.⁹ In addition to his coal and lumber properties, Albert owned numerous other businesses as well. For example, his nephew George B. Thompson recalled that Uncle Albert owned land near Buena Vista, Maryland, where he had a large plant to produce ice for railroad refrigeration cars. George claimed he "nearly froze to death there in the winter of 1918."[10]

After they left Davis and established their permanent residence in Philadelphia, Frank's sister, Sarah Maude, moved in with her parents and abandoned her career in music to assist her father with his businesses. Maude circulated within the city's prominent social circles, but a family friend suspected that "the Thompsons' wealth was a hindrance to marriage." When she did marry, however, she married well. On November 29, 1918, Maude and Admiral Gustav Kaemmerling took their wedding vows in Philadelphia. Sixteen years her senior, Kaemmerling was sixty while Maude was forty-four when they married. The admiral had graduated from the U.S. Naval Academy in 1881, and served aboard Admiral Dewey's flag ship, the *Olympia*, at the Battle of Manila Bay during the Spanish American War. When they met during World War I he was stationed at the Camden Yards, New Jersey, and had reached the rank of rear admiral.[11]

Because her husband was gone for prolonged periods of time, her parents' large home in Philadelphia became their permanent residence as well. By 1920 both of her parents were in declining health. Albert died on April 24, 1921, at Joseph Price Memorial Hospital in Philadelphia, from complications following gall stone surgery. His wife Mary followed him on November 12, 1925. Maude inherited the house and their substantial estate. According to the family, "she learned the business trade from her father and managed his estate and holdings the remainder of her life." Maude donated Frank's mausoleum to the cemetery to be used for storage, and constructed an even more splendid one where in death her brother and their parents were reunited.[12]

Maude and her husband, who had retired in 1922, built a home on Rock Island in Lake Pennesseewassee near her hometown of Norway, Maine, and spent their summers there. The admiral's health was declining by the early 1930s, and he died at their home in Philadelphia on July 28, 1934. To honor her family, and the town she loved, Maude became a generous benefactor, contributing many improvements, including a new library, and providing major financial assistance toward construction of the local hospital.[13]

In 1951, when she was seventy-seven years old, Sarah Maude Thompson Kaemmerling composed a detailed will in which she directed that the bulk of her estate should be distributed to institutions and associations "engaged exclusively in charitable, educational or scientific activities for the promotion of science, health, education, good citizenship and the well-doing and well-being of mankind."[14] In 1954, Maude amended her will and granted 3,149 acres of her property to the state of West Virginia for the formation of a state park, with the stipulation that the state match her donation by acquiring an additional three thousand acres. The state responded by acquiring more than thirty properties between 1964 and 1970, and the Canaan Valley Resort State Park was established in 1971. With this simple act of charity, one of many in her long and productive life, Maude accomplished more for the long-term economic development of Tucker County than perhaps any other single person. She also left a legacy to the people of West Virginia that will continue in perpetuity. Maude died in her Philadelphia home on March 29, 1957. Rather than rest in the mausoleum she had constructed, however, Maude's ashes were scattered on Rock Island where she and her husband had spent so many summers.[15]

250 EPILOGUE

Thompson Mausoleum, Pine Grove Cemetery, Norway, Maine. Courtesy of Mary Beausoleil.

The deadly confrontation between Robert Eastham and Frank Thompson and the ensuing trial have entered the folklore of Tucker County, but what happened to the memories of the two men in death was as different as were their lives. Frank died an early and violent death at only thirty-five, surrounded by doctors who tried to save him and caring friends. His body was transported to Norway, Maine, where his remains eventually joined his parents in a magnificent mausoleum. But he was soon forgotten in West Virginia where for a decade he had played a major role in the political economy of Tucker County, as well as in his Maine hometown where he was a stranger to most residents.

Robert Eastham lived on in Tucker County folklore long after he escaped his jail cell and returned to his old home place in

Virginia. Many know the story of the shoot-out between a former Mosby Ranger and a lumber tycoon. More particularly, however, his exploits as a woodsman are still legendary in a county dominated by the Canaan Valley State Park and Monongahela National Forest. A collection of local stories published in 1960 carries one entitled "The Mystery of Eastham's Riffles." It tells of a stranger who fished the riffles, which are just below the splash dam that Eastham dynamited, and are named after him. When it was nearly dark, according to the story, a menacing figure appeared out of nowhere to advise the fisherman on how to successfully land his fish before disappearing just as mysteriously. When he reported on the incident back at the Blackwater Hotel, everyone concurred that the apparition was the ghost of Robert Eastham.[16]

Back home in Rappahannock County, Virginia, Eastham was less mysterious but remained a well-known eccentric, admired for his Civil War exploits among people whose identity was shaped by that epic event that had engulfed their land. Yet his eccentricities also kept family and friends at arm's length. When he died in 1924, Eastham was buried in the family cemetery on Buena Vista farm next to his kin. Over time, the section of pasture below the house where the cemetery was located became overgrown, and then deteriorated rapidly after the property passed out of the Eastham family and was vandalized. Sometime around 1990, the gravestones of Robert, Mary, and their daughter Eliza were removed from the family cemetery by great nephew Thomas Eastham and are honorably preserved in the garden of his wife Louise's antebellum plantation house, "Ben Venue." A strange end to an enigmatic life.

When they died, Frank was thirty-five and Bob was eighty-two. Both were unique individuals, products of very different life experiences and, indeed, two different worlds. Eastham grew to adulthood in an America of separate regions and in a South that

Gravestones of Robert, wife Mary C., and daughter Eliza, at Ben Venue, Washington, Rappahannock County, Virginia. Photograph by Ronald Lewis, courtesy of Louise King Eastham.

had suffered the death and devastation of a civil war succeeded by the poverty of postwar reconstruction. Thompson came of age during the late nineteenth century when America was on its way to becoming a major industrial power, when American regions were incorporated into a national market system, and the drive for great wealth was palpable to many and possible for a few. Thompson represented the future, and Eastham the past. On the broad scale of history, the "old" nineteenth century seemed to gradually morph into the "new" twentieth century. On the stage where modern incorporators met traditional resisters, however, change was often traumatic and sometimes tragic. The Eastham-Thompson feud was both.

Ben Venue plantation where the gravestones of Robert Eastham and family have been preserved. Photograph by Ronald Lewis, courtesy of Louise King Eastham.

In the early 1980s, Robert W. Eastham III visited Frank's cousin Benjamin F. Thompson in the Canaan Valley. His home was within eyesight of the cabin Robert and Mollie Eastham built in 1876 when they arrived in West Virginia, although it had since become part of a newer house. The two men "drank a bit of bourbon to toast the end of the Eastham-Thompson feud" while sitting "beneath the uniformed portrait of Ben's ancestor who was a federal officer in the Civil War." Mr. Eastham later recollected that the meeting was amicable, but that they agreed to disagree about "the troubles." They did succeed in "burying the hatchet" while putting a sizable dent in a good bottle of bourbon. Old Bob Ridley would have approved.[17]

NOTES

INTRODUCTION

1. For the "moonshine wars," see for example, Wilbur R. Miller, *Revenuers and Moonshiners: Enforcing Federal Liquor Law in the Mountain South, 1865–1900* (Chapel Hill: University of North Carolina Press, 1991); and Bruce E. Stewart, "'These Big-Boned Semi-Barbarian People': Moonshining and the Myth of Violent Appalachia, 1870–1900," in *Blood in the Hills: A History of Violence in Appalachia*, ed. Bruce E. Stewart (Lexington: University Press of Kentucky, 2012), 180–206. For feuds, see for example, Altina L. Waller, *Feud: Hatfields, McCoys, and Social Change in Appalachia, 1860–1900* (Chapel Hill: University of North Carolina Press, 1988); John Ed Pearce, *Days of Darkness: The Feuds of Eastern Kentucky* (Lexington: University Press of Kentucky, 1994); Brandon Kirk, *Blood in West Virginia: Brumfield v. McCoy* (Gretna, LA: Pelican, 2014); and Dwight B. Billings and Kathleen M. Blee, *Road to Poverty: The Making of Wealth and Hardship in Appalachia* (New York: Cambridge University Press, 2000).
2. Anthony Harkins, *Hillbilly: A Cultural History of an American Icon* (New York: Oxford University Press, 2004), 29.
3. Ronald L. Lewis, *Transforming the Appalachian Countryside: Railroads, Deforestation, and Social Change in West Virginia, 1880–1920* (Chapel Hill: University of North Carolina Press, 1998), 103–29.
4. David Thelen, *Paths of Resistance: Tradition and Dignity in Industrializing Missouri* (New York: Oxford University Press, 1986), 11–43; Richard Maxwell Brown, *No Duty to Retreat: Violence and Values in American History and Society* (Norman: University of Oklahoma Press, 1991), 45–46.

5 Brown, *No Duty to Retreat*, 44.
6 Ibid., 45.
7 Ibid., 55–56.
8 For the construction of Appalachian stereotypes, see Henry D. Shapiro, *Appalachia on Our Mind: The Southern Mountains and Mountaineers in the American Consciousness, 1870–1920* (Chapel Hill: University of North Carolina Press, 1978); and Allen W. Batteau, *The Invention of Appalachia* (Tucson: University of Arizona Press, 1990).
9 For the mine wars, see James Green, *The Devil Is Here in These Hills: West Virginia's Coal Miners and Their Battle for Freedom* (New York: Atlantic Monthly Press, 2015).

I. THE INCORPORATION OF WEST VIRGINIA

1 Colin Woodard, *American Nations: A History of the Eleven Rival Regional Cultures of North America* (New York: Viking, 2011), describes eleven cultural regions; Richard Maxwell Brown, *No Duty to Retreat: Violence and Values in American History and Society* (Norman: University of Oklahoma Press, 1991); Alan Trachtenberg, *The Incorporation of America: Culture and Society in the Gilded Age* (New York: Hill and Wang, 1982).
2 David Thelen, *Paths of Resistance: Tradition and Dignity in Industrializing Missouri* (New York: Oxford University Press, 1986).
3 Quotations from Brown, *No Duty to Retreat*, 45; McKinney, "Industrialization and Violence in Appalachia in the 1890s," in *An Appalachian Symposium*, ed. by J. W. Williamson (Boone, NC: Appalachian State University Press, 1977), 131–44.
4 Thelen, *Paths of Resistance*, 13–16, quotation on 16.
5 *Manufacturer's Record* 50 (Oct. 1906): 338; Ronald L. Lewis, *Transforming the Appalachian Countryside: Railroads, Deforestation, and Social Change in West Virginia, 1880–1920* (Chapel Hill: University of North Carolina Press, 1998), 58.
6 *Wheeling Register*, Nov. 10, 1881.
7 Granville Davisson Hall, *The Rending of Virginia: A History* (Chicago: Mayer and Miller Press, 1902), 617.

8 Thelen, *Paths of Resistance*, 28.
9 Ibid., 29, 31; quotation from Brown, *No Duty to Retreat*, 45–46.
10 Thelen, *Paths of Resistance*, 201.
11 John Alexander Williams, *West Virginia and the Captains of Industry* (Morgantown: West Virginia University Library, 1976), 3, 5.
12 Ibid., quotation on 4, 8.
13 Ibid., 7–8, quotation on 10.
14 Ibid., 11.
15 Ibid., quotation on 12, 13.
16 Ibid., 15.
17 Benjamin F. G. Kline Jr., "The Nature of Logging Railroads of West Virginia," *Log Train* 2 (Jan. 1984): 12; Williams, *Captains of Industry*, 168; James Morton Callahan, *Semi-Centennial History of West Virginia* (Charleston: Semi-Centennial Commission of West Virginia, 1913), 306–7; "Map of West Virginia Showing Railroads," in Roy B. Clarkson, *Tumult on the Mountains: Lumbering in West Virginia, 1770–1920* (Parsons, WV: McClain, 1964), insert.
18 Callahan, *Semi-Centennial History*, quotation on 212, 213.
19 E. Lawrence Marquess, "The West Virginia Venture: Empire Out of Wilderness," *West Virginia History* 14 (1952): 7–11; Charles M. Pepper, *The Life and Times of Henry Gassaway Davis, 1823–1916* (New York: Century, 1920), 30–32; Thomas Richard Ross, *Henry Gassaway Davis: An Old-Fashioned Biography* (Parsons, WV: McClain, 1994), 141–43.
20 Pepper, *Henry Gassaway Davis*, 97–98; *Charter and By-Laws of the West Virginia Central and Pittsburgh Railway Company*, Manuscript, West Virginia and Regional History Center, West Virginia University, Morgantown (hereafter WVRHC), 85. Stockholders included Secretary of State James G. Blaine and Secretary of the Treasury William Windom, as well as senators Thomas F. Bayard, H. G. Davis, Arthur P. Gorman, Johnson N. Camden, former senator and Maryland governor William P. Whyte, and U. S. Grant Jr., son of the former president (Ross, *Henry Gassaway Davis*, 142).

21 Marquess, "West Virginia Venture," 12; *Charter and By-Laws of the West Virginia Central and Pittsburgh Railway Company*, 3, quotation on 5–6.

22 W. Raymond Hicks, "The West Virginia Central and Pittsburgh Railway," *Railway and Locomotive Historical Society Bulletin* 113 (1965): 6–8, 10–18; Marquess, "West Virginia Venture," 16–19.

23 Callahan, *Semi-Centennial History*, 210–11, quotation on 212.

24 Kline, "Nature of the Logging Railroads," 12; Marquess, "West Virginia Venture," 20.

25 William Price McNeel, *The Durbin Route: The Greenbrier Division of the Chesapeake and Ohio Railway* (Charleston, WV: Pictorial Histories Publishing, 1985), 13–14; Roy B. Clarkson, *On Beyond Leatherbark: The Cass Saga* (Parsons, WV: McClain, 1990), 18–29; Clarkson, *Tumult on the Mountains*, 31.

26 Clarkson, *Tumult on the Mountains*, 31; Brooks, *Forestry and Wood Products*, 20.

27 Kenneth Gilbert, ed., *Mountain Trace*, Book 2 (Charleston, WV: Jalamap, 1983), 44–45; Edith Kimmell Starkey, "Over the Mountain: Timbering at Braucher," *Goldenseal* 13 (Summer 1987): 34.

28 Inventory taken from Homer Floyd Fansler, *History of Tucker County, West Virginia* (Parsons, WV: McClain, 1962), 84–85; "Davis," typescript, Notebook 1, Folder 1, D. D. Brown Notebooks, WVRHC.

29 Clarkson, *Tumult on the Mountains*, 84–85; "Davis," typescript, Notebook 1, Folder 1, D. D. Brown Notebooks, WVRHC.

30 Pearle G. Mott, *History of Davis and Canaan Valley* (Parsons, WV: McClain, 1972), 3.

31 For the sale of Davis town lots, see the Tucker County Land Books and Deed Books, 1884–1894, Clerk's Office, Tucker County Court House, Parsons, West Virginia.

32 Fansler, *History of Tucker County*, 279–86; *West Virginia Central and Pittsburgh Railway Company* (promotional pamphlet); *Davis Industrial Edition*, Aug. 9, 1895.

33 Reproduced in Fansler, *History of Tucker County*, 288–89.

34 Lewis, *Transforming the Appalachian Countryside*, 195; Fansler, *History of Tucker County*, 366.

2. MODERNIZING THE LAW

35 *West Virginia Gazetteer and Business Directory, 1891–92*, vol. 4, quotation on 295.
36 The above discussion drawn from Lewis, *Transforming the Appalachian Countryside*, 185–209, and *West Virginia Gazetteer and Business Directories* for respective towns and years.

2. MODERNIZING THE LAW

1 Richard Orr Curry, *A House Divided: A Study of Statehood Politics and the Copperhead Movement in West Virginia* (Pittsburgh, PA: University of Pittsburgh Press, 1964), 137; John Alexander Williams, "The New Dominion and the Old: Ante-Bellum and Statehood Politics as the Background of West Virginia's 'Bourbon Democracy,'" *West Virginia History* 33 (1973): 355.
2 James Willard Hurst, *Law and Economic Growth: The Legal History of the Lumber Industry in Wisconsin, 1836–1915* (Cambridge, MA: Harvard University Press, 1964), 231.
3 West Virginia, *Acts of the Legislature*, 1877, Chapter 121, 178–89; 1881, 296–301; 1885, Chapter 12, 14–19.
4 Ibid., 1882, Chapter 118, 338–40.
5 Lawrence M. Friedman, *A History of American Law* (New York: Simon and Schuster, 1973), 410, 417; A. G. Roeber, *Faithful Magistrates and Republican Lawyers: Creators of Virginia Legal Culture, 1680–1810* (Chapel Hill: University of North Carolina Press, 1981); F. Thornton Miller, *Juries and Judges versus the Law: Virginia's Provincial Legal Perspective, 1783–1828* (Charlottesville: University Press of Virginia, 1994).
6 Miller, *Juries and Judges versus the Law*, 3–7, 14–15, 25, 103–04.
7 Morton J. Horwitz, *The Transformation of American Law, 1780–1860*, vol. 1 (Cambridge, MA: Harvard University Press, 1977), 74–80, 98–99; Jeff L. Lewin, "The Silent Revolution in West Virginia's Law of Nuisance," *West Virginia Law Review* 90 (Winter 1989–90): 244–46, 251; Ronald L. Lewis, *Transforming the Appalachian Countryside: Railroads, Deforestation, and Social Change in West Virginia, 1880–1920* (Chapel Hill: University of North Carolina Press, 1998), 114.

8. Lewin, "The Silent Revolution in West Virginia's Law," 252–53, 270.
9. Ibid., 245–46, 253–54, 270–72.
10. Ibid., 263–64.
11. Gaston v. Mace, 33 W.Va. 15–18 (1889).
12. Ibid.; Lewis, *Transforming the Appalachian Countryside*, 119.
13. "Ironheads" originally referred to the Regular Democrats of the northern and western counties who represented the iron interests, and "Agrarians" referred to "Bourbon Democrats" of the eastern and southern counties. See Charles H. Ambler and Festus P. Summers, *West Virginia: The Mountain State*, 2nd ed. (New York: Prentice-Hall, 1958), 400–401; and Williams, "New Dominion and the Old," 322. For the "Republican Party Army" see Gordon McKinney, *Southern Mountain Republicans, 1865–1900: Politics and the Appalachian Community* (Chapel Hill: University of North Carolina Press, 1978).
14. John Alexander Williams, "Class, Section, and Culture in Nineteenth-Century West Virginia Politics," in *Appalachia in the Making: The Mountain South in the Nineteenth Century*, ed. Mary Beth Pudup, Dwight B. Billings, and Altine L. Waller (Chapel Hill: University of North Carolina Press, 1995), 224.
15. Williams, "New Dominion and the Old," 349, quotations on 352.
16. Ibid., 368.
17. Homer Lloyd Fansler, *History of Tucker County, West Virginia* (Parsons, WV: McClain, 1962), 248–49.
18. Ibid., 252; Tucker County Election Book No. 1, 1–2, 9–11.
19. Fansler, *History of Tucker County*, 253–54, quotation on 253; Fansler, "The Tucker County Seat War," *Parsons Advocate*, April 16, 1959.
20. Fansler, *History of Tucker County*; "Tucker County Seat War."
21. *Wheeling Intelligencer*, Aug. 4, 1893; Fansler, *History of Tucker County*, 255; Fansler, "Tucker County Seat War."
22. Hamilton et al. v. Tucker County Court et al., 38 W.Va. 71–79.
23. Quotation from *Wheeling Intelligencer*, Aug. 4, 1893. The names were taken from Fansler, *History of Tucker County*, 249–51, 255–56. Fansler identifies these men as active in the movement. Their names were drawn from a list of petition captains who led the electoral districts in 1892–1893; men who pledged to cover the cost of the special election in 1893; men who offered the use of their

building in Parsons as a temporary courthouse; men who offered to provide land in Parsons for the site of a new courthouse; and others who served in various capacities as lawyers and organizers. A collective biography of this group was pieced together from diverse sources, but primarily from Fansler, *History of Tucker County*, Hu Maxwell, *History of Tucker County, West Virginia* (1884; reprint Kingwood, WV: Preston, 1971), and biographical directories, particularly *Men of West Virginia*, 2 vols. (Chicago: Biographical Publishing, 1903).

24 A collective biography of this group was pieced together from diverse sources, but primarily from Fansler, *History of Tucker County*; Maxwell, *History of Tucker County*; and biographical directories, particularly *Men of West Virginia*.

25 The preceding discussion is based on the collective biographies drawn from Fansler, *History of Tucker County*; Maxwell, *History of Tucker County*; and biographical directories, particularly *Men of West Virginia*. See also Lewis, *Transforming the Appalachian Countryside*, 222–24.

26 Donald L. Rice, *Bicentennial History of Randolph County, West Virginia, 1787–1987* (Elkins, WV: Randolph County Historical Society, 1987), 39, reprints the article citing the *Pittsburgh Leader*, May 15, 1899.

3. ROBERT W. EASTHAM, THE EARLY YEARS

1 Mary Elizabeth Hite, *My Rappahannock Story Book* (Richmond, VA: Dietz Press, 1950), 200–202; Byrd Eastham, *The Descendants of Franklin Dabney Eastham* (Charlottesville, VA, 1997). Their children were Robert Woodford, b. 1842; Franklin Dabney, b. 1843; Emma C., b. 1844; Philip Byrd, b. 1845; William B., b. 1847; John R., b. 1848; Edwin L., b. 1850; Ann M., b. 1852; Ada V., b. 1854; and Charles B., b. 1858.

2 Hite, *My Rappahannock Story Book*, 202. The roster of men in the 7th Virginia Cavalry alone nearly reach that total of Easthams.

3 Service Record, Eastham, Franklin Dabney, 6th Cavalry Regiment, http://ranger95.com/civil_war/virginia/cavalry/6va_cav/6th_cav

_rgt_rost_c_e.html (accessed July 25, 2016); Interview, Edwin I. Eastham, III, Sept. 11, 2014, Huntly, Rappahannock County, VA. Frank Dabney was his great grandfather.

4 Robert Woodford Eastham III, interview by Ronald Lewis, June 25, 1992, Flint Hill, VA (Mr. Eastham died in 1995); "Pvt Philip Byrd Eastham," Find A Grave Memorial, http://www.findagrave.com/cgi-bin/fg.cgi?page=gr&GRid=18078000 (accessed July 21, 2016); Williamson, *Mosby's Rangers: A Record of the Operations of the Forty-Third Battalion of Virginia Cavalry from its Organization to the Surrender*, 2nd ed. (1896; reprint New York: Sturgis & Walton, 1909), 534.

5 Elisabeth B. and C. E. Johnson Jr., *Rappahannock County, Virginia: A History* (Salem, WV: Walsworth, 1981), quotation on 414; Eastham, Woodford, Co. D, Mosby's Regiment Virginia Cavalry (Partisan Rangers), http://ranger95.com/civil_war/virginia/cavalry/43va_cav_bn_csa/43rd_cav_bn_rost_d.html (accessed July 25, 2016); Eastham, Robert Woodford, 6th Cavalry Regiment, http://ranger95.com/civil_war/virginia/cavalry/6va_cav/6th_cav_rgt_rost_c_e.html (accessed July 25, 2016); John H. Eicher and David J. Eicher, *Civil War High Commands* (Stanford, CA: Stanford University Press, 2001), 316. Much has been written about Jackson, but see James I. Robertson Jr., *Stonewall Jackson: The Man, The Soldier, The Legend* (New York: MacMillan, 1997).

6 McMichael, "Robert Woodford Eastham," 2; Eastham, Robert Woodford, 6th Cavalry Regiment, http://ranger95.com/civil_war/virginia/cavalry/6va_cav/6th_cav_rgt_rost_c_e.html (accessed July 25, 2016); Michael P. Musick, *6th Virginia Cavalry. The Virginia Regimental Histories Series* (H. E. Howard, 1990); Eicher and Eicher, *Civil War High Commands*, 316.

7 Hu Maxwell, *History of Tucker County, West Virginia* (Kingwood, WV: Preston, 1884), 399; Charles L. Dufour, *Gentle Tiger: The Gallant Life of Roberdau Wheat* (Baton Rouge: Louisiana State University Press, 1999). For General Field see *Generals in Gray: Lives of the Confederate Commanders* (Baton Rouge: Louisiana State University Press, 1959). For General Ewell see Donald C. Pfanz, *Richard S. Ewell: A Soldier's Life* (Chapel Hill: University of North Carolina Press, 1998).

8 Much has been written about J. E. B. Stuart, but see Jeffry D. Wert, *Cavalryman of the Lost Cause: A Biography of J. E. B. Stuart* (New York: Simon & Schuster, 2008).

9 George Ellis Moore, *A Banner in the Hills: West Virginia's Statehood* (New York: Appleton-Century-Crofts, 1963), 182–94; Boyd B. Stutler, *West Virginia in the Civil War* (Charleston, WV: Education Foundation, 1966), 204–9; William N. McDonald, *A History of the Laurel Brigade*, ed. by Bushrod C. Washington (Baltimore: Sun Job Printing Office by Mrs. Kate S. McDonald, 1907), 118–30.

10 Eastham, Robert Woodford, 6th Cavalry Regiment, http://ranger95.com/civil_war/virginia/cavalry/6va_cav/6th_cav_rgt_rost_c_e.html (accessed July 25, 2016). On Eastham's possibly having met Mosby prior to joining his partisans, see Robert Woodford Eastham III, "Robert Woodford ('Bob Ridley') Eastham, 1842–1924," unpublished, handwritten script, 31 pp., Rappahannock County Historical Society.

11 Hugh C. Keen and Horace Mewborn, *43rd Battalion Virginia Cavalry Mosby's Command* (Lynchburg, VA: H. E. Howard, 1993), 12; Jeffry D. Wert, *Mosby's Rangers* (New York: Simon and Schuster, 1990), 68–71. On Confederacy policies toward partisan groups see Daniel E. Sutherland, "Guerrilla Warfare, Democracy, and the Fate of the Confederacy," *Journal of Southern History* 68 (May 2002): 259–92.

12 John W. Munson, *Reminiscences of a Mosby Guerrilla* (New York: Moffat, Yard, 1906), 178–84 on uniforms; Hugh C. Keen and Horace Mewborn, *43rd Battalion Virginia Cavalry Mosby's Command* (Lynchburg, VA: H. E. Howard, 1993), 12.

13 John W. Munson quoted in Keen and Mewborn, *43rd Battalion Virginia Cavalry*, 17.

14 Munson, *Reminiscences of a Mosby Guerrilla* (1906; reprint Washington DC: Zenger, 1983), 23–25; Keen and Mewborn, *43rd Battalion Virginia Cavalry*, 15–16.

15 Johnson and Johnson, *Rappahannock County, Virginia*, 414. For lyrics of the song see, "Old Bob Ridley!" (bsvg200857) American Song Sheets, Duke Libraries, Duke University.

16 Letter to the Editor, *Northern Virginian* 4, no. 3 (summer–fall, 1933). To this day several of the Eastham descendants are noted horsemen.
17 Maxwell, *History of Tucker County*, 398.
18 Homer Floyd Fansler, *History of Tucker County, West Virginia* (Parsons, WV: McClain, 1962), 601.
19 Johnson and Johnson, *Rappahannock County, Virginia*, 414, gives the figure as $15,000, while Fansler, *History of Tucker County*, claims it was $5,000; Maxwell, *History of Tucker County*, quotation on 399.
20 Maxwell, *History of Tucker County*, 400.
21 Ibid., 400–401 (respectively).
22 Ibid., 402. This story was passed down in the family as well.
23 Williamson, *Mosby's Rangers*, 243.
24 Ibid., 243–44, quotation on 244.
25 Munson, *Reminiscences of a Mosby Guerrilla*, 254.
26 Williamson, *Mosby's Rangers*, 262.
27 J. Marshall Crawford, *Mosby and His Men: A Record of the Adventures of That Renowned Partisan Ranger, John S. Mosby* (New York: G. W. Carleton, 1867), 331.
28 Williamson, *Mosby's Rangers*, 206–12; Wert, *Mosby's Rangers*, 190–93.
29 Williamson, *Mosby's Rangers*, quotations on 210; Wert, *Mosby's Rangers*, 192–93.
30 Quoted in John S. Mosby, *The Memoirs of Colonel John S. Mosby*, ed. Charles Wells Russell (Bloomington: Indiana University Press, 1959), 365–67, quotation on 367.
31 Ibid., 365.
32 "Marlbrough s'en va-t-en guerre," https://en.wikipedia.org; "Malbrook Has Gone to the War," *Arthur's Ladies' Magazine of Elegant Literature and the Fine Arts* (1844), 8, http://search.proquest.com/docview/124533760; Munson, *Reminiscences*, 107–9.
33 Crawford, *Mosby and His Men*, 332–33; McMichael, "Robert Woodford Eastham," 4, citing John Scott, *Partisan Life with Colonel John Mosby* (New York: Harper and Brothers, 1876).
34 Jimmy DeBerg, interview by Ronald Lewis, Sept. 11, 2014, near Flint Hill, VA.

35 Williamson, *Mosby's Rangers*, 392; Wert, *Mosby's Rangers*, quotations on 288–89.
36 Maxwell, *History of Tucker County*, 403; quotation from, "Duel on a Train," *Washington Times*, March 20, 1897.
37 Keen and Mewborn, *43rd Battalion Virginia Cavalry*; Robert Woodford Eastham, Family History Report, Rappahannock County Historical Society; Wert, *Mosby's Rangers*, 290.
38 Records of the Assistant Commissioner for the State of Virginia Bureau of Refugees, Freedmen, and Abandoned Lands, 1865–1869, National Archives Microfilm Publications M1048, Roll 59 "Narrative Reports of Criminal Cases Involving Freedmen, Mar. 1866–Feb. 1867," Freedmen's Bureau Online, www.freedmensbureau.com/virginia/crimcases2.htm (accessed July 21, 2016).
39 "Eastham Trial Drags Slowly," *Grafton Sentinel Weekly*, Dec. 3, 1897.
40 Maxwell, *History of Tucker County*, 403; http://trees.ancestrylibrary.com/tree/12875899/person/1140043866.

4. EASTHAM IN WEST VIRGINIA

1 Roy B. Clarkson, *Tumult on the Mountains: Lumbering in West Virginia, 1770–1920* (Parsons, WV: McClain, 1964), 3–4; Ronald L. Lewis, *Transforming the Appalachian Countryside: Railroads, Deforestation, and Social Change in West Virginia, 1880–1920* (Chapel Hill: University of North Carolina Press, 1998), 17.
2 Robert W. Eastham III, interview by Ronald Lewis, June 25, 1992, Flint Hill, VA; Ruth Cooper Allman, *Canaan Valley and the Black Bear* (Parsons, WV: McClain, 1976), 28–29; Pearle G. Mott, *History of Davis and Canaan Valley* (Parsons, WV: McClain, 1972), 481.
3 Jack Waugh, "Lumbering before Pinchot: The Short, Loud Death of the Canaan Valley," *American Heritage* 42 (Feb.–Mar. 1991): 93–94.
4 David Hunter Strother, *Virginia Illustrated, Containing a Visit to the Canaan, and the Adventures of Porte Crayon and His Cousins* (New York: Harper and Brothers, 1871), 30.
5 Quoted in Waugh, "Lumbering Before Pinchot," 93.

NOTES TO CHAPTER 4

6 Tucker County Land Book, 1872–1880; Deed Book 3, 1876, 527; Homer Floyd Fansler, *History of Tucker County, West Virginia* (Parsons, WV: McClain, 1962), 595, states that they settled on 500 acres that he purchased from A. W. Read.
7 Fansler, *History of Tucker County*, 594–95; Allman, *Canaan Valley and the Black Bear*, 9–10; Maxwell, *History of Tucker County, West Virginia* (1884; reprint, Kingwood, WV: Preston, 1971), quotations on 403.
8 Tucker County Deed Book 5, 339; Myrtle Cooper Wiseman, "My Memories of the Cortland Community, Canaan Valley," in Mott, *History of Davis and Canaan Valley*, 480–87, quotation on 481.
9 Wiseman, "My Memories of the Cortland Community," 481.
10 Allman, *Canaan Valley and the Black Bear*, 1–2, quotation on 5.
11 Wiseman, "My Memories of the Cortland Community," 482, quotation on 483; Allman, *Canaan Valley and the Black Bear*, 5.
12 Fansler, *History of Tucker County*, 279; Mott, *History of Davis and Canaan Valley*, 4–5.
13 Election results reproduced in Maxwell, *History of Tucker County*, 571.
14 Tucker County Deed Book 8, 213–14; Deed Book 9, 351 and 487; Mott, *History of Davis and Canaan*, 6; Fansler, *History of Tucker County*, 280; Maxwell, *History of Tucker County*, 404; Davis Industrial Edition, *Tucker County Republican*, Aug. 9, 1895.
15 George B. Thompson, "Facts Concerning the Town of Davis," typescript, Sarah Thompson Fletcher Family Papers; Wiseman, "My Memories of the Cortland Community," quotation on 483. This probably referred to another of Eastham's numerous surveying projects.
16 "Bob Eastham, Deer Hunter and Guide," *Graphic News* 6 (Sept. 18, 1886): 197 (photo) and 198 (article).
17 Edwin I. Eastham III, interview by Ronald Lewis, Sept. 11, 2014, Huntly, VA; "Depositions for the Defendant, January–February 1896," Blackwater Lumber Company v. R. W. Eastham, Law Box 40, Case #775 A, Tucker County Circuit Court.
18 William B. Maxwell and wife, deed to R. W. Eastham, October 5, 1894, Tucker County Deed Book 14, 278.

19 Ibid.
20 Maxwell, *History of Tucker County*, 531; Fansler, *History of Tucker County*, 280n394, quotation on 601.
21 Maxwell, *History of Tucker County*, 403.
22 Fansler, *History of Tucker County*, 601.
23 Indictment, R. W. Eastham, Misdemeanor, May Term 1881, Law Box 7, Tucker County Circuit Court.
24 Fansler, *History of Tucker County*, 536; Mott, *History of Davis and Canaan*, 67. A bandsaw is a continuous steel strip with sawing teeth and differs from the circular saw which is a disk with a cutting edge.
25 Bruce Dalton, "Robert Eastham, A Transplanted Virginian," *Chronicles of the Tucker County Highlands History and Education Project* 26 (Aug. 2009), four pages unnumbered; Dave Lesher, "Sarah Maude Kaemmerling and Canaan Valley State Park," *Chronicles of the Tucker County Highlands History and Education Project* 60 (Aug. 2015), five pages unnumbered.
26 Plaintiff's Charge, Mar. 1888, R. W. Eastham v. J. L. Rumbarger Lumber Company, Law Box 14, Case #1215, Tucker County Circuit Court.
27 "Deposition of D. C. Van Buskirk," Feb. 20, 1889, R. W. Eastham v. J. L. Rumbarger Lumber Company, Law Box 14, Case #1215, Tucker County Circuit Court.
28 "Order," ibid.
29 State v. Eastham and Mouser, Law Box 24, Tucker County Circuit Court.
30 Town of Davis v. Davis, decided Apr. 6, 1895, 40 *West Virginia Reports*, 464–80, quotation on 477.
31 Quotation from Law Order Book 5, 79, July 14, 1893, Tucker County Circuit Court; Law Order Book 5, June 14, 1894, Tucker County Circuit Court.

5. WHO WERE THE THOMPSONS?

1 George B. Thompson to Ruth Moon, Mar. 20, 1932, Sarah Thompson Fletcher Family Papers.

2 Charles Foster Whitman, *A History of Norway, Maine: From the Earliest Settlement to the Close of the Year 1922* (Lewiston, ME: Lewiston Journal Printshop and Bindery, 1924), 518; Dave Lescher, "Sarah Maude Kaemmerling and Canaan Valley State Park: A Legacy That Almost Didn't Happen," *Chronicles of the Tucker County Highlands History and Education Project* 60 (Aug. 2015): 1–5.

3 Thompson to Moon, Mar. 20, 1932, Sarah Thompson Fletcher Family Papers; Whitman, *History of Norway*, 520.

4 Thompson to Moon, Mar. 20, 1932, and Ruth Anderson Eleson, "Thompson-Wheeler Roots," typescript, Sarah Thompson Fletcher Family Papers; U.S. Census of Population, 1850 and 1860; George Benjamin Thompson, interview by O. D. Lambert, Robert F. Munn, and Verl Z. Garster, Canaan Valley, Tucker County, WV, Apr. 13, 1956; *History of the Counties of McKean, Elk and Forest, Pennsylvania* (Chicago: J. H. Beers, 1890), 742–43. For a history of Berlin during these early years, and the prominent role played by Benjamin and Samuel in the town's affairs, see, *Berlin, New Hampshire Centennial, 1829–1929: A Series of Articles Compiled to Commemorate the Date of Incorporation of the Town of Berlin* (n.p.: Printed by Smith and Town, 1929).

5 George Benjamin Thompson, interview; Adeline (Clark) D'Entremont, "Regarding the Name of Hosea's and Lucy's 2nd Son and Notes Regarding the Thompson Family of Norway, Maine (also Philadelphia)," typescript, and his business card indicating his office was located at "No. 2 Beal's Block, Norway Village, ME," Sarah Thompson Fletcher Family Papers; Obituary, Mrs. Gustav Kaemmerling, newspaper copy provided courtesy of Dave Lesher.

6 New Hampshire, Marriage Records Index, 1637–1947, at Ancestry.com; Whitman, *History of Norway*, 519; quotation from D'Entremont, "Regarding the Name."

7 1880 federal census, Ancestry.com; *Rules of the Senate and House of Representatives of the State of New Hampshire, 1873* (Concord: Printed for the State, June 1873), 15, and *Rules of the Senate and House of Representatives of the State of New Hampshire, 1875*, 16; *History of the Counties of McKean, Elk and Forest*, 742–43.

8 D'Entremont, "Regarding the Name"; *History of the Counties of McKean, Elk and Forest*, quotation on 742–43; West Virginia Deaths Index, 1853–1973, at AncestryLibrary.com; Whitman, *History of Norway*, 201.
9 Whitman, *History of Norway*, 519.
10 U.S. Passport Applications, 1795–1925, June 23, 1898, and Sept. 3, 1903, both at Ancestry.com; quotation from D'Entremont, "Regarding the Name"; Whitman, *History of Norway*, 519.
11 D'Entremont, "Regarding the Name."
12 1850, 1860, 1870, 1880, 1900, and 1910 U.S. federal censuses, New Hampshire Marriage Records Index, 1637–1947, Find A Grave Memorial, all at Ancestry.com; Homer Floyd Fansler, *History of Tucker County, West Virginia* (Parsons, WV: McClain, 1962), 540–41; George B. Thompson, *History of the Lumber Business at Davis, West Virginia, 1886–1924* (Parsons, WV: McClain, 1974), 12–13.
13 Obituary prepared by George B. Thompson, Sarah Thompson Fletcher Family Papers.
14 1850, 1860, 1880, 1920, and 1930 U.S. federal censuses, at Heritage.com; Whitman, *History of Norway*, 359–60; Thompson, *History of the Lumber Business*, 13; Fansler, *History of Tucker County*, 10, 13.
15 Fansler, *History of Tucker County*, 537, n752; George Benjamin Thompson, interview; Albert Thompson to George B. Thompson, May 28, 1893, Sarah Thompson Fletcher Family Papers.
16 Fansler, *History of Tucker County*, 240; Thompson, *History of the Lumber Business*, 16; Appointments of U.S. Postmasters, 1832–1971, vol. 99, 1904–1930, at Ancestry.com.
17 Fansler, *History of Tucker County*, 536; Thompson, *History of the Lumber Business*, 2–3 (quotation on 3).
18 Fansler, *History of Tucker County*, quotation on 538; Thompson, *History of the Lumber Business*, 4.
19 Fansler, *History of Tucker County*, 538; Thompson, *History of the Lumber Business*, 4–5; George B. Thompson, "Babcock Lumber and Boom Company," typescript, Sarah Thompson Fletcher Family Papers.
20 George B. Thompson, "History of Dry Fork Railroad," typescript, Sarah Thompson Fletcher Family Papers.

21 "W. H. Osterhout," *Elk County Genealogy, Biographical Sketches, Ridgway Township and Burough of Ridgway*, chap. 17, http://www.pa-roots.com/elk/history/chapter17.html (accessed July 21, 2016).

22 Fansler, *History of Tucker County*, 538; Thompson, *History of the Lumber Business*, 5–6; George B. Thompson, "Rape of a Virgin Forest," typescript, Sarah Thompson Fletcher Family Papers, WVRHC.

23 Thompson, *History of the Lumber Business*, 7–10, 13, 16; Dave Lesher, "Sarah Maude Kaemmerling," 2. For Albert Thompson's purchase of the Eastham land, see Albert Thompson to George B. Thompson, Jan. 5, 1907, Sarah Thompson Fletcher Family Papers. For Albert Thompson's reassertion of control in the company, see his letters to George B. Thompson, Jan. 1, May 28, June 22, Nov. 9, 1907, Sarah Thompson Fletcher Family Papers.

24 Fansler, *History of Tucker County*, 539–41; Thompson, *History of the Lumber Business*, 7–10, 13, 16.

25 Obituary prepared by George B. Thompson, Sarah Thompson Fletcher Family Papers; Thompson, *History of the Lumber Business*, 14–15; 1900 and 1910 U.S. federal censuses, 1916 and 1932, Long Beach, CA, City Directories, and U.S., Find A Grave Index, 1600-Current, all on Ancestry.com.

26 1850, 1860, 1870, 1880, 1900, and 1910 U.S. federal censuses, New Hampshire Marriage Records Index, 1637–1947, Find A Grave Memorial, all at Ancestry.com; Fansler, *History of Tucker*, 540–41; Thompson, *History of the Lumber Business*, 12–13; Obituary, "Sumner W. Thompson," unidentified newspaper clipping, Sarah Thompson Fletcher Family Papers.

27 Whitman, *History of Norway*, quotation on 359–60; 1910 U.S. Federal Census, 1930 U.S. Federal Census, and U.S. Find A Grave Index, 1600s-Current, all at Ancestry.com.

28 Fansler, *History of Tucker County*, 541–42; Thompson, *History of the Lumber Business*, 16; Thompson, "Babcock Lumber and Boom Company."

6. SETTING THE STAGE FOR TROUBLE

1. "Bill of Complaint," May 9, 1895, Blackwater Lumber Company v. R. W. Eastham, Law Box 40, Case # 775A, Circuit Court of Tucker County.
2. C. Powell Grady to Robert Eastham, Nov. 5, 1887, ibid.
3. Grady to Eastham, May 20, 1889, ibid.
4. Hiram Woods to Robert Eastham, Dec. 26, 1891, ibid.
5. Grady to Eastham, Mar. 3, June 22, Dec. 5, 1893, ibid.
6. Eastham to Woods, Feb. 16, 1894, ibid.
7. Woods to Eastham, Feb. 20, 1894, ibid.
8. Eastham to Woods, Feb. 23, 1894, ibid.
9. Grady to Eastham, Jan. 4, 1894, ibid.
10. Eastham to Woods, Feb. 23, 1894, ibid.
11. Grady to Eastham, Mar. 5, 1894, ibid.
12. Woods to Eastham, Feb. 22, 1895, ibid.
13. Woods to Eastham, Nov. 15, 1895, ibid.
14. Grady to Woods, Oct. 10, 1895, ibid.
15. *Law Order Book 5*, 137; R. W. Eastham v. Blackwater Lumber Company, case files, Law Box 24, Case 1734, Tucker County Circuit Court.
16. Notices published in the *Tucker Democrat*, case files, R. W. Eastham v. Blackwater Lumber Company, case files, Law Box 24, Case 1734, Tucker County Circuit Court.
17. "Order," Nov. 28, 1895, case files, ibid.
18. "Agreement," Eastham and Blackwater Boom and Lumber Co., Mar. 1, 1892, case files, ibid.
19. "Transcription of the evidence taken at the November term, 1895," ibid.
20. Letter filed with deposition, Frank E. Thompson to William H. Bumgardner, Feb. 26, 1896, Blackwater Lumber Company v. R W. Eastham, Law Box 40, Case 775A, Tucker County Circuit Court.
21. "Depositions," Feb. 26, 1896, ibid.
22. Frank Thompson's deposition in, "Depositions for Plaintiff," undated, taken between Sept. 20 and Oct. 26, 1896, ibid.
23. Quotation from Notice, Oct. 5, 1894, ibid; Notice, Jan. 7, 1895, ibid.

272 NOTES TO CHAPTER 7

24 Notice, Apr. 13, 1895, ibid.
25 "Plaintiff's Exhibit C," Aug. 8, 1888, case files, and "Plaintiff's Exhibit D," Apr. 15, 1895, ibid.
26 "Plaintiff's Exhibit E," Jan. 31, 1891, and "Bill of Complaint," May 9, 1895, ibid.
27 Plaintiff's "Exhibit D," Apr. 15, 1895, ibid; quotations from "Response of R. W. Eastham to the bill exhibited against him in this court by the Blackwater Lumber Company, plaintiff," ibid.
28 "Summons," May 9, 1895, and "Injunction Bond," May 9, 1895, case files, ibid.

7. THE STRUGGLE FOR CONTROL

1 "Bill of Contempt," Blackwater Lumber Company v. R. W. Eastham, Law Box 40, Case 775A, Tucker County Circuit Court.
2 "Brief for Defendant," Mar. 10, 1896, ibid. Counsel cited the precedents of *Cooley Con. Lim.*, 557; Morgan v. King, 18 Barb. 284; Gardner v. Newberg, 2 John. Chy. 162. For the law regulating river booms see *Code of West Virginia*, 3rd ed. (1891), 1004.
3 "Brief of Defendant," Mar. 10, 1896, citing Constitution W.Va., Art. 3, Sec. 9, and *Code West Virginia*, Ch. 42, Sec. 1.
4 "Brief for the Defendant," Mar. 10, 1896. Counsel citing Gaston v. Mace, 33 W.Va. 14 on a "floatable" stream, and *Code of West Virginia*, 3rd ed. (1894), sect. 20, clause 4, 1011 on boomage charges, and sect. 25, 1014, on right to break a jam.
5 "Brief for Defendant," Apr. 14, 1896, Blackwater Lumber Company v. R. W. Eastham, Law Box 40, Case 775A, Tucker County Circuit Court.
6 "Depositions of Defendant," ibid.
7 "Depositions of A. Thompson, F. E. Thompson, and Others," Aug. 26, 1895, ibid.
8 Eastham's deposition was given Feb. 11 thru 13, 1896, "Depositions, January–February, 1896," ibid.
9 "Depositions on Behalf of the Defense," Nov. 15, 1895, ibid.
10 "Depositions of A. Thompson, F. E. Thompson, and Others," Aug. 26, 1895, ibid.

11 "Depositions for the Plaintiff," Feb. 28, 1896, ibid.
12 "Depositions of A. Thompson, F. E. Thompson, and Others," Aug. 26, 1895, ibid.
13 "Depositions, Jan.–February, 1896," ibid.
14 "Deposition of Dave Lambie," Jan. 9, 1896, ibid.
15 "Depositions of A. Thompson, F. E. Thompson, and others," Aug. 26, 1895, ibid.
16 "Depositions of C. W. Propst and Others," Feb. 28, 1896, ibid.
17 "Depositions of A. Thompson, F. E. Thompson, and others," Aug. 26, 1895, ibid.
18 Eastham's deposition was taken on Feb. 10, "Depositions, Jan.-February, 1896," ibid.
19 "Depositions, Jan.–February, 1896," ibid.
20 George B. Thompson, "Forest Fires in Davis Area," typescript, Sarah Thompson Fletcher Family Papers.
21 "Depositions, Jan.-February 1896," Blackwater Lumber Company v. R. W. Eastham, Law Box 40, Case 775A, Tucker County Circuit Court.
22 "Depositions on Behalf of Defendant, Jan.–February, 1896," ibid.

8. THE SHOOT-OUT AND "LAWYERS BY THE DOZEN"

1 Homer Floyd Fansler, *History of Tucker County, West Virginia* (Parsons, WV: McClain, 1962), 602; Elizabeth Williams v. Karl Degler, Law Order Book 6, 12, 136, 147, Tucker County Circuit Court.
2 Fansler, *History of Tucker County*, quotation on 602; Homer F. Fansler, "Echoes of the Past-Tucker County's Greatest Murder Case," *Parsons Advocate*, Aug. 28, 1958; "In Contempt of Court," *Parsons Advocate*, March 19, 1897; "Duel on a Train," *Washington Times*, Mar. 20, 1897; "Shooting After Court," *New York Sun*, Mar. 20, 1897. For the placard's message, see Robert Woodford Eastham III, "Bob Ridley Eastham: Ranger Followed Trail of Adventure," Part 2, *Rappahannock News*, Jan. 5, 1985, 5.
3 "Deposition of Thomas Wheeler," filed Apr. 3, 1897, State v. R. W. Eastham, Law Box 38, Tucker County Circuit Court.

4 Fansler, *History of Tucker County*, 601; quotation from Fansler, "Echoes of the Past,"; "Eastham Case: A Famous Murder Trial," *Parkersburg Sentinel*, Nov. 1897.
5 Eastham, "Bob Ridley Eastham," 5; "Deposition of Dr. B. M. Smith," filed Apr. 3, 1897, State v. R. W. Eastham, Law Box 38, Tucker County Circuit Court.
6 "Deposition of Dr. B. M. Smith."
7 "Deposition of Dr. C. R. Foutch," filed Apr. 3, 1897, and "Deposition of Dr. Johnston," filed Apr. 3, 1897, State v. R. W. Eastham, Law Box 38, Tucker County Circuit Court.
8 "Deposition of Dr. C. R. Foutch."
9 Fansler, *History of Tucker County*, 601; "Eastham's Victim Dead," *Evening Times* (Washington, DC), March 20, 1897; "Deposition of Dr. C. R. Foutch." See also, "Deposition of Dr. Johnston."
10 George B. Thompson, "Mar. 18, 1930," handwritten recollection on ledger paper, Sarah Thompson Fletcher Family Papers.
11 Warrant, Mar. 25, 1895, case files, ibid.
12 Security Bond, case files, ibid.
13 Thomas Richard Ross, *Henry Gassaway Davis: An Old-Fashioned Biography* (Parsons, WV: McClain, 1994), 230–33; Festus P. Summers, *William L. Wilson and Tariff Reform* (New Brunswick, NJ: Rutgers University Press, 1953), 190–225.
14 James Morton Callahan, *History of West Virginia, Old and New* (Chicago: American Historical Society, 1923), 2:586.
15 "Lawyers by the Dozen," *Evening Times* (Washington, DC), Aug. 4, 1897; "Col. Eastham Indicted," *Alexandria Gazette*, June 21, 1897.
16 Callahan, *History of West Virginia*, 3:403–4; "Alston G. Dayton," in *West Virginia Encyclopedia*, ed. Ken Sullivan (Charleston: West Virginia Humanities Council, 2006), 188; "Col. Eastham Indicted," *Alexandria Gazette*, June 21, 1897.
17 George W. Atkinson, *Bench and Bar of West Virginia* (Charleston, WV: Virginian Law Book Company, 1919), 176–78; "William Gustavus Conley," in *West Virginia Encyclopedia*, 160–61.
18 "Absalom M. Cunningham," in Atkinson, *Bench and Bar of West Virginia*, 338–39.

19 "William Carroll Howard, Wheeling," from *West Virginians* (published by West Virginia Biographical Association, 1928; submitted by Linda Fluharty), http://www.wvgenweb.org/ohio/howard.htm (accessed July 21, 2016).
20 Callahan, *History of West Virginia*, 3:284; "Copperhead Movement," in *West Virginia Encyclopedia*, 168. For more, see Richard Orr Curry, *A House Divided: A Study of Statehood Politics and the Copperhead Movement in West Virginia* (Pittsburgh, PA: University of Pittsburgh Press, 1964).
21 George W. Atkinson and Alvaro F. Gibbens, *Prominent Men of West Virginia* (Wheeling, WV: W. L. Callin, 1890), 853–54; Hu Maxwell, *History of Tucker County, West Virginia* (Kingwood, WV: Preston, 1884), quotation on 200.
22 1900 census; Fansler, *History of Tucker County*, 463.
23 Fansler, *History of Tucker County*, 235, 255, 385, 389, 409, 434–35.
24 Atkinson, *Bench and Bar of West Virginia*, 129–30; Ross, *Davis*, 252, 310n31; John Alexander Williams, *West Virginia and the Captains of Industry* (Morgantown: West Virginia University Library, 1976), 34, 42–43, 200–201, 211–16, 221, 227.
25 Callahan, *History of West Virginia*, 3:488–89.
26 Atkinson and Gibbens, *Prominent Men of West Virginia*, 567–68.
27 "John T. McGraw," in *West Virginia Encyclopedia*, 467; Summers, *Wilson and Tariff Reform*, 44.
28 Callahan, *History of West Virginia*, 3:559.
29 "Holmes Conrad," U.S. Department of Justice, www.justice.gov/osg/bio/holmes-conrad (accessed July 21, 2016).
30 Atkinson, *Bench and Bar of West Virginia*, 336–37.
31 Clement A. Evans, *Confederate Military History, Extended Edition* (Wilmington, NC: Broadfoot, 1987), 142–44.
32 Atkinson, *Bench and Bar of West Virginia*, 336–37.
33 Gleaned from online sources and "James Marshall McCormick," in *Some Old Families of Clarke County, Virginia*, ed. Lorraine F. Myers, Stuart E. Brown, Jr., and Eileen M. Chappel (Berryville, VA: Virginia Book Company, 1994), 31.
34 Chris Doxzen, "Legal Legends of Rappahannock County," *Rappahannock News*, Aug. 8, 2013; Eastham, "Bob Ridley Eastham," 5;

"Henry H. Downing," http://www.wikiwand.com/en/Henry_H._Downing (accessed July 25, 2016); "Henry H. Downing," Find a Grave Memorial, http://www.findagrave.com/cgi-bin/fg.cgi?page=gr&GRid=24042573 (accessed April 17, 2015).
35 Reproduced in Pearle G. Mott, *History of Davis and Canaan Valley* (Parsons, WV: McClain, 1972), 128.
36 Ibid., 126; *Journal of the House of Delegates of the State of West Virginia for the Twenty-Fourth Regular Session*, commencing Jan. 11, 1899 (Charleston, WV: Press Butler, 1899), vi.
37 Ross, *Davis*, 110; Williams, *West Virginia and the Captains of Industry*, 136.
38 Callahan, *History of West Virginia*, 3:189–90.

9. JURY SELECTION AND THE APPEAL

1 Taken from "Eastham Case," *Parkersburg Sentinel*, Nov. 24, 26, 1897; "Trial of Col. Eastham," *Alexandria Gazette*, Aug. 4, 1897; "Col. Eastham's Case," *Alexandria Gazette*, Aug. 5, 1897; State v. R. W. Eastham, Law Box 38, Tucker County Circuit Court, "Exceptions 3, 6, 9," Nov. 23, 1897; "Proposed Charges for the Grand Jury," n.d. [Aug. 1897], Folder 3, Box 32, Alston G. Dayton Papers, WVRHC.
2 "Col Eastham's Case," *Alexandria Gazette*, Aug. 5, 1897
3 West Virginia Supreme Court of Appeals, Order Books, Robert Eastham v. John Homer Holt, Judge, Charleston, WV. Thanks to Professor Robert Bastress for his assistance and Supreme Court clerk Rory Perry for providing the documents.
4 "The Eastham Case," *Alexandria Gazette*, Sept. 4, 1897, and "The Eastham Case," *Alexandria Gazette*, Sept. 14, 1897.
5 Robert W. Eastham v. John Homer Holt, Judge, September Term, 1897, 43, *West Virginia Reports*, quotation on 636. For full documentation, see ibid., 599–637; Supreme Court of Appeals of West Virginia, Ex parte Eastham, Sept. 14, 1897, 43 W. Va. 637, 27 S.E. 896; and West Virginia Supreme Court of Appeals, Order Books, Robert W. Eastham v. John Homer Holt, Judge, Sept. 2, Sept. 3, Sept. 16, Nov. 2, 24, 27, 1897, Charleston, WV. See also, "Judge

Dent's Apology," *Parsons Advocate*, Dec. 3, 1897, quoting from *Eastham v. Holt*, 636.
6 John Phillip Reid, *An American Judge: Marmaduke Dent of West Virginia* (New York: New York University Press, 1968), 47–48.
7 Ibid., quotation on 181–82, 186.
8 Ibid., 188–89.
9 Ibid., 189, quotation on 191.
10 Ibid., 191–92.
11 *Eastham v. Holt*, 43; *W.Va. Reports*, 624.
12 Ibid., 625–26.
13 Ibid., 627–28.
14 Ibid., 630–31.
15 Ibid., 632–33.
16 Ibid., 634–35.
17 Ibid., 635.
18 Ibid., 602–3.
19 Ibid., 604–7, quotations on 604 and 607 respectively.
20 Ibid., 607–8.
21 Ibid., 611.
22 Ibid., 615.
23 Ibid., 616.
24 Ibid., 617–18.
25 Ibid., 621–22.
26 Ibid., 620.
27 Homer Floyd Fansler, "Tucker County's Greatest Murder Case," *Parsons Advocate*, Aug. 28, 1958, quote directly from the Dec. 24, 1897 issue of the same paper.
28 "Trial of Col. Eastham," *Alexandria Gazette*, Aug. 4, 1897.
29 Fansler, "Tucker County's Greatest Murder Case."
30 "The Eastham Case," *Parsons Advocate*, Nov. 23, 1897.
31 Fansler, "Tucker County's Greatest Murder Case."
32 "Eastham Trial," *Wheeling Daily Intelligencer*, Nov. 26, 1897.
33 "Eastham Trial Drags Slowly," *Grafton Sentinel Weekly*, Dec. 3, 1897.
34 Orders, entered Nov. 27, 1897 and Nov. 29, 1897, State v. R. W. Eastham, Law Box 38, Tucker County Circuit Court; quotation from

"Eastham Trial," *Wheeling Daily Intelligencer*, Nov. 26, 1897; "Eastham Trial," *Wheeling Daily Intelligencer*, Nov. 27, 1897.
35 "Eastham Trial Drags Slowly," *Grafton Sentinel Weekly*, Dec. 3, 1897.
36 Ibid. Camden Lipscomb was a Parsons attorney, a former mayor of the city, and friendly with Eastham.
37 "On Trial for His Life," *Parsons Advocate*, Dec. 3, 1897.
38 "Eastham Trial Drags Slowly," *Grafton Sentinel Weekly*, Dec. 3, 1897.
39 Ibid.
40 Quotation from "Panel Secured," *Wheeling Daily Intelligencer*, Dec. 2, 1897; "Eastham Trial On," *Wheeling Daily Intelligencer*, Dec. 3, 1897; *Parkersburg Sentinel*, Dec. 7, 1897.

10. ON TRIAL FOR MURDER

1 "Eastham Trial," *Wheeling Daily Intelligencer*, Dec. 7, 1897.
2 "On Trial for His Life," *Parsons Advocate*, Dec. 3, 1897.
3 "Eastham Trial." *Wheeling Daily Intelligencer*, Dec. 7, 1897.
4 Transcript of Trial Testimony, n.d., F. S. Landstreet, State v. R. W. Eastham, Law Box 38, Tucker County Circuit Court. For a brief version see "On Trial for His Life," *Parsons Advocate*, Dec. 3, 1897.
5 "Witness List and Summary of Their Testimony," n.d., Folder 1, Box 36, Alston G. Dayton Papers, WVRHC.
6 "Eastham's Trial," *Wheeling Daily Intelligencer*, Dec. 4, 1897.
7 "Witness List and Summary of Their Testimony," n.d., Folder 1, Box 36, Alston G. Dayton Papers, WVRHC.
8 Ibid.
9 "On Trial for His Life," *Parsons Advocate*, Dec. 10, 1897. Hoke attended the proceedings for six days and the court reimbursed him $116 for his travel expenses (State v. R. W. Eastham, December 16, 1897, Law Order Book 6, 286).
10 "On Trial for His Life," *Parsons Advocate*, Dec. 10, 1897, and "No Politics in It," *Wheeling Daily Intelligencer*, Dec. 6, 1897.
11 "Eastham's Trial," *Wheeling Daily Intelligencer*, Dec. 9, 1897.

NOTES TO CHAPTER 10   279

12 "On Trial for His Life," *Parsons Advocate*, Dec. 10, 1897; "Eastham the Aggressor," *Wheeling Daily Intelligencer*, Dec. 8, 1897.
13 "Eastham the Aggressor"; "On Trial for His Life," *Parsons Advocate*, Dec. 10, 1897.
14 "Eastham's Trial," *Wheeling Daily Intelligencer*, Dec. 9, 1897.
15 "On Trial for His Life," *Parsons Advocate*, Dec. 10, 1897.
16 "The Eastham Trial," *Grafton Sentinel Weekly*, Dec. 10, 1897.
17 "Transcript of Testimony," John W. Hockman, State v. Robert W. Eastham, Law Box 38, Tucker County Circuit Court Records.
18 "Transcript of Trial Testimony," J. A. Houston and J. M. Reed, ibid.
19 "Transcript of Trial Testimony," J. M. Reed, ibid.
20 "Vacation Order" (Petition to take deposition of Thomas Burger), entered Nov. 2, 1897, ibid.; "The Case of Col. Eastham," *Alexandria Gazette*, Nov. 11; quotation from "The Eastham Case," *Alexandria Gazette*, Nov. 12, 1897.
21 *West Virginia Senate Journal*, 1911, appendix C, 29–30.
22 "The Defense Opens," *Wheeling Daily Intelligencer*, Dec. 10, 1897.
23 "Involuntary Manslaughter," *Parsons Advocate*, Dec. 17, 1897.
24 Ibid.
25 "Eastham Takes the Stand Himself," *Parkersburg Sentinel*, Dec. 17, 1897. See also "Eastham's Story," *Wheeling Daily Intelligencer*, Dec. 14, 1897.
26 "Eastham Case," *Wheeling Daily Intelligencer* (Rep.), Dec. 15, 1897; "Will Decide the Eastham Case," *Parkersburg Sentinel* (Dem.) Dec. 15, 1897.
27 "Involuntary Manslaughter," *Wheeling Daily Intelligencer*, Dec. 17, 1897 "Involuntary Manslaughter," *Parsons Advocate*, Dec. 17, 1897.
28 Law Order Book 6, 285–86, Dec. 16, 1897, Tucker County Circuit Court; Verdict, State v. R.W. Eastham, Law Box 38, Tucker County Circuit Court.
29 Charles E. Hogg, *Hogg's West Virginia Code*, vol. 3 (St. Paul, MN: West Publishing, 1914), sect. 5152, 2835; *Michie's Jurisprudence of Virginia and West Virginia*, vol. 9B, LexisNexis; State v. Cain, 20 W. Va. 679 (1882).

30 Quotations from "Involuntary Manslaughter," *Parkersburg Sentinel*, Dec. 17, 1897. See also "Involuntary Manslaughter," *Wheeling Daily Intelligencer*, Dec.17, 1897; "End of Eastham Case," *Roanoke Times*, Dec. 18, 1897.
31 "Two Years in Jail," *Roanoke Times*, Dec. 19, 1897.
32 "Col. Eastham's Case," Charles Town, WV, *Spirit of Jefferson*, Jan. 4, 1898; Quotation from *Randolph Enterprise* (Elkins), Dec. 29, 1897.
33 "Defendant's Bill of Exception No. 5," State v. R. W. Eastham, Jan. 24, 1898, Law Box 38, Tucker County Circuit Court.
34 "Defendant's Bill of Exception No. 2," ibid.
35 "Defendant's Bill of Exception No. 5," ibid.
36 Item, Charles Town, WV, *Spirit of Jefferson*, Feb. 8, 1898.
37 "Two Years," *Parkersburg Sentinel*, Dec. 18, 1897.
38 Ibid.
39 "What Holt Said," *Grafton Sentinel Weekly*, Dec. 24, 1897.
40 "From Tragedy to Fame," *Grafton Sentinel Weekly*, Dec. 31, 1897, reprinted from *Elkins Mountain Echo*.
41 "No Politics in It," *Wheeling Daily Intelligencer*, Dec. 6, 1897.
42 *Randolph Enterprise* (Elkins), Dec. 29, 1897.
43 "The Result of the Eastham Case," *Grafton Sentinel Weekly*, Jan. 7, 1898, reproduced from *West Virginia Bar*.
44 See for example, "Trial of Col. Eastham," *Alexandria Gazette*, Aug. 4, 1897; "Col. Eastham's Case," Charles Town, WV, *Spirit of Jefferson*, Jan. 4, 1898.
45 "Mosby's Men," *Alexandria Gazette*, Oct. 14, 1897.
46 "Reunion of Mosby's Command," *Alexandria Gazette*, Oct. 14, 1897.
47 This letter was framed on the wall in the home of Eastham's great nephew and namesake, Robert Woodford Eastham, of Flint Hill, VA. I copied it by hand during a visit with him in 1992.
48 Quotations from "Bob Eastham Paralyzed," *Grafton Sentinel Weekly*, Feb. 4, 1898; *Alexandria Gazette*, Feb. 2, 1898.
49 Quotation from "Col. Eastham Breaks Jail," *Washington Times*, May 14, 1898. See also "Thompson's Slayer Escapes," *Scranton Tribune*, May 12, 1898, and *Staunton Spectator and Vindicator*, May 19

and June 2, 1898. General Fitzhugh Lee was a commander of cavalry during the Civil War, served as governor of Virginia (1886–1890), and held the post of Consul General of Havana when the Spanish-American War broke out in 1898. He became Major General of Volunteers, VII Army Corps. There is no evidence that Eastham attempted to join Lee's corps. See Harry Warren Readnour, "General Fitzhugh Lee: A Biographical Study" (Ph.D. diss., University of Virginia, 1971).

50 Quotation from "The Eastham Case," *Alexandria Gazette*, June 10, 1898; "Case Against Eastham Dismissed," *Alexandria Gazette*, Sept. 16, 1898.

51 Elisabeth B. and C. E. Johnson Jr., *Rappahannock County, Virginia: A History* (Salem, WV: Walsworth, 1981), 415; Robert Woodford Eastham III, "Bob Ridley Eastham: Ranger Followed Trail of Adventure," Part 2, *Rappahannock News*, Jan. 5, 1985, 5.

52 Johnson and Johnson, *Rappahannock County, Virginia*, 415. See also Chris Doxzen, "The Legal Legends of Rappahannock County," *Rappahannock News*, Aug. 8, 2008, http://www.rappnews.com/2013/08/08/the-legal-legends-of-rappahannock-county/123403/.

EPILOGUE

1 Tucker County Deed Book 16, May 1, 1897; Deed Book 17, Oct. 6, 1898; and Deed Book 23, July 8, 1903, Tucker County Circuit Court.

2 Sara Maude (Thompson) Fletcher, interview by Ronald L. Lewis, Oct. 31, 2014, Davis, West Virginia; Robert Woodford Eastham III, "Bob Ridley Eastham: Ranger Followed Trail of Adventure," Part 2, *Rappahannock News*, Jan. 5, 1985, 5, 10.

3 "Winchester Fair A Great Success," *Richmond Times Dispatch*, Oct. 23, 1908.

4 Elisabeth B. and C. E. Johnson Jr., *Rappahannock History, Virginia: A History* (Salem, WV: Walsworth, 1981), 195–96; Photographs in author's possession.

5 Eastham, "Bob Ridley Eastham," 5, 10.

6 Edwin I. "Butch" Eastham interview by Ronald L. Lewis, Sept. 11, 1014, Huntly, VA.

7. Eastham, "Bob Ridley Eastham," 10; Edwin Eastham, interview.
8. Robert W. Eastham III, interview by Ronald L. Lewis, June 25, 1992, Flint Hill, VA; Virginia Birth, Marriage, and Death Records, Ancestry.com; Virginia Death Records, Ancestry.com; Bruce Dalton, "Robert Eastham, A Transplanted Virginian and a Challenger of the Canaan Establishment," *Chronicles of Tucker County Highlands History and Education Project* 26 (Aug. 2009): 4. The inventory and appraisal of his personal effects was reproduced in Dora Lee McMichael, "Robert Woodford Eastham," unpublished paper, Rappahannock County Historical Society.
9. "A. Thompson Dies in Philadelphia," obituary, unidentified newspaper clipping, Sarah Thompson Fletcher Family Papers. See also, Obituary, Albert Thompson, *Lumberman's Review*, Sept. 1921 (courtesy of Dave Lesher), and Obituary, "Albert Thompson," *Philadelphia Evening Public Ledger*, Apr. 25, 1921.
10. G. B. Thompson to W. R. Hicks, June 8, 1952, and Feb. 5, 1953, Sarah Thompson Fletcher Family Papers.
11. Adeline (Clark) D'Entremont, "Regarding the Name of Hosea's and Lucy's 2nd Son and Notes Regarding the Thompson Family of Norway, Maine and Philadelphia," typescript (quotation), Sarah Thompson Fletcher Family Papers; Charles Foster Whitman, *A History of Norway Maine: From the Earliest Settlement to the Close of the Year 1922* (Lewiston, ME: Lewiston Journal Printshop and Bindery, 1924), 519.
12. Quotation from D'Entremont, "Regarding the Name," Sarah Thompson Fletcher Family Papers; "Last Will and Testament of Albert Thompson," Will Book 2, 216, Tucker County Clerk's Office, Parsons, WV; Certificate of Death, Albert Thompson, Commonwealth of Pennsylvania, Department of Health, Bureau of Vital Statistics, file 44253. Courtesy of Dave Lesher; "A Town's Memorial—Norway Pine Grove," Norway Historical Society, March 20, 2012, http://norwayhistoricalsociety.org/PineGrove.php.
13. Dave Lesher, "Sarah Maude Kaemmerling and Canaan Valley State Park: A Legacy That Almost Didn't Happen," *Chronicles of Tucker County Highlands History and Education Project* 60 (Aug. 2015): 3; Obituary, Mrs. Gustav Kaemmerling, Norway, Maine, newspaper

clipping, copy courtesy of Dave Thresher; Quotation from D'Entremont, "Regarding the Name," Sarah Thompson Fletcher Family Papers; Norway Historical Society, "Interesting Places," http://www.norwayhistoricalsociety.org/InterestingPlaces.php (accessed July 21, 2016), and "History of Norway Memorial Library," http://www.norway.lib.me.us/History.html (accessed July 21, 2016).
14 Tucker Community Foundation, Sarah Thompson Kaemmerling Fund, http://www.tuckerfoundation.whatsupwv.com/endowed-funds/grants/sarah-thompson-kaemmerling (accessed July 21, 2016).
15 Will Book No. 4, p. 343, and Land Book, 1961, Dry Fork District, 18, Tucker County Circuit Court; Fansler, *History of Tucker County, West Virginia* (Parsons, WV: McClain, 1962), 537n752; Lesher, "Sarah Maude Kaemmerling," 4–5; Obituary, Mrs. Maude Kaemmerling, Norway newspaper clipping, courtesy Dave Lesher.
16 Jack Preble, *Land of Canaan: Plain Tales from the Mountains of West Virginia* (Parsons, WV: McClain, 1960), 99–105.
17 Eastham, "Bob Ridley Eastham," 5; Robert W. Eastham III, interview.

BIBLIOGRAPHY

LEGAL DOCUMENTS

Blackwater Lumber Company v. R. W. Eastham. Law Box 40. Case #775 A. Tucker County Circuit Court.
Code of West Virginia. 3rd ed. (1891), 1004, (1894), sect. 20, 1011, sect. 25, 1014.
Elizabeth Williams v. Karl Degler. Tucker County Circuit Court v. Karl Degler. Law Order Book 6, 12, 136, 147. Tucker County Circuit Court.
Gaston v. Mace. 33 W.Va. 15–18 (1889).
Hamilton et al. v. Tucker County Court et al. 38 W.Va. 71–79.
Hogg, Charles E. *Hogg's West Virginia Code.* Vol. 3. St. Paul, MN: West Publishing, 1914.
Indictment. R. W. Eastham. Misdemeanor. May term 1881. Law Box 7. Tucker County Circuit Court.
Law Order Book 5. Tucker County Circuit Court.
Michie's Jurisprudence of Virginia and West Virginia. Vol. 9B, 2012 replacement (Lexis Nexis).
Robert W. Eastham v. John Homer Holt, Judge. September Term, 1897. 43 *West Virginia Reports*, 599–637.
R. W. Eastham v. Blackwater Lumber Company. Law Box 24. Case 1734. Tucker County Circuit Court.
R. W. Eastham v. J. L. Rumbarger Lumber Company. Law Box 14. Case 1215. Tucker County Circuit Court.
State v. R. W. Eastham. Law Box 7. Tucker County Circuit Court.
———. Law Box 38. Tucker County Circuit Court.
Supreme Court of Appeals of West Virginia. *Ex parte Eastham.* Sept. 14, 1897. 43 W. Va. 637. 27 S.E. 896.

Town of Davis v. Davis. Apr. 6, 1895. 40 *West Virginia Reports*, 464–80.
West Virginia Supreme Court of Appeals. Order Books. *Robert Eastham* v. *John Homer Holt, Judge*, Charleston, WV.
———. Order Books. *Robert W. Eastham v. John Homer Holt, Judge.* Sept. 2, 3, 16, Nov. 2, 24, 27, 1897. Charleston, WV.

GOVERNMENT DOCUMENTS

Journal of the House of Delegates of the State of West Virginia. Twenty-Fourth Regular Session, commencing Jan. 11, 1899. Charleston, WV: Press Butler Printing, 1899.
"Narrative Reports of Criminal Cases Involving Freedmen, Mar. 1866–Feb. 1867." Freedmen's Bureau Online, www.freedmensbureau.com/virginia/crimcases2.htm.
Records of the Assistant Commissioner for the State of Virginia Bureau of Refugees, Freedmen, and Abandoned Lands, 1865–1869. National Archives Microfilm Publications M1048, Roll 59.
Tucker County Election Book No. 1. Tucker County Clerk's Office, Parsons, WV.
Tucker County Land Books, 1897–1898, 1899–1900. Tucker County Clerk's Office, Parsons, WV.
Tucker County Land Books and Deed Books, 1884–1894. Tucker County Clerk's Office, Parsons, WV.
Tucker County Will Book 2. Tucker County Clerk's Office, Parsons, WV.
West Virginia. *Acts of the Legislature.* 1877.
———. *Acts of the Legislature.* 1882.
———. *Senate Journal.* 1911.

MANUSCRIPTS

Brown, D. D. Notebooks. West Virginia and Regional History Center. West Virginia University. Morgantown, WV.
Charter and By-Laws of the West Virginia Central and Pittsburgh Railway Company. West Virginia and Regional History Center, West Virginia University, Morgantown, WV.

Davis, Henry Gassaway, Papers. Series 6, 9, and 10. West Virginia and Regional History Center. West Virginia University. Morgantown, WV.

Dayton, Alston G., Papers. West Virginia and Regional History Center. West Virginia University. Morgantown, WV.

Eastham, Robert Woodford, III. Handwritten Biography of Robert Woodford ("Bob Ridley") Eastham, 1842–1924. Thirty-one-page typescript. Rappahannock County Historical Society. Washington, VA.

Eastham Files. Rappahannock County Historical Society, Washington, VA.

Fletcher, Sarah Maude (Thompson), Family Papers. Canaan Valley. Tucker County, West Virginia and Regional History Center, West Virginia University, Morgantown, WV.

McMichael, Dora Lee. "Robert Woodford Eastham." Typescript. Soldier Project. 1996. Rappahannock County Historical Society, Washington, VA.

INTERVIEWS

Eastham, Edwin I., III. Interview by Ronald L. Lewis. Sept. 11, 2014. Huntly, Rappahannock County, VA. In author's possession.

Eastham, Louise King. Interview by Ronald L. Lewis. Sept. 22, 2015. Ben Venue, Washington, VA. In author's possession.

Eastham, Robert Woodford, III. Interview by Ronald L. Lewis. June 25, 1992. Flint Hill, Rappahannock County, VA (Mr. Eastham died in 1995). In author's possession.

Fletcher, Sarah Maude (Thompson). Interview by Ronald L. Lewis. Oct. 31, 2014 and Oct. 14, 2015. Canaan Valley. Tucker County, WV. In author's possession.

Thompson, George B. Interview by O. D. Lambert, Robert F. Munn, and Verl Z. Garster. April 13, 1956. Oral History Collection 6. West Virginia and Regional History Center. West Virginia University. Morgantown, WV.

ONLINE SOURCES

Decennial Censuses of the United States, 1830–1930. Ancestry.com.
Eastham, Franklin Dabney. Service Record. 6th Cavalry Virginia Regiment. http://ranger95.com/civil_war/virginia/cavalry/6va_cav/6th_cav_rgt_rost_c_e.html.
"Eastham, Pvt. Philip Byrd." http://www.findagrave.com/cgi-bin/fg.cgi?page=gr&GRid=18078000.
Eastham, Robert Woodford. Service Record. 6th Cavalry Regiment. http://ranger95.com/civil_war/virginia/cavalry/6va_cav/6th_cav_rgt_rost_c_e.html. See also, www.fold3.com/image/#7218049 through 7218059.
Eastham, Woodford. Co. D. Mosby's Regiment Virginia Cavalry (Partisan Rangers), http://ranger95.com/civil_war/virginia/43va_cav_bn_csa/43rd_cav_bn_rost_d.html.
"Henry H. Downing." *Find a Grave Memorial*. http://www.findagrave.com/cgi-bin/fg.cgi?page=gr&GRid=24042573.
———. http://www.wikiwand.com/en/Henry_H._Downing.
"Marlbrough s'en va-t-en guerre." https://en.wikipedia.org/wiki/Marlbrough_s%27en_va-t-en_guerre.
"Osterhout, W. H." *Elk County Genealogy, Biographical Sketches, Ridgway Township and Burough of Ridgway*, chap. 17. http://www.pa-roots.com/elk/history/chapter17.html.
"A Town's Memorial—Norway Pine Grove." Norway Historical Society. March 20, 2012. http://norwayhistoricalsociety.org/PineGrove.php.
Tucker Community Foundation. Sarah Thompson Kaemmerling Fund. http://www.tuckerfoundation.whatsupwv.com/endowed-funds/grants/sarah-thompson-kaemmerling.
West Virginia Deaths Index, 1853–1973. Ancestry.com.

NEWSPAPERS

Alexandria (VA) Gazette
Charles Town (WV) Spirit of Jefferson
Cincinnati (OH) Graphic News

Elkins (WV) Randolph Enterprise
Grafton (WV) Sentinel Weekly
Lumberman's Review
Manufacturers Record
New York Sun
Parkersburg (WV) Sentinel
Parsons (WV) Advocate
Rappahannock (VA) News
Richmond (VA) Times Dispatch
Roanoke (VA) Times
Scranton (PA) Tribune
St. George and Parsons (WV) Tucker County Democrat
St. George (WV) Tucker County Pioneer
Staunton (VA) Spectator and Vindicator
Tucker County Republican, Davis Industrial Edition
Washington (DC) Evening Times
Washington (VA) Rappahannock News
Washington (DC) Times
Wheeling (WV) Daily Intelligencer
Wheeling (WV) Register

BOOKS AND ARTICLES

Allman, Ruth Cooper. *Canaan Valley and the Black Bear*. Parsons, WV: McClain, 1976.

Ambler, Charles H., and Festus P. Summers. *West Virginia: The Mountain State*. 2nd ed. New York: Prentice-Hall, 1958.

Atkinson, George W. *Bench and Bar of West Virginia*. Charleston, WV: Virginian Law Book Company, 1919.

Atkinson, George W., and Alvaro F. Gibbens. *Prominent Men of West Virginia*. Wheeling, WV: W. L. Callin, 1890.

Batteau, Allen W. *The Invention of Appalachia*. Tucson: University of Arizona Press, 1990.

Berlin, New Hampshire Centennial, 1829–1929: A Series of Articles Compiled to Commemorate the Date of Incorporation of the Town of Berlin. N.p.: Printed by Smith and Town, 1929.

Billings, Dwight B., and Kathleen M. Blee. *Road to Poverty: The Making of Wealth and Hardship in Appalachia*. New York: Cambridge University Press, 2000.

Brown, Richard Maxwell. *No Duty to Retreat: Violence and Values in American History and Society*. Norman: University of Oklahoma Press, 1991.

Callahan, James Morton. *History of West Virginia, Old and New*. 3 vols. Chicago: American Historical Society, 1923.

———. *Semi-Centennial History of West Virginia*. Charleston: Semi-Centennial Commission of West Virginia, 1913.

Clarkson, Roy B. *On Beyond Leatherbark: The Cass Saga*. Parsons, WV: McClain, 1990.

———. *Tumult on the Mountains: Lumbering in West Virginia, 1770–1920*. Parsons, WV: McClain, 1964.

Crawford, J. Marshall. *Mosby and His Men: A Record of the Adventures of That Renowned Partisan Ranger, John S. Mosby*. New York: G. W. Carleton, 1867.

Curry, Richard Orr. *A House Divided: A Study of Statehood Politics and the Copperhead Movement in West Virginia*. Pittsburgh, PA: University of Pittsburgh Press, 1964.

Dalton, Bruce. "Robert Eastham, A Transplanted Virginian." *Chronicles of the Tucker County Highlands History and Education Project* 26 (Aug. 2009): 1–4.

Daughtry, Mary. *Gray Cavalier: The Life and Wars of General W. H. F. "Rooney" Lee*. Cambridge, MA: Da Capo Press, 2002.

Dufour, Charles L. *Gentle Tiger: The Gallant Life of Roberdau Wheat*. Baton Rouge: Louisiana State University Press, 1999.

Eastham, Byrd. *The Descendants of Franklin Dabney Eastham [1843–1915]*. Charlottesville, VA: privately printed, 1997.

Eastham, Robert Woodford, III. "Bob Ridley Eastham: Ranger Followed Trail of Adventure." Part 1. *Rappahannock News*, Dec. 29, 1984, 5.

———. "Bob Ridley Eastham: Ranger Followed Trail of Adventure." Part 2. *Rappahannock News*, Jan. 5, 1985, 5, 10.

Eicher, John H., and David J. Eicher. *Civil War High Commands*. Stanford: Stanford University Press, 2001.

Evans, Clement A. *Confederate Military History Extended Edition.* Wilmington, NC: Broadfoot, 1987.

Fansler, Homer Floyd. *History of Tucker County, West Virginia.* Parsons, WV: McClain, 1962.

Friedman, Lawrence M. *A History of American Law.* New York: Simon and Schuster, 1973.

Gilbert, Kenneth, ed. *Mountain Trace.* Book 2. Charleston, WV: Jalamap, 1983.

Green, James. *The Devil Is Here in These Hills: West Virginia's Coal Miners and Their Battle for Freedom.* New York: Atlantic Monthly Press, 2015.

Hall, Granville Davisson. *The Rending of Virginia: A History.* Chicago: Mayer and Miller Press, 1902.

Harkins, Anthony. *Hillbilly: A Cultural History of an American Icon.* New York: Oxford University Press, 2004.

Hicks, W. Raymond. "The West Virginia Central and Pittsburgh Railway." *Railway and Locomotive Historical Society Bulletin* 113 (1965): 6–31.

History of the Counties of McKean, Elk and Forest, Pennsylvania. Chicago: J. H. Beers, 1890.

Hite, Mary Elizabeth. *My Rappahannock Story Book.* Richmond, VA: Dietz Press, 1950.

Horwitz, Morton J. *The Transformation of American Law, 1780–1860.* Cambridge, MA: Harvard University Press, 1977.

Hurst, James Willard. *Law and Economic Growth: The Legal History of the Lumber Industry in Wisconsin, 1836–1915.* Cambridge, MA: Harvard University Press, 1964.

Johnson, Elisabeth B., and C. E. Johnson Jr. *Rappahannock County, Virginia: A History.* Salem, WV: Walsworth, 1981.

Keen, Hugh C., and Horace Mewborn. *43rd Battalion Virginia Cavalry, Mosby's Command.* Lynchburg, VA: H. E. Howard, 1993.

Kirk, Brandon. *Blood in West Virginia: Brumfield v. McCoy.* Gretna, LA: Pelican, 2014.

Kline, Benjamin F. G., Jr. "The Nature of Logging Railroads of West Virginia." *Log Train* 2 (Jan. 1984): 12–15.

Lesher, Dave. "Sarah Maude Kaemmerling and Canaan Valley State Park." *Chronicles of the Tucker County Highlands History and Education Project* 60 (Aug. 2015): 1–5.

Lewin, Jeff L. "The Silent Revolution in West Virginia's Law of Nuisance." *West Virginia Law Review* 90 (winter 1989–90): 235–353.

Lewis, Ronald L. *Transforming the Appalachian Countryside: Railroads, Deforestation, and Social Change in West Virginia, 1880–1920.* Chapel Hill: University of North Carolina Press, 1998.

"Malbrook Has Gone to the War." *Arthur's Ladies' Magazine of Elegant Literature and the Fine Arts* (1844): 8. http://search.proquest.com/docview/124533760.

Marquess, E. Lawrence. "The West Virginia Venture: Empire Out of Wilderness." *West Virginia History* 14 (1952): 5–27.

Maxwell, Hu. *History of Tucker County, West Virginia.* 1884. Reprint, Kingwood, WV: Preston, 1971.

McDonald, William N. *A History of the Laurel Brigade.* Edited by Bushrod C. Washington. Baltimore: Sun Job Printing Office for Mrs. Kate S. McDonald, 1907.

McKinney, Gordon. *Southern Mountain Republicans, 1865–1900: Politics and the Appalachian Community.* Chapel Hill: University of North Carolina Press, 1978.

McNeel, William Price. *The Durbin Route: The Greenbrier Division of the Chesapeake and Ohio Railway.* Charleston, WV: Pictorial Histories Publishing, 1985.

Men of West Virginia. 2 vols. Chicago: Biographical Publishing, 1903.

Miller, F. Thornton. *Juries and Judges versus the Law: Virginia's Provincial Legal Perspective, 1783–1828.* Charlottesville: University Press of Virginia, 1994.

Miller, Wilbur R. *Revenuers and Moonshiners: Enforcing Federal Liquor Law in the Mountain South, 1865–1900.* Chapel Hill: University of North Carolina Press, 1991.

Moore, George Ellis. *A Banner in the Hills: West Virginia's Statehood.* New York: Appleton-Century-Crofts, 1963.

Mosby, John S. *The Memoirs of Colonel John S. Mosby.* 1917. Reprint edited by Charles Wells Russell, Bloomington: Indiana University Press, 1959.

Mott, Pearle G. *History of Davis and Canaan Valley*. Parsons, WV: McClain, 1972.

Munson, John W. *Reminiscences of a Mosby Guerrilla*. New York: Moffat, Yard, 1906.

Myers, Lorraine F., Stuart E. Brown Jr., and Eileen M. Chappel. *Some Old Families of Clarke County, Virginia*. Berryville, VA: Virginia Book Company, 1994.

Pearce, John Ed. *Days of Darkness: The Feuds of Eastern Kentucky*. Lexington: University Press of Kentucky, 1994.

Pepper, Charles M. *The Life and Times of Henry Gassaway Davis, 1823–1916*. New York: Century, 1920.

Pfanz, Donald C. *Richard S. Ewell: A Soldier's Life*. Chapel Hill: University of North Carolina Press, 1998.

Readnour, Harry Warren. "General Fitzhugh Lee: A Biographical Study." Ph.D. diss. University of Virginia, 1971.

Reid, John Phillip. *An American Judge: Marmaduke Dent of West Virginia*. New York: New York University Press, 1968.

Rice, Donald L. *Bicentennial History of Randolph County, West Virginia, 1787–1987*. Elkins, WV: Randolph County Historical Society, 1987.

Robertson, James I., Jr. *Stonewall Jackson: The Man, The Soldier, The Legend*. New York: MacMillan, 1997.

Roeber, A. G. *Faithful Magistrates and Republican Lawyers: Creators of Virginia Legal Culture, 1680–1810*. Chapel Hill: University of North Carolina Press, 1981.

Ross, Thomas Richard. *Henry Gassaway Davis: An Old-Fashioned Biography*. Parsons, WV: McClain, 1994.

Rules of the Senate and House of Representatives of the State of New Hampshire, 1873, and 1975. Concord: Printed for the State, June 1873 and 1875.

Starkey, Edith Kimmell. "Over the Mountain: Timbering at Braucher." *Goldenseal* 13 (summer 1987): 34–39.

Stewart, Bruce E. "'These Big-Boned Semi-Barbarian People': Moonshining and the Myth of Violent Appalachia, 1870–1900." In *Blood in the Hills: A History of Violence in Appalachia*, edited by Bruce E. Stewart, 180–206. Lexington: University Press of Kentucky, 2012.

Strother, David Hunter. *Virginia Illustrated, Containing a Visit to the Canaan, and the Adventures of Porte Crayon and His Cousins.* New York: Harper and Brothers, 1871.

Stutler, Boyd B. *West Virginia in the Civil War.* Charleston, WV: Education Foundation, 1966.

Sullivan, Ken, ed. *The West Virginia Encyclopedia.* Charleston: West Virginia Humanities Council, 2006.

Summers, Festus P. *William L. Wilson and Tariff Reform.* New Brunswick, NJ: Rutgers University Press, 1953.

Sutherland, Daniel E. "Guerrilla Warfare, Democracy, and the Fate of the Confederacy." *Journal of Southern History* 68 (May 2002): 259–92.

Thompson, George B. *History of the Lumber Business at Davis, West Virginia, 1886–1924.* Parsons, WV: McClain, 1974.

Trachtenberg, Alan. *The Incorporation of America: Culture and Society in the Gilded Age.* New York: Hill and Wang, 1982.

Waller, Altina L. *Feud: Hatfields, McCoys, and Social Change in Appalachia, 1860–1900.* Chapel Hill: University of North Carolina Press, 1988.

Warner, Ezra J. *Generals in Gray: Lives of the Confederate Commanders.* Baton Rouge: Louisiana State University Press, 1959.

Waugh, Jack. "Lumbering Before Pinchot: The Short, Loud Death of the Canaan Valley." *American Heritage* 42 (Feb.–Mar. 1991): 93–94.

Wert, Jeffry D. *Cavalryman of the Lost Cause: A Biography of J. E. B. Stuart.* New York: Simon & Schuster, 2008.

———. *Mosby's Rangers.* New York: Simon & Schuster, 1990.

Whitman, Charles Foster. *A History of Norway, Maine: From the Earliest Settlement to the Close of the Year 1922.* Lewiston, ME: Lewiston Journal Printshop and Bindery, 1924.

Williams, John Alexander. "The New Dominion and the Old: Ante-Bellum and Statehood Politics as the Background of West Virginia's 'Bourbon Democracy.'" *West Virginia History* 33 (1973): 317–407.

———. *West Virginia and the Captains of Industry.* Morgantown: West Virginia University Library, 1976.

Williamson, James J. *Mosby's Rangers: A Record of the Operations of the Forty-Third Battalion of Virginia Cavalry from Its Organization to the Surrender*. 1896. Reprint, New York: Sturgis & Walton, 1909.

Woodward, Colin. *American Nations: A History of the Eleven Rival Regional Cultures of North America*. New York: Viking, 2011.

INDEX

"Agrarian" Democrats, 15–16
Ambler, Charles, 42
Anderson, H. H., 158–59
Arnett, William Willey, 186–87, 227
Atkinson, George W., 170, 173, 177

Berryville (VA) Wagon Train Raid, 67–71
Blackman, Silas, 241
Blackwater Boom and Lumber Co., 23
Blackwater Lumber Co., 23, 96, 110, 114, 129–34
Blackwater Lumber Co. v. R.W. Eastham: Eastham served injunction, 129–34; charges and countercharges, 135–40; Eastham's land flooded, 140–44; splash dam dynamited, 144–47; shooting at the splash dam, 147–57; splash dam burned, 157–60
Blake, Charles G., 96, 103–4, 111–12
"Bourbon" Democrats, 33
Brannon, Judge Henry, 194–97, 201–5
Brown, Dr. William A., 163
Brown, Richard, and "Western Civil War of Incorporation," 6–8
Bumgardner, William, 126–27
Burger, Thomas, 225

Callahan, James Morton, 19, 21, 178
Camden, Johnson Newlon, 14–21
Canaan Valley, 78–79
Carr, George A., 155, 215
Cayton, William M., 45, 180–81, 191–92, 201–2, 240
Chidester, H. L., 142
Clayton, William C., 189
Cole, H. D., 163–64, 218
Conley, William G., 174, 176, 191, 193, 228
Conrad, Holmes, 185–86
Cooper, Frank, 159
Cooper, Henry Jackson, 80–81, 140, 143, 145–46, 212–13, 215, 243
Cosner, Christopher C., 209
Cosner, Harrison, 123
Cunningham, Absalom M., 177, 193
Cupp, Will E., 46, 93

Dailey, C. Wood, 182, 227, 241
Dailey, Thomas, 144, 215–16
Davis, Henry Gassaway, and Eastham's defense, 2, 181–82; economic development, 19–22, 24, 82; establishes town of Davis, 82–84; state politics, 14–17; Tucker Co. courthouse war, 51
Davis, John James, 15, 178–79, 228
Davis, Rebecca Harding, 79
Davis, Thomas B., 20, 24, 82, 215

Davis, William R., 82
Davis, WV, 24–30
Dayton, Alston G., 167–69, 171–75, 215, 217, 227
Degler, Karl, 161–62
Dent, Judge Marmaduke H., 194–201, 203, 210–11
Downing, Henry Hawkins, 188
Durkin, Edward P., 180

Eastham, Benjamin Franklin "Captain Frank," 53, 64
Eastham, Charles B. "Charlie," 61, 243
Eastham, Edwin I. "Butch," III, 244–45
Eastham, Franklin Dabney, 54
Eastham, Louise King, viii, 251
Eastham, Mary Catharine "Mollie" Read, 77, 81, 243, 245
Eastham, Philip Byrd, 54–55, 66, 86
Eastham, Robert W. v. John Homer Holt, Judge, 194–205
Eastham, Robert Woodford, III, vii, 253
Eastham, Robert Woodford "Bob Ridley": ancestry, 52–53; in the Civil War, 53–73 passim; enlisted, 55; in Major Chatham Wheat's "Louisiana Tigers," 56; in Brig. Gen. William E. Jones's raid into West Virginia, 56–58; with Mosby's Rangers, 58–74; known as "Bob Ridley," 60–61; war-time exploits, 62–73; paroled, 74; Freedmen's Bureau charges, 74–76; roamed post-war South, 77; marries, 77; moves to Canaan Valley, WV, 78–80; establishing town of Davis, 82–84; as famous outdoorsman, 84–87; property holdings, 88; physical altercations, 88–89, 92; origins of feud with Frank Thompson, 2, 90, 11518; other legal disputes, 91–93; as land agent, 114–18; *Eastham v. Blackwater Lumber Co.*, 118–25; opens Blackwater's boom, 125–29; served with injunction, 129–34; Eastham's land flooded, 140–44; splash dam dynamited, 144–47; shooting at the splash dam, 147–57; deposition, 154–55; splash dam burned, 157–60; gunfight at Parsons depot, 162–69; prosecuting attorneys, 173–80; defense attorneys, 180–90; grand jury selection, 191–94; *Eastham v. Holt*, 194–205; petit jury selection, 205–11; testimony for the defense, 225–30; defense files bills of exception, 230–32, 239; press response to trial and verdict, 232–36; sentenced, 229–30, 239; sends regrets to Mosby Rangers reunion organizers, 236–37; receives letter from John S. Mosby, 237–38; escapes from jail, 238–41; sells land in West Virginia, 242–43; back in Virginia, 243–47, 251–52; death and burial, 245, 251; enters Tucker County folklore, 250–51

INDEX 299

Eastham, R.W. v. Blackwater Lumber Company, 118–25, 216
Elkins, Stephen B., 15–17, 20–21, 24
English, Judge John, 194–95, 197, 210–11

Fansler, Homer, 88–89, 162
Fernando, Peter, 146, 152
Fletcher, Sarah Thompson, viii
Forty-Third Battalion, Virginia Cavalry, Mosby's Rangers, 58–73 passim
Foutch, Dr. C. R., 166–67

Gaston v. Mace, 40–41
Grady, C. Powell, 114–18, 148
Groghan, S.W., 218

Hamilton et al. v. Tucker County Court et al., 46–47
Hansford, Lloyd, 93, 181
Harper, (sheriff) Riley, 48, 49, 169, 240
Harper, C. S., 143
Harper, E. A., 143
Hockman, John W., 219–20
Hoke, Judge Joseph T., 93, 130–33, 216
Holt, Judge John Homer, 163, 169, 172–73, 189–90; announced verdict and sentence in *State v. Eastham*, 229, 239; charges of bias against, 232–36; decisions appealed, 194–205 passim; defense files bills of exception, 230–32; petit jury selection, 206, 210
Houston, J. A., 221–22

Houston, J. E., 232
Howard, John Andrew, 177–78, 194

Johnson, George H., 231
Johnston, Dr. Joseph, 166–67
Jones, Brigadier General William E. "Grumble," 56–58

Kaemmerling, Admiral Gustav, 248–49
Kaemmerling, Sarah Maude Thompson, 97, 100, 247; builds mausoleum, 247–50; donates land for Canaan Valley Resort and State Park, 249
"Kanawha Ring" Democrats, 16
Keplinger, David, 146–47, 153, 215

Lambie, Dave, 149
Landstreet, Fairfax S., 213–14
Lipscomb, Camden, 209
Lipscomb, William F., 169

"Malbrook has gone to the Wars" (fiddle tune), 68–69, 71
Marshall Coal and Lumber Co., 24
Mauck, W. K., 142–43, 148–49, 213
Maxwell, Hu, 61–63, 64, 88
Maxwell, Wilson Bonnifield, 119, 125, 136, 138–40, 181, 184–85, 194, 220
McCormick, James Marshall, 187–88, 194, 217, 227
McCrea, D. A., 217
McGraw, John T., 183–84
McWhorter, Henry C., 194–95, 197, 201
Menifus, Minor, 75

300 INDEX

Mick, Alfred, 215
Minear, Adam C., 45
Moffett, Horatio Gates, 188
Mosby, Colonel John Singleton (Mosby's Rangers), 58–73 passim, 237–38

"Old Bob Ridley" (minstrel tune), 60–61
Osterhout, William, 90, 101

Parsons, Adonijah B., 179, 181
Parsons, Frank A., 231
Parsons, Ward, 45–46, 47, 49
Parsons, WV, 30–31, 45–47

"Redeemer" Democrats, 15
Reed, Dr. Adolphus W., 77
Reed, J. M., 222–23
Reed, Mary A., 77
"Regular" Democrats, 16
Reynolds, Francis Marion, 189, 211
Rumbarger, Jacob L., 23, 89, 106–7
Rumbarger Lumber Co., 89

Scott, James Porter, 180
Silver, William, 226
Smith, Dr. Benjamin M., 164–65, 219–20
State v. R. W. Eastham, and the "war of incorporation," 169–73; a contentious trial, 205–11; defense attorneys, 180–90; defense files bills of exception, 230–32; grand jury selection, 191–94; state's attorneys, 173–80; petit jury selection, 205–11; press response to trial and verdict, 232–36; testimony for the defense, 225–30; testimony for the state, 212–24; verdict and sentence announced, 229, 239; WV supreme court hears appeal, 239–40
St. George, WV, 45–46
Strieby, Cyrus O., 48, 49, 182–83, 202, 220
Strother, David Hunter, 79

Thompson, 167–69
Thompson, Albert, 97–99; and Blackwater Boom & Lumber Co., 23, 106–11; and son Frank's death, 167–69; testifies at trial, 217; described, 247–48; died, 248
Thompson, Benjamin F., vii
Thompson, Frank E., family of, 94–96, 99–100; general manager of Blackwater Lumber Co., 110; origins of feud with Eastham, 2, 90, 11518; serves Eastham with injunction, 129–34; Eastham's land flooded, 140–44; shooting at splash dam, 147–57; splash dam dynamited, 14447; splash dam burned, 157–60; gunfight at Parsons depot, 162–69; died, 167–69; prosecuting attorneys, 173–80; grand jury selection, 191–94; petit jury selection, 205–11; testimony in trial for murder of, 212–24; state rests its case, 224; verdict and sentence, 229; burial, 247, 250
Thompson, George B., 84, 95–96, 104–6, 108, 111, 113, 243; and death of Frank

Thompson, 167–169
Thompson, John F., 101, 103, 111
Thompson, Mary Elizabeth Blake, 97; and death of son Frank, 167–69; died, 248
Thompson, Sarah Maude. *See* Sarah Maude Kaemmerling
Thompson, Sumner W., 96, 101, 111, 123–24, 147; testimony of, 149–52
Thompson Lumber Co., 23, 96; established, 103; sold, 103, 113, 243
Tolbard, Frank, 145, 147
Trachtenberg, Alan, and "the incorporation of America," 11–12
Tucker County, WV, and courthouse war in, 41–51

Valentine, Arthur Jay, 49

Wagoner, Howard J., 188–89
western wars of incorporation. *See* Brown, Richard, and "Western Civil War of Incorporation"
West Virginia: "incorporation" of, 12–14; legal revolution in, 32–41; politics of industrialization in, 41–44
West Virginia Central & Pittsburgh Railroad (WVC&P), 20–21, 23, 44–45; completed to Davis, 50, 84, 89
West Virginia Pulp and Paper Co., 24
Wheeler, Thomas, 146
Whitmer, Robert F., 109
Williams, Alice, 161–62
Williams, Elizabeth v. Karl Degler, 161–62, 222
Williams, John A., 16–17, 42
Williamson, James J., 65
Wilmoth, T. W., 228
Wilson, J. F., 225
Wilson, William L., 171
Wiltshire, Charles B., 66–67
Woods, Hiram, 114–18, 148

www.ingramcontent.com/pod-product-compliance
Lightning Source LLC
Chambersburg PA
CBHW071736150426
43191CB00010B/1592